SCHOLASTIC

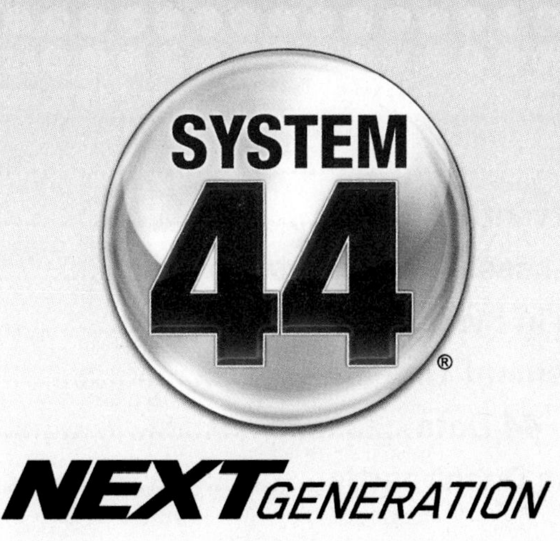

NEXT GENERATION

Screening, Assessment, and Reporting Guide

- Screening and Placement
- Progress Monitoring
- Summative Assessment

Photo Credits: p. 90tl: © Nivek Neslo/Getty Images; p. 91tr: © Bob Daemmrich/Photo Edit; p. 98tl: © Bob Daemmrich/Photo Edit; p. 99tr: © Nivek Neslo/Getty Images; p. 110tr: Jeffrey Vock © Scholastic Inc.; pp. 130tl and 131tr: Jeffrey Vock © Scholastic Inc.; p. 140tr: Jeffrey Vock © Scholastic Inc.; p. 150tr: Jeffrey Vock © Scholastic Inc.

ISBN-13: 978-0-545-50112-5
ISBN-10: 0-545-50112-1

1 2 3 4 5 6 7 8 9 10 08 22 21 20 19 18 17 16 15 14 13

Text pages printed on 10% PCW recycled paper.

Contents

About This Guide

This guide provides teachers and school- and district-level administrators with an overview of the assessment and reporting components in *System 44*.

Use this guide to:

- Screen appropriate students into *System 44.*
- Place students at an individualized point of entry.
- Group students for instruction according to their specific skill needs.
- Monitor progress for students, groups, classes, and schools.
- Use data to inform instruction and to communicate with administrators and families.

This guide has five key sections:

1. **Assessment** Explains how to use two assessments to screen appropriate students into *System 44:*
   - *Scholastic Reading Inventory* (SRI), an assessment of reading comprehension which is also an indicator of need for intensive phonics and decoding instruction.
   - *Scholastic Phonics Inventory* (SPI), an assessment of basic letter recognition, decoding skills, and sight word knowledge.

   This section also explains how to continually monitor student progress using SPI, reports data, Progress Monitoring Tests, and Summative Assessments.
2. **Administering Assessment** Describes how to prepare students for taking *System 44* assessments, how to administer them, and how to score and interpret results.
3. **Reporting in *System 44*** Presents detailed information about each report in the program, as well as how and when to use class, group, and individual reports to monitor progress and to guide data-driven instruction. The guide also provides a recommended timeline for using *System 44* reports.
4. **Data-Driven Decision Making** Includes information about grading, monitoring oral reading fluency, and using skill-based criteria for exiting *System 44.*
5. **Administrator Reports** Provides detailed information about each administrator report in the program, as well as how to use the Leadership Dashboard to monitor progress.

Response to Intervention

What Is Response to Intervention?

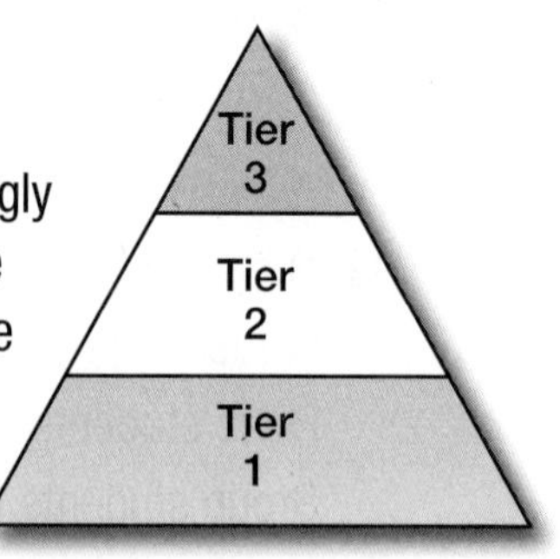

Response to Intervention (RTI) is the systematic practice of providing increasingly intensive educational interventions, measuring student progress, and using the resulting data to make key educational decisions. Research indicates that close progress monitoring such as that which RTI requires can potentially result in more students correctly placed in intervention (Cortiella, 2005; Duffy, 2008; Fuchs & Fuchs, 2007).

RTI is a data-driven framework that enables teachers to continually screen students' skills, identify achievement targets, collect data, monitor students' progress, and calibrate instruction to meet all students' needs. By revealing students' strengths and unveiling opportunities for improvement, RTI can help educators harness and allocate resources more effectively to ensure every child is a confident, capable lifelong learner. See page 474 of *Resources for Differentiated Instruction* for a complete overview of RTI.

RTI in *System 44*

***System 44* and the assessments it includes use data to guide instruction to meet key principles of RTI and support district-level RTI initiatives.**

- **Universal Screening Measures** The Administering Assessment section of this guide (pp. 55–67) explains how to use the *Scholastic Reading Inventory* (SRI) and the *Scholastic Phonics Inventory* (SPI) to place students in the program. The purpose of the SRI is to measure the reading comprehension proficiency of students in Grades K–12. The purpose of the SPI is to identify elementary, middle, and high school students who lack basic decoding skills, and to determine whether *System 44* is the appropriate intervention for these students.
- **Frequent Progress Monitoring** The *System 44* Assessment section of this guide (pp. 17–54) explains how to monitor student progress. Administer SPI three times per year, at least five weeks apart, to reassess students' reading skills. (See information about the SPI Student Progress Report on pp. 84–85.) The *System 44* software continually monitors student progress by collecting data within software activities, as well as at the end of each Topic. As students move through the instruction, the software collects data on mastery of the scope and sequence in relation to time spent on the software and monitors how well students maintain skills. (See information about the Response to Intervention Report on pp. 92–93 and the Student Software Performance Report on pp. 96–97.)
- **Data-Driven Decision Making** The *System 44* software is adaptive and continuously adjusts instruction and practice to meet the unique needs of each student. Pacing is differentiated and content is individualized for each student depending on his or her rate of success.

Comprehensive Assessment in *System 44*

Assessment is an essential component of effective teaching and learning. Meaningful assessment provides detailed feedback on student performance that can inform instruction and enable teachers to target individual student needs.

System 44 includes multiple assessment measures that provide an ongoing picture of student progress and performance. Assessment results are actionable and can be used by teachers, administrators, parents, and students for a number of purposes.

Diagnostic Screening and Placement

The *Scholastic Reading Inventory* (SRI) is designed to:

- Measure students' reading levels.
- Identify students for additional screening with *Scholastic Phonics Inventory* (SPI).

The *Scholastic Phonics Inventory* (SPI) is designed to:

- Measure students' decoding skills.
- Screen and place appropriate students into *System 44* instruction at the appropriate level.
- Generate diagnostic, baseline performance data for each student.
- Report baseline information for teachers, administrators, students, and families.

Progress Monitoring

SPI is also designed to:

- Monitor students' decoding progress at key points throughout the program.
- Inform grouping and differentiated instruction.
- Provide progress information for teachers, administrators, and families.

Actionable reports based on data from the *System 44* software may be used to monitor class, group, subgroup, and individual progress and to:

- Group and regroup students for differentiated instruction.
- Provide performance data for grading needs.
- Share meaningful progress information with students, parents, and administrators.

Fast-Tracks are embedded software assessments that:

- Ensure students focus instructional time on areas of need, rather than on areas already mastered.
- Individualize student pacing through the instruction.

Progress Monitoring Tests and Summative Assessments

***System 44* print-based assessments may be used to:**

- Measure how well students maintain previously taught skills and content.
- Ensure transfer and application of maintained skills to the reading of printed text.

Assessment Data in *System 44*

***System 44* provides six types of assessment data that can be used to monitor progress, diagnose strengths and weaknesses, and inform instruction.**

Purpose	Assessment	What It Assesses	When
Diagnostic Screening/ Placement FOR appropriate screening and initial placement into *System 44*	***Scholastic Reading Inventory* (SRI)**	• Baseline reading comprehension level	• Before placement into *System 44*
	***Scholastic Phonics Inventory* (SPI)**	• Baseline decoding and sight word reading fluency	• After SRI and prior to beginning *System 44*
Diagnostic FOR diagnosing student strengths and weaknesses	***System 44* Software**	• Phonemic Awareness • Decoding • Sight Words • Spelling • Comprehension	• Ongoing data collection occurs on a daily basis.
Progress Monitoring FOR monitoring of performance over time, usage, and grouping for differentiated instruction	***Scholastic Phonics Inventory* (SPI)**	• Letter Names • Sight Words • Nonsense Words	• At the middle and end of the school year
	***System 44* Software**	• Decoding Accuracy • Decoding Fluency • Spelling • Comprehension • Oral Reading Fluency	• Ongoing data collection occurs on a daily basis.
	***Scholastic Reading Counts!® (SRC!)* Quizzes**	• Reading Comprehension • Independent Reading	• As students complete books from the *System 44* Library
	***System 44* Progress Monitoring Tests**	• Phonemic Awareness and Phonics • Sight Words and Spelling • Morphology	• Five times throughout the program
Differentiated Placement FOR data-driven, adaptive placement to accelerate the pace of learning	**Fast-Tracks**	• Decoding • Morphology • Word-Level Fluency	• Occurs automatically for appropriate students before a new Series on the software (approximately every 1–2 weeks)
Informal Assessment FOR teacher-directed observational evaluation of students' skills	***System 44* Informal Assessment**	• Decoding • Word Recognition • Meaning/Context	• As part of each direct-instruction lesson
Summative Assessment FOR evaluating transfer of newly acquired skills	***System 44* Midyear and End-of-Year Tests**	• Phonemic Awareness and Phonics • Word Recognition and Spelling • Morphology	• Twice (Midyear and End-of-Year)

<table>
<tr><th>What the Data Show</th><th>Informing Instruction</th></tr>
<tr><td>Screening and Placement Report
• Percent accurate and fluent in Letter Names, Sight Words, and Nonsense Words
• Description of the Decoding Diagnoses (See pages 33 and 81)
• Recommended Placement (See page 81)</td><td>If student is a Pre- or Beginning Decoder:
• Enroll in System 44 software, Series 1
If student is a Developing Decoder:
• Enroll in System 44 software, Series 4
If student is an Advancing Decoder:
• Enroll in READ 180</td></tr>
<tr><td>Student Software Performance Report
• Scope and sequence completion
• Fast-Tracked Topics
• Number of cycles to mastery
• Software scores
• Success and Writing Strands performance</td><td>If a student requires three software cycles to achieve mastery or is provisionally promoted:
• Note the Topic and provide one-to-one intervention
If a student's Topic scores are below 70%:
• Review the score type (Sound, Word, Spelling, or Comprehension) to determine where the student is struggling, and provide remediation</td></tr>
<tr><td>Summary Progress Report
• SPI fluency scores
• SPI decoding status
Reading Progress Report
• Current progress
• Software usage
• Cumulative performance
Scholastic Reading Counts! Reading Progress Report
• Quizzes passed successfully
• Number of books read
System 44 Progress Monitoring Test: Answer Key & Score Sheet
• Number of items correct for each part and for the entire test</td><td>If a student's SPI fluency score is not improving:
• Review student-level reports data to adjust teacher-led instruction and provide additional practice
If a student has a Median Session Time of less than 15 minutes:
• Ensure each student gets adequate time on the software
If a student's software scores are below 70%:
• Provide remediation in areas of skill need during the small-group instruction rotation
If students are not meeting individualized reading goals:
• Encourage students to choose books at appropriate Lexile® levels
• Adjust students' reading goals or the percent required to pass a quiz to encourage success
If a student does not pass a Progress Monitoring Test:
• Consider review and reteaching for skills not maintained over time
• Regroup for teacher-led instruction</td></tr>
<tr><td>Response to Intervention Report
• Number of Topics Fast-Tracked
• Individual student's RTI
• Median RTI

Student Software Performance Report
• Which Topics the student has Fast-Tracked</td><td>If a student Fast-Tracked 10 or more Topics:
• System 44 software is meeting the needs of students who have already mastered certain skills
• Student's RTI will likely be above the median RTI
If a student's progress and mastery is consistently below the median RTI:
• Review student-level reports data to adjust teacher-led instruction and provide additional practice
• Determine if student Fast-Tracked any Topics
If a student Fast-Tracked a Topic:
• Note the content covered in that Topic
• Monitor the student's performance in class to ensure he/she continues to demonstrate mastery in those skills</td></tr>
<tr><td>Resources for Differentiated Instruction
• Cloze item performance at the end of each direct-instruction lesson</td><td>If a student is struggling with lesson content:
• Provide opportunities for one-to-one support
• Review relevant reports data to understand performance on the software</td></tr>
<tr><td>System 44 Midyear and End-of-Year Test: Answer Key & Score Sheet
• Number of items correct for each part and for the entire test</td><td>If a student does not pass the Summative Assessment (see pp. 66–67):
• Consider review and reteaching for skills not maintained over time
• Regroup for teacher-led instruction</td></tr>
</table>

System 44 Assessment Timeline

This timeline recommends when to administer *System 44* assessments throughout the course of a school year.

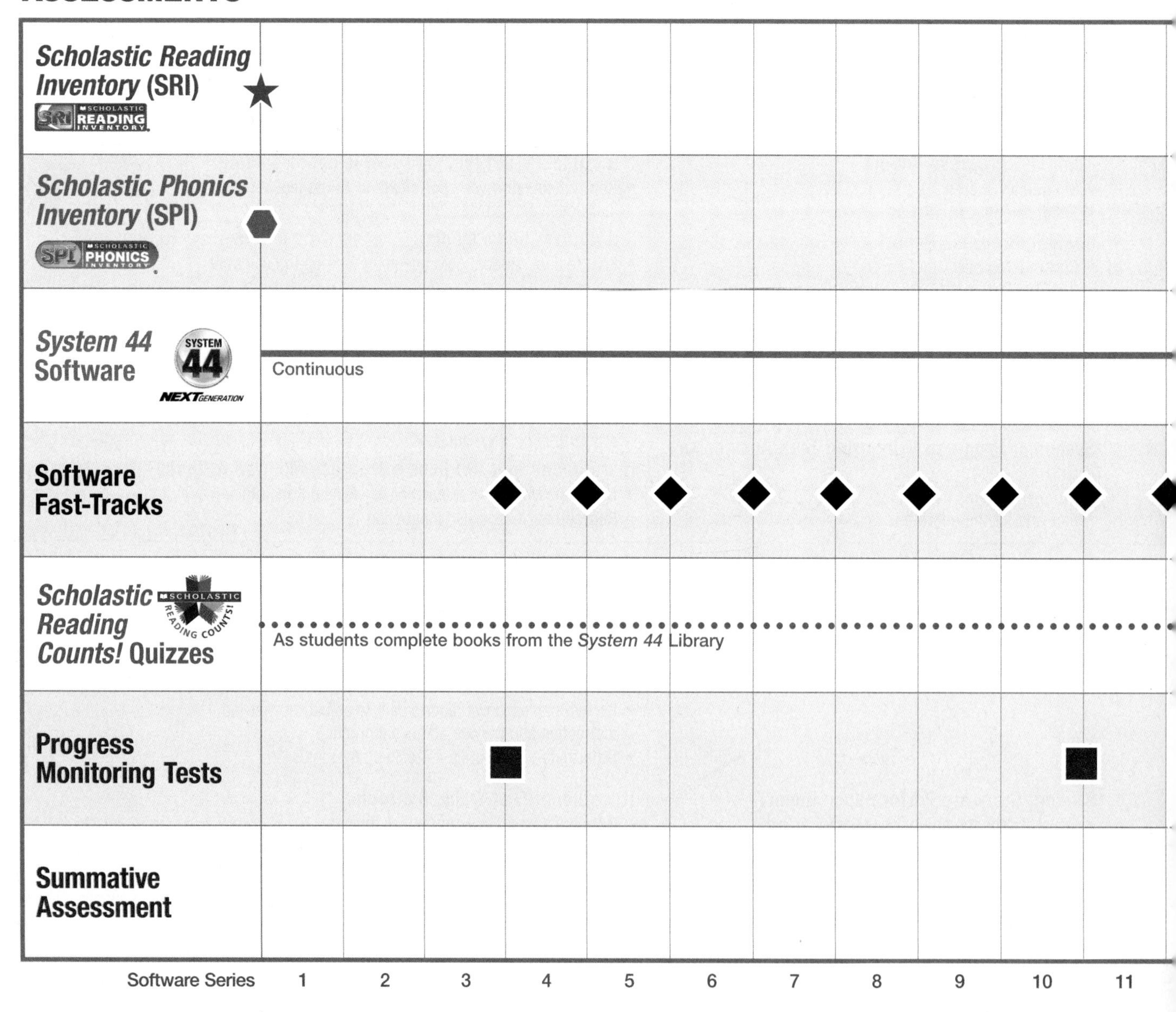

Interpreting the *System 44* Assessment Timeline

Assessment	Purpose	Timeline Symbol
Scholastic Reading Inventory	Screening and Placement	★
Scholastic Phonics Inventory	Screening, Placement, and Progress Monitoring	⬢
***System 44* Software**	Progress Monitoring and Diagnostic Assessment	⟶
Software Fast-Tracks	Ongoing Differentiated Placement	◆
***Scholastic Reading Counts!* Quizzes**	Progress Monitoring	·······▶
***System 44* Progress Monitoring Tests**	Progress Monitoring	■
***System 44* Midyear Test and End-of-Year Test**	Summative Assessment	●

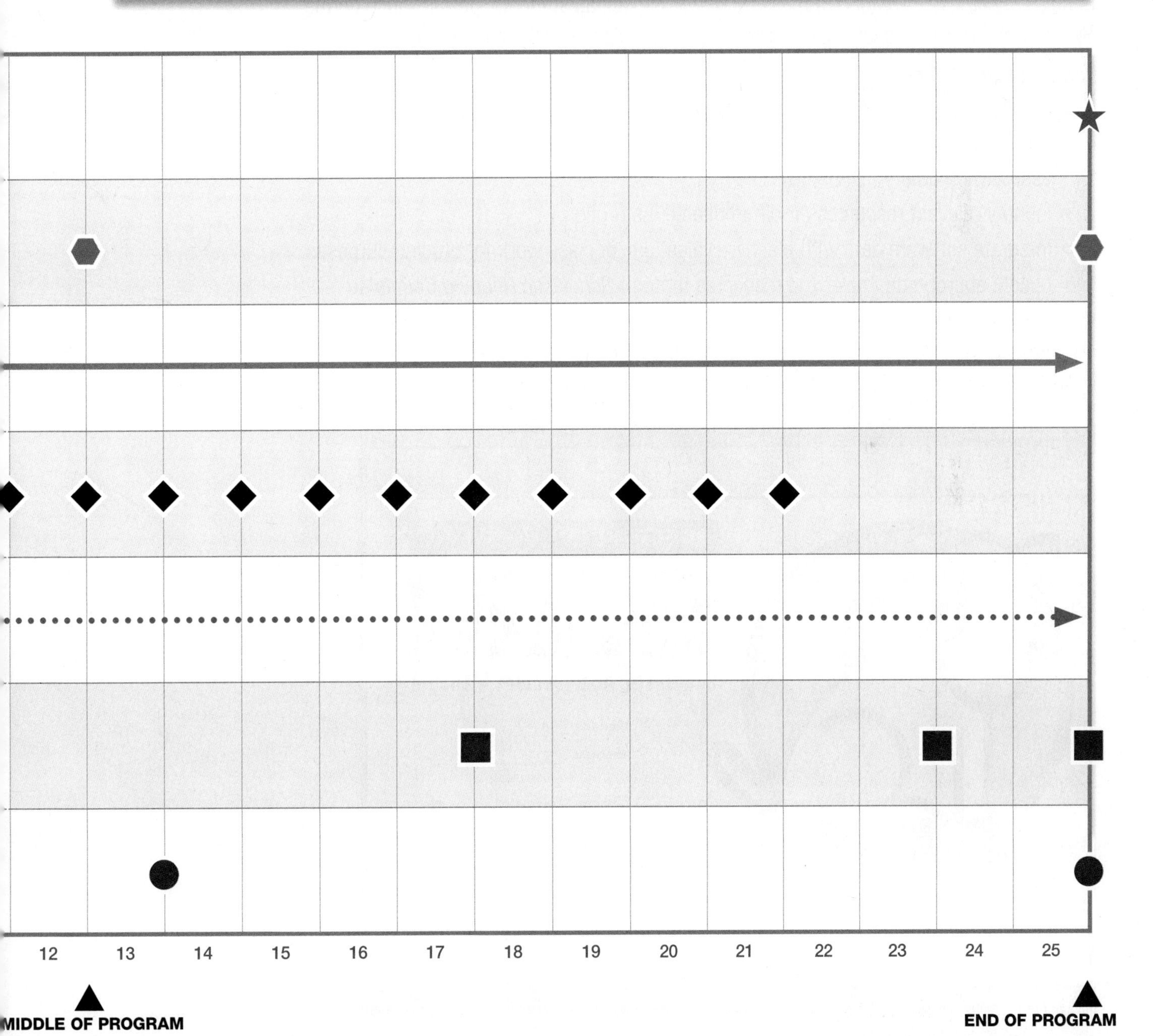

Managing *System 44* Data

The *System 44* software collects and analyzes data that enables teachers to monitor progress and target instruction to meet students' specific needs.

Scholastic Achievement Manager (SAM) Overview

Teachers and administrators may access student performance data on the program's technology-based instructional and assessment components through the Scholastic Achievement Manager (SAM). SAM is a computer-based management and reporting system that gathers usage and performance data from the *Scholastic Reading Inventory* (SRI) and *Scholastic Phonics Inventory* (SPI) assessments, as well as students' performance on the *System 44* software. Results are presented and organized in actionable reports.

You can use SAM to:

- Enroll students in the *System 44* software, as well as the SRI and the SPI assessments.
- Individualize instruction by accessing reports containing performance and assessment data.
- Identify relevant resources for differentiated instruction.
- Integrate software data with teacher evaluations of class work for grading purposes.
- Locate appropriate books and resources through *Scholastic Reading Counts!* to tailor instruction.
- Access the SAM Student Digital Portfolio to set and track academic and behavioral goals, access and grade fluency recordings, and assess student writing.

Accessing Information Through SAM

The SAM Home Page includes a "SmartBar" that lists the students currently enrolled in *System 44*. A message center on the Home Page generates *reminders* about when to run reports containing key assessment data and generates *alerts* if students are not progressing as expected. Use the five main buttons—Roster, Reports, Resources, Books, and Portfolio—to access each area of SAM.

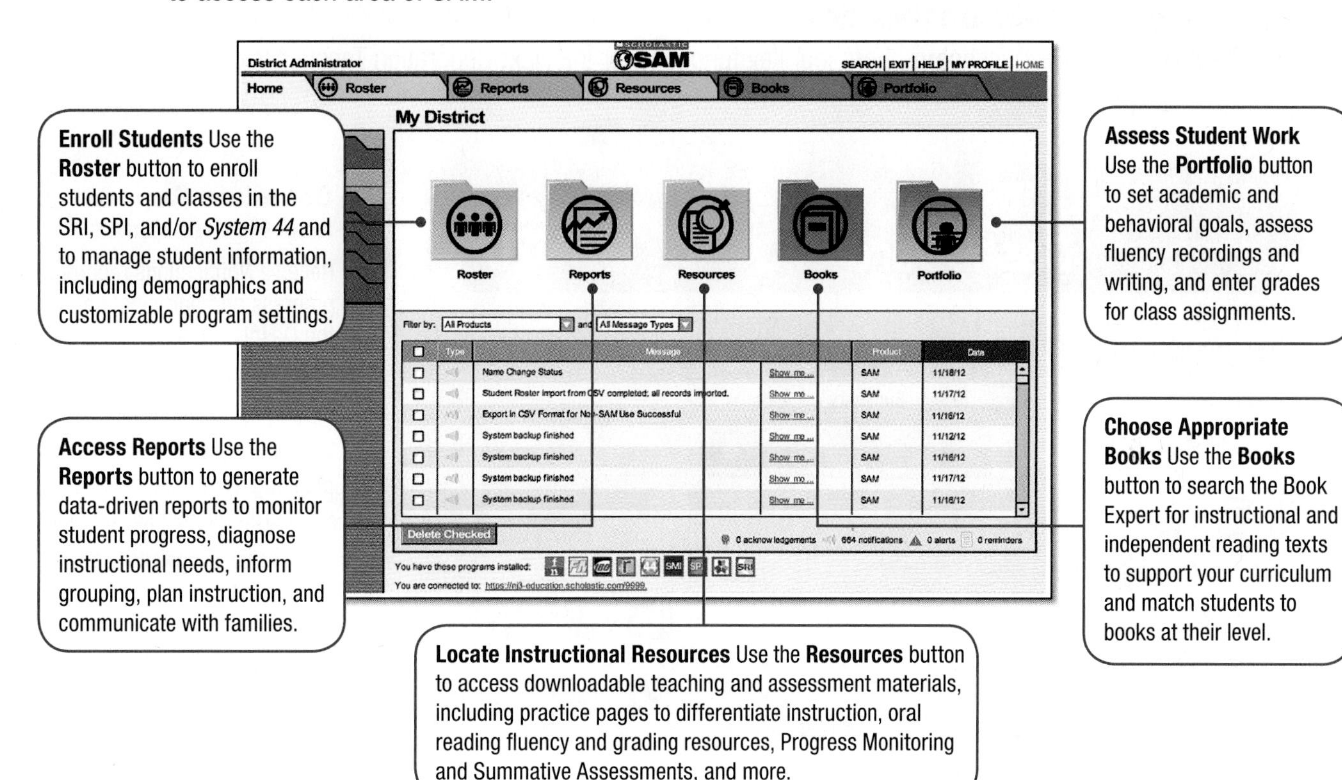

Enroll Students Use the **Roster** button to enroll students and classes in the SRI, SPI, and/or *System 44* and to manage student information, including demographics and customizable program settings.

Access Reports Use the **Reports** button to generate data-driven reports to monitor student progress, diagnose instructional needs, inform grouping, plan instruction, and communicate with families.

Locate Instructional Resources Use the **Resources** button to access downloadable teaching and assessment materials, including practice pages to differentiate instruction, oral reading fluency and grading resources, Progress Monitoring and Summative Assessments, and more.

Assess Student Work Use the **Portfolio** button to set academic and behavioral goals, assess fluency recordings and writing, and enter grades for class assignments.

Choose Appropriate Books Use the **Books** button to search the Book Expert for instructional and independent reading texts to support your curriculum and match students to books at their level.

SAM also includes a **Student Digital Portfolio** for assessing oral reading fluency with engaging and instructional-level text found in the Success Passages. Student recordings may be evaluated for pacing (WCPM), phrasing, and prosody. Teachers can also assess students' writing.

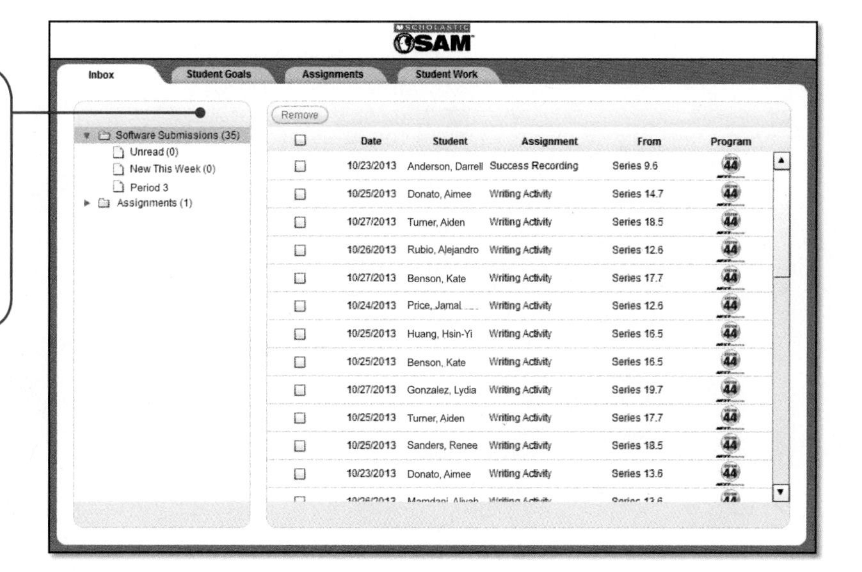

You can find step-by-step instructions on how to strategically use SAM in the *System 44* Software Manual (**SAM Keyword:** 44 Software Manual).

Understanding the Dashboards

The Teacher Dashboard, Leadership Dashboard, and Student Dashboard provide teachers, leaders, and students with resources and data needed for daily engagement, data-driven differentiated instruction, and successful implementation.

System 44 Teacher Dashboard

The *System 44* Teacher Dashboard offers four key functions for the Next Generation Teacher:

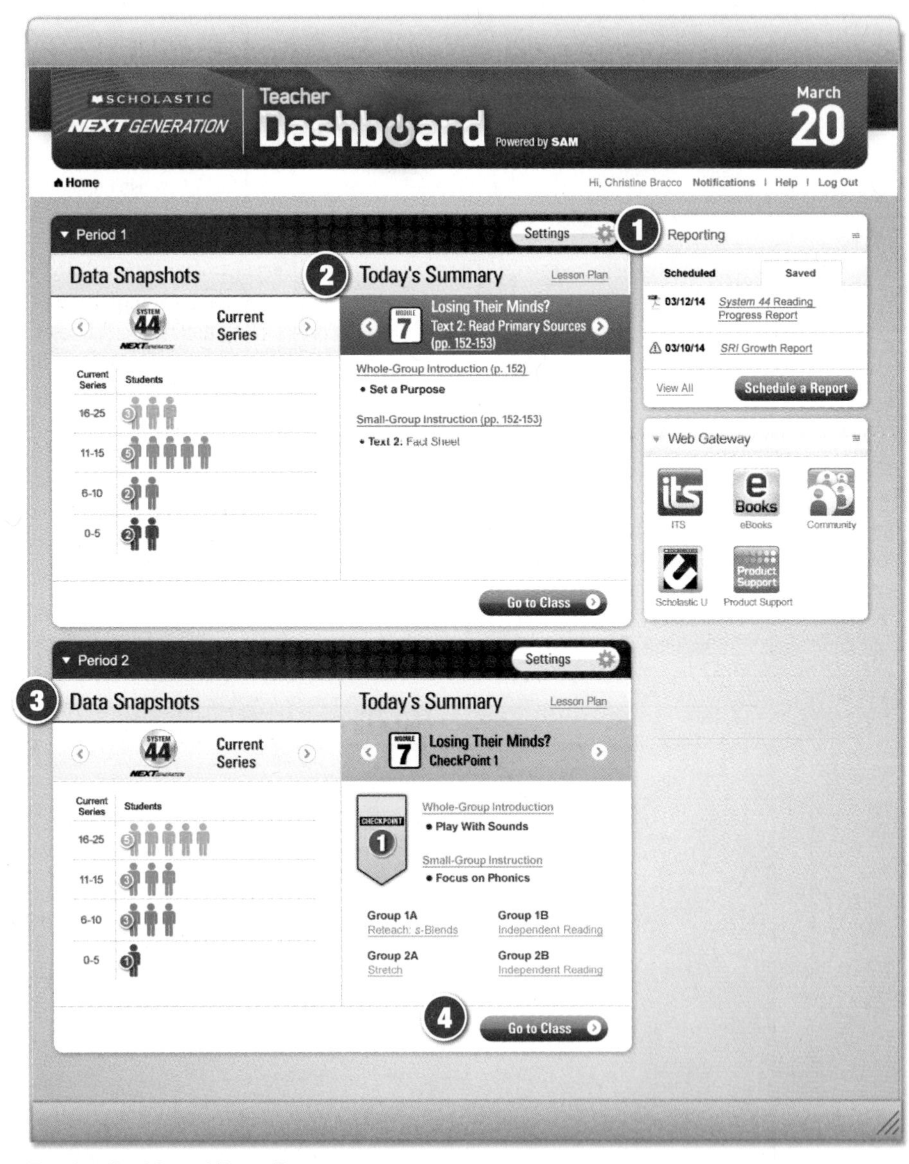

Teacher Dashboard Home Page

1 Schedule Reports and Notifications

Receive Notifications regarding student progress and participation. Schedule the Dashboard to run SAM reports.

2 Plan Instruction

Link to the *System 44* Interactive Teaching System (ITS) for daily planning. Generate, save, and print standards-aligned lesson plans.

3 Review Performance Results

Monitor student progress in each software component and plan appropriate intervention.

4 Group Students

Use the Groupinator® to form dynamic groups and differentiate instruction based on student performance results. Professional Development resources are also available on each Class Page.

Navigating the Teacher Dashboard Home Page

Use your SAM login information to log in to the Teacher Dashboard. The Home Page features student results and accompanying lesson plans for each class period.

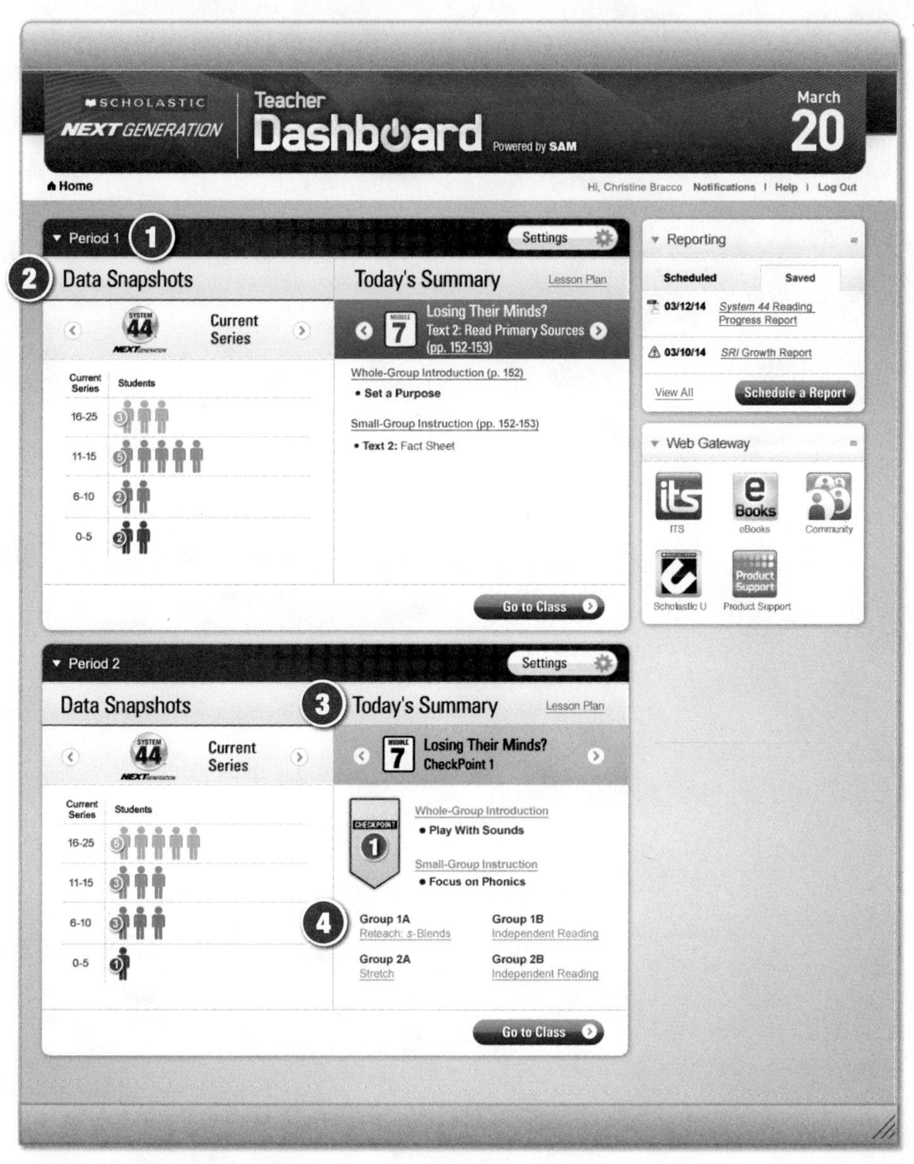

Teacher Dashboard Home Page

1 Class Digest

Each class has its own digest that provides overviews of performance results and daily *44Book* instruction. Establish standard class naming conventions in SAM to ensure relevant class names appear on the Teacher Home Page.

2 Data Snapshots

At-a-glance views of class performance help drive instructional planning and pacing. *System 44* Average Daily Use is the default Data Snapshot. Click the left and right arrows to review usage and performance results from SPI, SRI, and *SRC!*

3 Today's Summary

Whole- and Small-Group overviews provide a summary of the day's instruction. The summary links directly to the Interactive Teaching System. Click on Settings to select the *44Book* used with each class. Use the left and right arrows to advance through a *44Book* Module.

4 Groups

Student groups are generated by the Groupinator and are included on the Today's Summary at each *44Book* CheckPoint. The Summary links directly to accompanying lessons on the Interactive Teaching System.

Assessment

Screening Overview

***System 44* includes two screening measures to help you effectively identify students who will most benefit from *System 44* software instruction:**

- *Scholastic Reading Inventory* (SRI)
- *Scholastic Phonics Inventory* (SPI)

Identifying Students

Struggling readers vary in their particular strengths and challenges. It is important to screen students for entry into *System 44* to ensure that the instruction is appropriate for their specific skill needs. Students who are candidates for *System 44* may struggle with:

- Basic phonemic awareness.
- Decoding and word recognition.
- Word-level fluency.
- Strategies for reading unfamiliar words.
- Reading text two or more years below grade level.

Screening Into *System 44*

The flowchart below demonstrates the two primary paths for screening students into *System 44*, using the *Scholastic Reading Inventory* and the *Scholastic Phonics Inventory.*

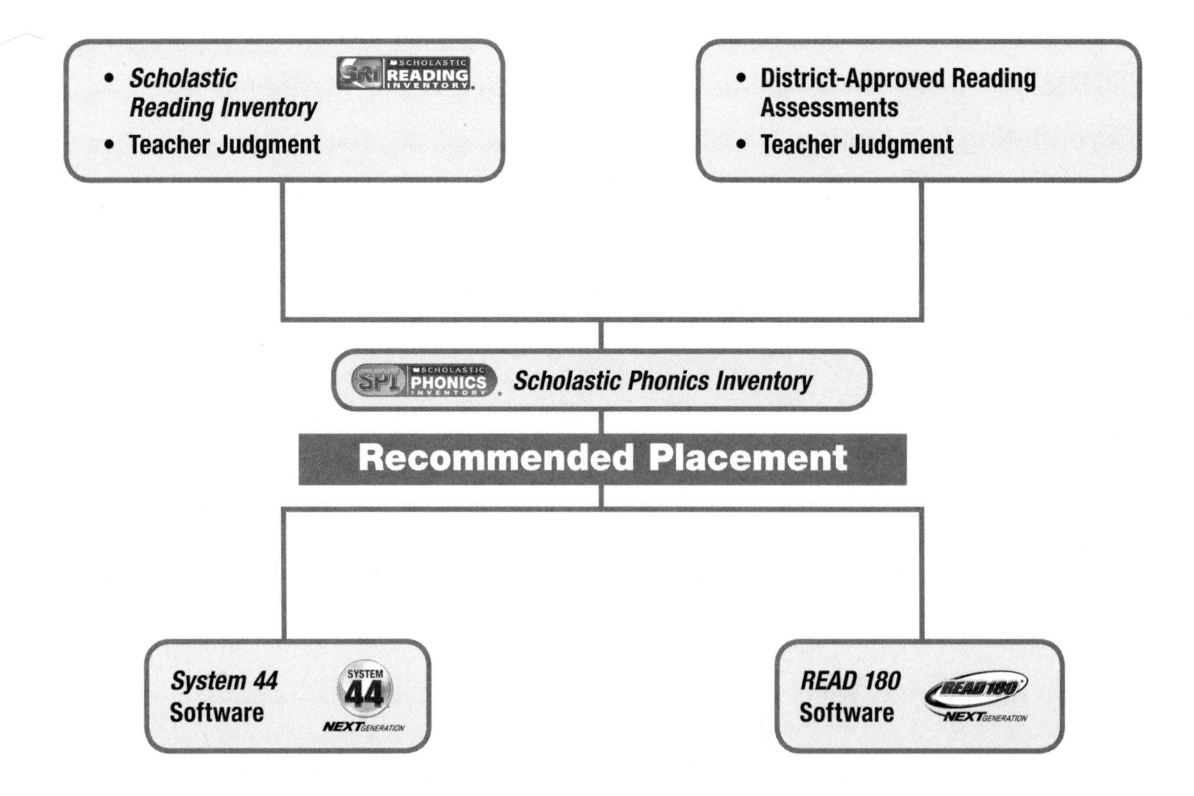

Scholastic Reading Inventory (SRI)

Performance on the *Scholastic Reading Inventory* (SRI) may be used as the first indication of a need for *System 44* instruction. The SRI is a computer-adaptive assessment that provides an objective measure of students' reading comprehension skills on the Lexile Framework®.

The SRI can be administered at the beginning of the school year to determine each student's baseline reading level. This will enable you to:

- Form initial small groups based on reading levels.
- Identify students for additional screening with SPI.

The Scholastic Achievement Manager (SAM) records each student's SRI result as a Lexile. Students with Lexile measures of BR–400L may lack decoding skills and should take the *Scholastic Phonics Inventory* (SPI) for possible screening into *System 44*.

How the SRI Works

During an SRI test, students read brief passages from literature and nonfiction and answer questions about what they have read. Each test screen contains a passage and a question.

Computer-Adaptive Assessment

As a computer-adaptive test, the SRI adjusts item difficulty to students' responses. As students progress through the assessment, the difficulty levels of questions change according to students' performance. As the student correctly answers questions, the Lexile of each question increases. When the student answers a question incorrectly, the next question presented is at a lower Lexile level. The assessment stops once the student has answered a sufficient number of questions to determine an accurate Lexile measure.

Sample Student SRI Performance

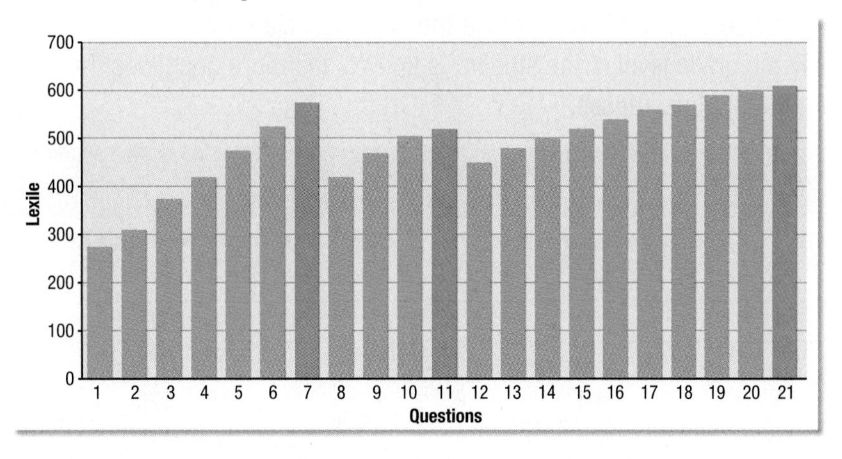

The bar graph above represents a sample student's performance on one SRI test. Each question is numbered. Questions answered correctly are blue; incorrect answers are orange. Note how the level of test items adjusts to the student's responses. This graph is only a sample. The number of questions and the Lexile of each question depends on individual student performance.

The Research Behind the SRI

The SRI is a research-based assessment that has been field-tested and validated to ensure that it is a reliable indicator of reading comprehension.

Field Testing

The SRI is based on the Lexile Framework for Reading. A linking study between the SRI and the Lexile Framework developed normative information based on a sample of 512,224 students from a medium-to-large state. The sample's distributions of scores on norm-referenced and other standardized measures of reading comprehension are similar to those reported for national distribution.

Reliability

Assessment results should be reliable—stable, accurate, and dependable. A test's accuracy is estimated by a number called the standard error of measurement (SEM). The SEM provides information about how accurately a test is able to measure a student's ability. Once the SEM is known, it can be taken into account when reviewing test results. In reality, all test scores include some measure of error, or level of uncertainty.

The SRI computer algorithm uses a statistical procedure designed to estimate each student's ability to comprehend text. The algorithm uses prior information about students' levels to control the selection of questions and the calculation of each student's reading ability after they respond to each question. When students take a computer-adaptive test, they all receive approximately the same raw score, or number of items answered correctly. This occurs because the questions are targeted for each student's unique ability.

Because each student takes a unique test, the SEM associated with any one score or student is also unique. The initial SEM, or uncertainty, for an SRI score is shown in the table below. When students are appropriately targeted, using both grade level and initial reading level, students can respond to fewer test questions and not increase the error associated with the measurement process. When only the grade level of the student is known, the more questions the student answers, the more the SEM decreases.

Mean SEM on SRI by Extent of Prior Knowledge

Number of Items	SEM, Grade Level Known	SEM, Grade and Reading Level Known
15	104L	58L
16	102L	57L
17	99L	57L
18	96L	57L
19	93L	57L
20	91L	56L
21	89L	56L
22	87L	55L
23	86L	54L
24	84L	54L

Validity

Validity indicates whether the test measures what it is supposed to measure. There are several ways to examine the validity of a test like SRI. Each type of validation asks an important question about the test.

- **Content Validity** Does the test sample important content related to what the test is supposed to measure?
- **Construct Validity** Does the test measure the theoretical construct (or trait) it claims to measure?
- **Criterion-Related Validity** Does the test adequately predict the test-taker's behavior in a specific situation?

Content Validity

The SRI consists of short passages and questions that measure comprehension by focusing on skills readers use when studying written materials from a variety of content areas. These skills include identifying details, drawing conclusions, and making comparisons, which are the component skills of reading comprehension.

Passage Selection

SRI passages are selected from authentic texts that students encounter both in and out of the classroom, such as textbooks, literature, magazines, and newspapers. Passage topics span a variety of interest areas. No prior knowledge is required to understand a passage.

Item Format

Each test question, or item, has a statement and four answer choices. This is considered an embedded completion item format, which has been shown to accurately measure the ability to draw inferences and establish logical connections between ideas.

Statements are written to enable students to arrive at the correct answer by comprehending the passage. All four answer choices are plausible when the statement is read independently of the text. Item reading levels are controlled to be easier than the most difficult word in the passage.

Below are sample items at various Lexile levels that might appear on an SRI test.

Sample Item	Lexile
Q. When I was talking to Donny Thunderbird, he told me about his relatives all over the reservation. He has cousins with no mother or father, but because they are members of the tribe, they will never be without a home. They will always belong to something. **The tribe is ______________.** **A.** lost **B.** huge **C.** famous **D.** supportive	**700L–850L**
Q. Cody's room at home looked like a tornado had hit it. Boxes were piled everywhere. Some were open, with things falling out. Others were still taped shut. **The room was ______________.** **A.** messy **B.** small **C.** empty **D.** bright	**400L–550L**
Q. He broke records every week. No one in the state had ever caught more passes. Or gained more yards. Or scored more touchdowns. **He was a ______________ player.** **A.** great **B.** slow **C.** new **D.** last	**100L–250L**

Construct Validity

SRI was examined for construct validity using several measures, including developmental changes in test scores and correlation with similar tests that measure reading comprehension.

Developmental Nature of SRI

Reading is a skill that typically develops with age—as students read more, their skills improve, and they are able to access more complex texts. Because growth in reading is uneven, with the greatest growth usually taking place in earlier grades, SRI measures should show a similar trend of decreasing gains as grade level increases. Multiple studies indicate that performance on SRI increases with grade level. These studies also demonstrate that the growth is not a straight-line slope; that is, the growth in earlier grades is steeper than growth in later grades, which supports the construct validity of the SRI.

The graph below displays growth by grade level.

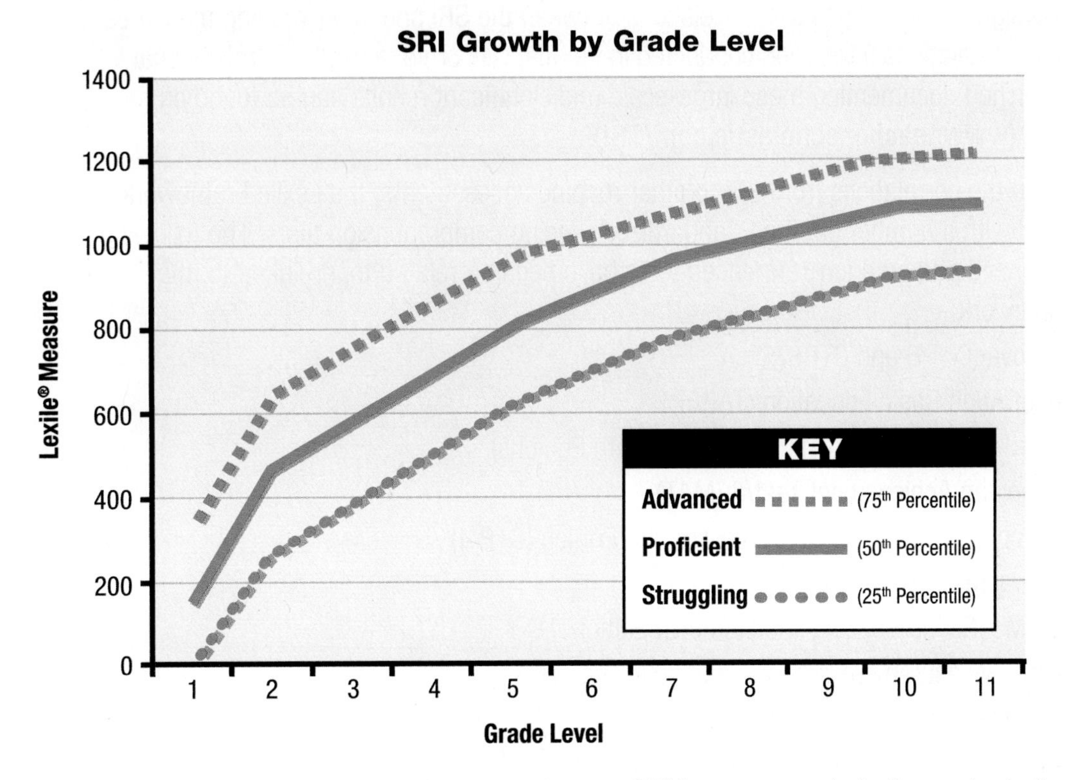

In addition to the changes in growth expectations on SRI from one grade to the next, studies reveal that older struggling readers receive lower scores on the SRI than their peers who are reading at grade level, which is also reflected in their performance results on state assessments. This discrepancy between results for struggling readers and grade-level readers further supports the construct validity of SRI.

The studies indicate that while growth for grade-level readers decreases as students move to higher grade levels, this should not be the case for older struggling readers who receive reading intervention. When compared to grade-level readers, struggling readers should demonstrate greater growth from one SRI test to the next.

See **Appendix 1** to review the correlation between SRI Lexile levels and their equivalent grade levels.

SRI has been directly correlated with numerous state assessments. All studies reveal statistically significant and positive correlations between the SRI and other reading measures. Large-scale correlations have been conducted in Florida, California, and Ohio. Professional Papers published documenting these large-scale and significant results can be found on the SRI website **(www.teacher.scholastic.com/SRI)**.

In addition to the correlations from SRI to other reading assessments, the Lexile Framework is correlated with a number of other standardized reading comprehension tests. The following norm-referenced and criterion-referenced tests have been correlated to, or linked to, the Lexile Framework:

- TerraNova (CAT/6 and CTBS/5)
- Tests of Adult Basic Education (TABE)
- Stanford Achievement Tests (Ninth and Tenth Editions)
- Metropolitan Achievement Test/8 (MAT)
- ERB: Comprehensive Testing Program, 4th Edition (CTP 4)
- The Iowa Tests (ITBS and ITED)
- Gates-MacGinitie Reading Tests, Fourth Edition
- Dynamic Measurement Group: Dynamic Indicators of Basic Early Literacy Skills (DIBELS)
- Test of English as a Foreign Language (TOEFL)

Many state assessments link to the Lexile Framework, and SRI provides extrapolated cut scores for these states. This allows for customized performance standards alignment to state outcome expectations. See **Appendix 2** to review the list of assessments currently aligned to the Lexile Framework.

Criterion-Related Validity

The criterion-related validity of a test indicates the test's effectiveness in predicting an individual's behavior in a specific situation. Convergent validity examines those situations in which test scores are expected to be influenced by behavior. Conversely, discriminate validity examines those situations in which test scores are not expected to be influenced by behavior. For example, because targeted reading intervention programs are specifically designed to improve students' reading comprehension, an effective intervention would be expected to improve students' reading test scores. Research shows that there is a positive relationship between SRI scores and enrollment in reading intervention. Similarly, studies indicate that SRI measures reading ability and is not influenced by gender, ethnicity, socioeconomic status, special education status, or English language learner status.

How SRI Results Are Reported

Teachers administer the SRI for screening at the beginning of the school year. They may also administer it to measure progress at the end of the school year. Results can be compared against the original (norm) group that took the test. SAM reports for individual students, classes, schools, or districts display SRI results with the following metrics:

Normative Data

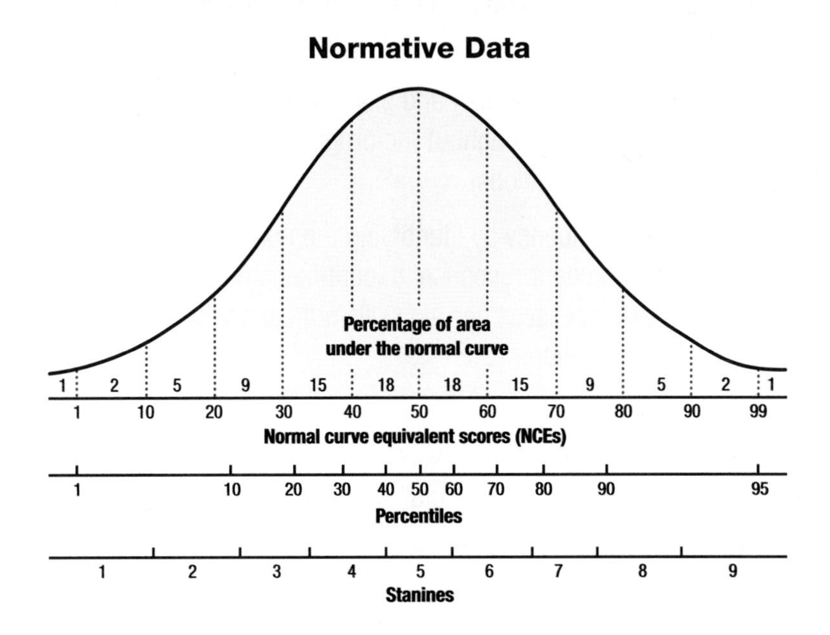

Percentile Rank A student's percentile rank is a score that tells the percent of students in a particular group that received lower scores on a test than the student did. It shows the student's relative position, or rank, in a group of students who are in the same grade. For example, if a student scores at the 65th percentile, it means that the student performed as well as or better than 65 percent of the norm group.

Stanine A stanine is a standardized score ranging from 1 to 9. Unlike percentile rank, stanine scores are equally distributed across the entire bell curve for all grade levels. Stanines represent a range of scores. Stanines of 1–3 are considered below average, stanines of 4–6 are considered average, and stanines of 7–9 are considered above average. Like percentiles, stanines indicate a student's standing in comparison with the norm group.

Normal Curve Equivalent (NCE) The NCE is a way of measuring where a student falls along a normal bell curve. NCEs range from 1 to 99. If a student was to make exactly one year of progress after one year of instruction, his NCE score would remain the same and his NCE gain would be zero, even though his Lexile would increase. Students who make more than a year's progress will have made a larger gain, resulting in a larger NCE score.

Grade Level The grade level indicates how close to grade-level proficiency a student's reading level is, based on Lexile measure and associated grade-level Lexile range. Grade-level equivalencies range from Far Below Grade Level to Far Above Grade Level.

Performance Standard A performance standard associates a student's Lexile with one of four performance standards: Below Basic, Basic, Proficient, and Advanced. These performance standards include a range of Lexile measures which vary by grade level.

Scholastic Phonics Inventory (SPI)

The *Scholastic Phonics Inventory* (SPI) is a software-based test of basic letter recognition, decoding skills, and sight word knowledge.

The SPI is designed to identify older struggling readers who require systematic and explicit phonics instruction to strengthen foundational skills necessary for fluency and reading comprehension.

SPI contains three equivalent test forms to screen and place students into *System 44* and to help monitor their progress at key points throughout the program. SPI also includes reports and resources, as well as test accommodations.

The SPI measures both accuracy and fluency by identifying the number of correct answers as well as the speed (or latency) of student response. It identifies students who may lack decoding skills, as well as those who possess certain skills but cannot apply or transfer them effectively or quickly enough to comprehend text.

The assessment is brief (10–12 minutes) and can be administered to multiple students concurrently. It consists of four sections:

- **Practice Test** (11 items), a warm-up activity that orients students to the interface.
- **Letter Recognition** (11 items), assessing students' ability to identify letters read aloud.
- **Sight Word Recognition** (30 items), assessing students' knowledge of high-frequency sight words.
- **Nonsense Word Decoding** (30 items), assessing pure decoding in a decontextualized setting.

How the SPI Works

Practice Test

The SPI begins with a series of 11 items that give students a chance to "warm up." The student is presented with a series of four circles and is instructed to click on the one that is different as quickly as possible. The student may pause the test, if necessary, by clicking the *Pause* button.

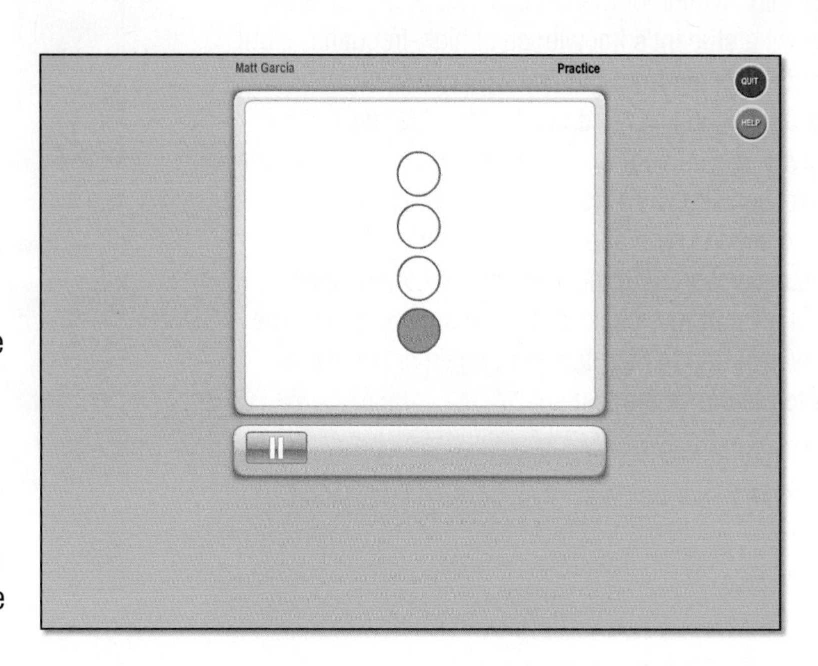

The student's performance on this task is used to ensure that his or her cognitive and/or motor skills do not interfere with the efficacy of the test and to introduce him or her to the test interface.

Letter Recognition

The second section of the SPI consists of 11 items that survey the student's ability to recognize letter names. The student hears a letter name and must click on the corresponding letter from a list of four choices. The test includes lowercase letters as target items and distractors. The student may click the *Replay* button to hear the letter name again. The student may pause the test by clicking the *Pause* button.

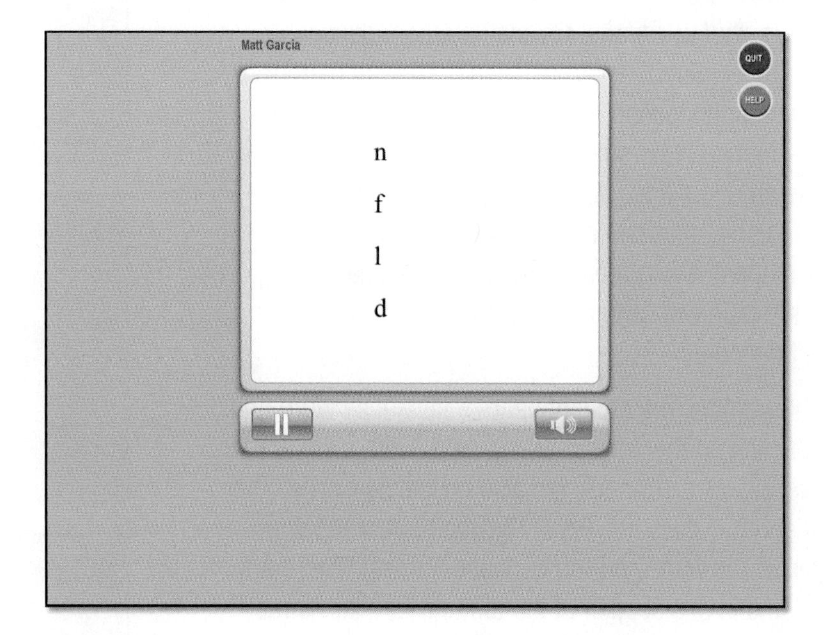

The student's performance on this task is used to measure his or her alphabet recognition skills.

Sight Word Recognition

The third section of the SPI consists of 30 items that assess a student's knowledge of high-frequency sight words selected from the first 300 words on the Dolch and Fry Word Lists. In the first type of activity, the student hears a word and must select the corresponding word from a list of four choices. In the second type of activity, the student hears a high-frequency word and must select the correct spelling from a list of four choices. The student may click the *Replay* button to hear the word again or the *Pause* button to pause the test.

The student's performance on this task is used to measure his or her level of sight word knowledge.

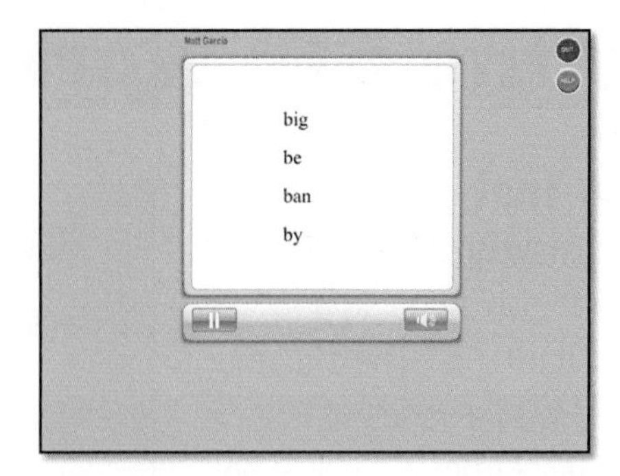

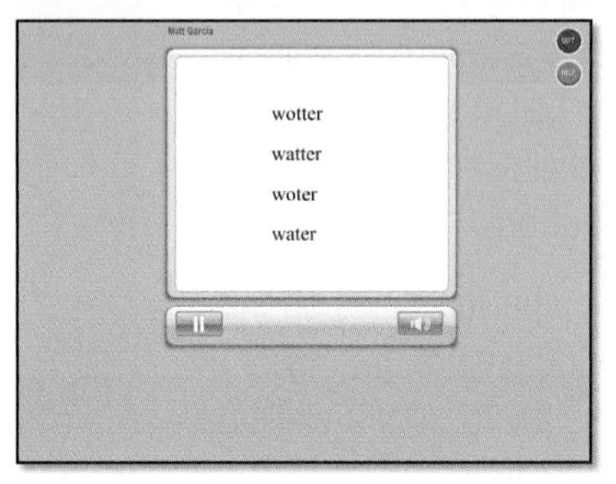

Nonsense Word Decoding

This final section of the SPI assesses the student's decoding ability using nonsense words: nonwords that follow the conventions of the English language (e.g., *jit, thut, wob*), thereby making them decodable while preventing them from being read from memory. The use of nonsense words is particularly important when testing older struggling readers as many of these students have developed extensive sight word vocabularies that can mask decoding deficiencies. The student may appear to be a fluent reader, but still struggle with unfamiliar words that he or she can't decode.

In this section, the student hears a nonsense word and must click on the corresponding word from a list of four choices—all distractors are also nonsense words. The student may click the *Replay* button to hear the word again or the *Pause* button to pause the test. There are 30 items in this section of the test, divided into three subtests of progressive difficulty.

The student's performance on this task is used to measure his or her ability to decode in a decontextualized setting.

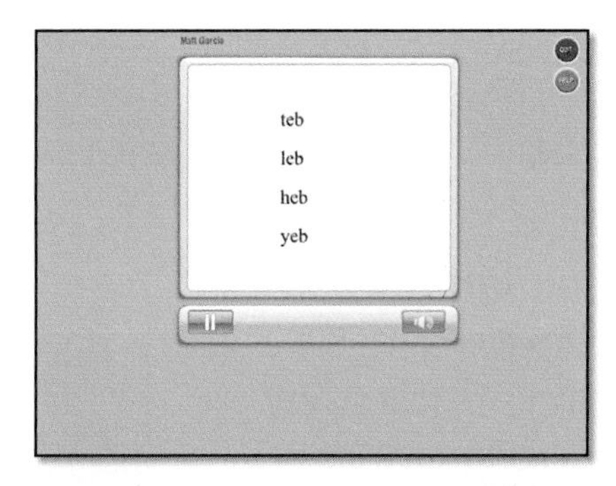

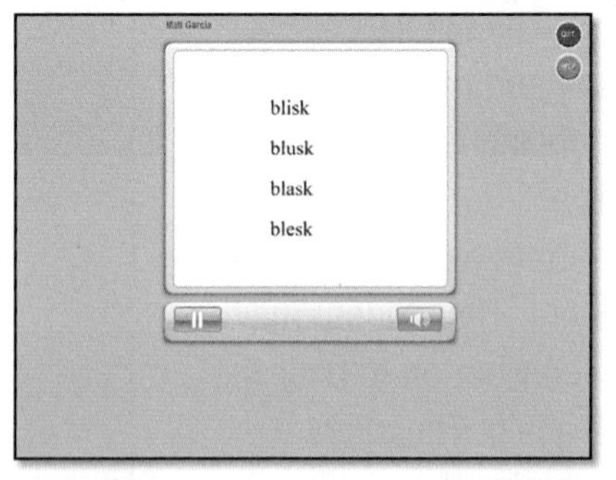

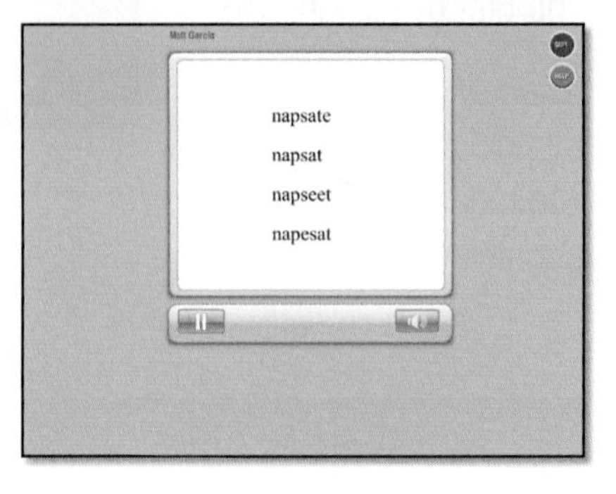

The Research Behind the SPI

Overview

The SPI was developed under the guidance of Dr. Marilyn Jager Adams, a leader in the field of reading research and instruction, and Dr. Ted Hasselbring of Vanderbilt University, a pioneer in the use of technology in education.

Dr. Richard K. Wagner of the Florida Center for Reading Research devised the scoring algorithm and evaluated the reliability and validity of SPI. Dr. Wagner's work is based on analyses conducted with 192 ninth graders in the Southwest, 217 fifth, seventh, and ninth graders in the Southeast, and 182 seventh and eighth graders in the Northeast.

Scoring

SPI measures both the accuracy and fluency of student responses. A response is scored as "accurate" if the student selects the correct answer; it is scored as "fluent" if the student selects the correct answer within the established time limit for the item, known as the fluency threshold.

Fluency thresholds were determined empirically for each item by analyzing the response times of students known to differ in levels of decoding and word recognition. The thresholds were set to optimize differentiation between students with weaknesses in decoding and word recognition and those with adequate decoding and word recognition skills.

Reliability

Reliability refers to the degree to which an assessment produces consistent scores. Two types of reliability were measured for SPI.

Internal consistency reliability refers to the degree to which all items in a test measure the same thing. Internal consistency reliability coefficients for the three forms of SPI range from .85 to .86, the highest possible value being 1.0.

Alternate-form reliability refers to the consistency of scores produced by different test forms. Alternate-form immediate reliability coefficients for SPI range from .78 to .86. The magnitude of these results supports both the internal consistency of SPI and the equivalence of the three test forms.

Validity

Validity refers to whether an assessment measures what it claims to measure. Several types of validity are relevant to SPI.

- **Content Validity:** Does the test content represent the scope of knowledge or skills being measured?
- **Construct Validity:** Does the test measure the theoretical construct it is supposed to measure?
- **Criterion-Related Validity:** Does the test predict the behavior or performance it is intended to predict?

Content Validity

SPI assesses three foundational reading skills. The items in each test form represent the scope of these skills.

- **Letter Recognition:** All 26 letters of the alphabet are represented, either as targets (correct answers) or distractors (incorrect answer choices). Only lowercase letters are used, as they are generally considered more challenging than uppercase letters and more appropriate for assessing older readers.
- **Sight Word Reading:** In some items, the targets come from the first 300 words on the Dolch and Fry Word Lists and the distractors are common words that look similar to the target. In other items, the targets come from the first 5,000 words in the *American Heritage Word Frequency Book*—a comprehensive list of words found in grade school texts—and the distractors are misspellings of the target.
- **Decoding:** All answer choices are nonwords that follow the conventions of English. The items represent the breadth of spelling patterns taught in most phonics programs and align to the *System 44* scope and sequence. Targets and distractors work together to assess individual sound-spellings and require students to attend to differences among spelling patterns. The items were carefully generated to avoid proper nouns, Spanish words, nonwords that sound like real words, and items that may be difficult for speakers of certain dialects, including African-American Vernacular English, to distinguish phonologically.

Throughout the development process, all items were reviewed by an esteemed group of reading and assessment experts, and replacements were made as necessary to ensure content validity.

Construct Validity

SPI was examined for construct validity by evaluating whether the test effectively distinguishes between students who are known to differ in levels of decoding and word recognition.

To accomplish this, Dr. Wagner compared differences in SPI performance to differences in performance on comparable measures—the Sight Word Efficiency and Phonetic Decoding Efficiency subtests of the *Test of Word Reading Efficiency* (TOWRE) and the Letter-Word Identification and Word Attack subtests of the *Woodcock-Johnson III Tests of Achievement*—for a group of students identified as poor decoders and a group of students identified as adequate decoders.

The two groups of students were found to differ substantially and significantly on all three forms of SPI. Moreover, the magnitude of these differences exceeded those of both the TOWRE and the Woodcock-Johnson.

Criterion-Related Validity

To examine the criterion-related validity of SPI, students' SPI fluency scores were correlated to their scores on the TOWRE and the Woodcock-Johnson. Correlations ranged from .50, which is acceptable, to .85, indicating that SPI is as effective as comparable measures at determining a student's level of decoding and word reading proficiency.

For additional information about SPI research, see the *Scholastic Phonics Inventory Technical Guide*, available online at **www.scholastic.com/spi/productsupport**.

Test Accommodations

SPI offers accuracy-only scoring for students who are unable to manipulate a mouse efficiently due to motor impairments, attention difficulties, or other issues. Teachers can enable this feature for individual students in the Scholastic Achievement Manager (SAM). For instructions, see *SAM Settings and Reports for Scholastic Phonics Inventory*, available online at **www.scholastic.com/spi/productsupport**.

About Accuracy-Only Scoring

SPI measures both the accuracy and fluency, or speed, of student responses. This facilitates identification of students who lack decoding and word recognition skills, as well as those who possess certain skills but cannot apply them efficiently enough to support comprehension. Students must respond correctly within a given time limit to earn credit for each item.

Students who are unable to manipulate a mouse efficiently due to motor impairments or other issues require special administration of the test so that response time does not adversely affect their scores. You may activate accuracy-only scoring to allow a student's score to be based only on the accuracy of his or her responses. The number and types of test items remain the same. Depending on how difficult it is for the student to move a mouse, you may choose to have an assistant do this for him or her.

The decision to use accuracy-only scoring should be made by the student's teacher or someone who is knowledgeable of the student's ability to manipulate a mouse. **Note that scores based on accuracy alone are not as predictive as those based on accuracy *and* fluency. Enable this feature only when a student is unable to manipulate a mouse efficiently.**

For details about the reliability and validity of accuracy-based scores, see the *Scholastic Phonics Inventory Technical Guide*, available online at **www.scholastic.com/spi/productsupport**.

How SPI Results Are Reported

Individual student results on the SPI are reported through SAM in the Screening and Placement Report. The report indicates the appropriate entry level for decoding instruction for each student.

Screening and Placement Report

CLASS: PERIOD 2

SPI SCHOLASTIC PHONICS INVENTORY

School: Cesar Chavez Middle School
Teacher: Mercedes Cole
Grade: 7

Time Period: 08/24/11 – 02/02/12

STUDENT	DATE OF SPI PLACEMENT TEST	% ACCURATE AND FLUENT ON SPI SUBTESTS: LETTER NAMES ACCURACY	SIGHT WORDS ACCURACY	SIGHT WORDS FLUENCY	NONSENSE WORDS ACCURACY	NONSENSE WORDS FLUENCY	SPI FLUENCY SCORE	SPI DECODING STATUS	SRI SCORE (LEXILE®)
Anderson, Darrell	09/04/11	100%	80%	13%	60%	17%	9	Beginning Decoder	BR
Benson, Kate	09/07/11	100%	90%	40%	77%	27%	20	Developing Decoder	350
Donato, Aimee	09/04/11	100%	80%	37%	70%	13%	15	Developing Decoder	220
Gonzalez, Lydia	09/04/11	55%	10%	N/A	7%	N/A	5*	Pre-Decoder	BR
Huang, Hsin-Yi	09/04/11	100%	80%	13%	80%	17%	9	Beginning Decoder	150
Lee, Andrea	09/08/11	100%	97%	80%	90%	77%	47	Advancing Decoder	450
Mamdani, Aliyah	09/07/11	100%	70%	13%	80%	43%	17	Developing Decoder	280
Molina, Robert	09/04/11	100%	83%	37%	83%	23%	18	Developing Decoder	330
Price, Jamal	09/07/11	100%	63%	27%	57%	20%	14	Developing Decoder	250
Rubio, Alejandro	09/04/11	100%	90%	33%	80%	37%	21	Developing Decoder	300
Sanders, Renee	09/22/11	91%	63%	13%	53%	13%	8	Beginning Decoder	BR
Turner, Aiden	09/10/11	73%	20%	7%	10%	3%	3	Pre-Decoder	BR
Young, Kevin	09/04/11	100%	80%	17%	67%	17%	10	Beginning Decoder	200

SPI FLUENCY SCORE	DECODING STATUS	RECOMMENDED INSTRUCTION AND PLACEMENT
0–10	Pre-Decoder	Phonemic awareness, letter names, letter-sound correspondence
0–10	Beginning Decoder	Foundational Phonics
11–22	Developing Decoder	Targeted phonics remediation
23–60	Advancing Decoder	Vocabulary, comprehension, fluency

* Student received accommodations during this test administration.

Using This Report

Purpose: This report details the performance of a class or group of students on the SPI placement test.

Follow-Up: Use SPI results and other evaluation data to place each student into an appropriate intervention. If you are using Scholastic programs, Pre- and Beginning Decoders are recommended for Series 1 of *System 44*, Developing Decoders are recommended for Series 4 of *System 44*, and Advancing Decoders are recommended for *READ 180*.

% Accurate and Fluent on SPI Subtests reports a student's performance on each of the five subtests. Students are expected to be both accurate and fluent to be considered proficient in a skill.

SRI Score (Lexile) reports the student's most recent score on the *Scholastic Reading Inventory*.

Decoding Status identifies a student as a Pre-, Beginning, Developing, or Advancing Decoder.

Placement recommendations suggest whether students should start with Series 1 or 4 of *System 44* or place into *READ 180*.

Criteria for SPI Decoding Statuses

SPI is a criterion-referenced test. Criterion-referenced results indicate student performance in relation to an established set of skills.

SPI reports describe students' foundational reading skills in terms of four levels of Decoding Status. Results are based on the accuracy of student responses in the Letter Names subtest, and both the accuracy and fluency (i.e., speed) of student responses in the Sight Words and Nonsense Words subtests. To receive credit for a fluent response, students must select the correct answer within a given time limit. Response time cutoffs differ by item, based on research conducted with students known to differ in levels of decoding and word recognition. For details of the study, see the *Scholastic Phonics Inventory Technical Guide*, available online at **www.scholastic.com/spi/productsupport**.

The chart below details the criteria used to establish each Decoding Status for both the fluency- and accuracy-based versions of the test. **Note that scores based on accuracy alone are not as predictive as those based on accuracy and fluency and should only be used when students require test accommodations because they are unable to manipulate a mouse efficiently.**

Decoding Status	Description	General Criteria	Criteria for Accuracy-Only Scoring
Pre-Decoder	A student with little or no knowledge of letter names or letter-sound correspondences.	• SPI Fluency Score: 0–10 • Letter Names: less than 70% accuracy • Nonsense Words: less than 50% accuracy on items that assess consonants and short vowels	• Accuracy Score: 0–45 • Letter Names: less than 70% accuracy • Nonsense Words: less than 50% accuracy on items that assess consonants and short vowels
Beginning Decoder	A student who can identify letter names but cannot decode fluently.	• SPI Fluency Score: 0–10 • Letter Names: at least 70% accuracy • Nonsense Words: at least 50% accuracy on items that assess consonants and short vowels	• Accuracy Score: 0–45 • Letter Names: at least 70% accuracy • Nonsense Words: at least 50% accuracy on items that assess consonants and short vowels
Developing Decoder	A student who can fluently decode words with consonants and short vowels but cannot fluently decode more complex words.	• SPI Fluency Score: 11–22	• Accuracy Score: 46–49
Advancing Decoder	A student who can decode with adequate fluency.	• SPI Fluency Score: 23–60	• Accuracy Score: 50–60

Note: The above criteria are based on data collected to date and may be updated based on future research.

Multiple Points of Entry

The software allows for multiple and customized points of entry into *System 44* instruction. Instruction in the *System 44* software is divided into 25 Series. Each Series is made up of 5–8 Topics, or lessons. (For a complete listing of Series and Topics, see the Summary of *System 44* Topics in *Resources for Differentiated Instruction*, p. 556.)

- **Series 1:** Students who need the full scope of phonics instruction begin with the first software Series.
- **Series 4:** Students who have demonstrated mastery of consonants and short vowels may begin with Series 4.
- **Fast-Tracks:** Students who are placed in Series 4 take one or more Fast-Track assessments to determine an individualized point of entry based on demonstrated proficiency.

Diagnostic Placement

Students take a series of brief skill-checks known as Fast-Tracks at the beginning of each of the 25 Series of instruction excluding 1–3, 24, and 25. These embedded software assessments are similar in structure to the SPI, but are targeted to the specific phonics skills within a Series of software instruction. Fast-Tracks are designed to identify decoding strengths and weaknesses through the use of both nonsense and real word items. Students who demonstrate proficiency in a Topic Fast-Track through it, only spending time on the Topics that require further instruction. This allows ongoing differentiated placement for each student. Students cannot Fast-Track Topics in the Sight Words or Success strands.

SPI Decoding Status determines recommended placement. Pre- and Beginning Decoders start with Series 1. Developing Decoders start with Series 4. Advancing Decoders place into *READ 180*.

SPI FLUENCY SCORE	SPI DECODING STATUS	SRI SCORE (LEXILE®)
9	Beginning Decoder	BR
20	Developing Decoder	350
15	Developing Decoder	220
5*	Pre-Decoder	BR
9	Beginning Decoder	150
47	Advancing Decoder	450
17	Developing Decoder	280

Screening and Placement Report (detail)

Differentiating Instruction in *System 44*

System 44 supports differentiated instruction that targets individual student needs in all rotations. Software results are used to group students, select books, and adjust instruction to support varying student needs.

Differentiating Instruction With Instructional Software

System 44 software gives students intensive, individualized instruction and skills practice. As students work independently on the computer, the software automatically and continuously collects student performance data. Two entry points and Fast-Track assessments tailor instruction to student needs for personalized learning. The Student Dashboard allows students to track their overall progress and build executive function skills.

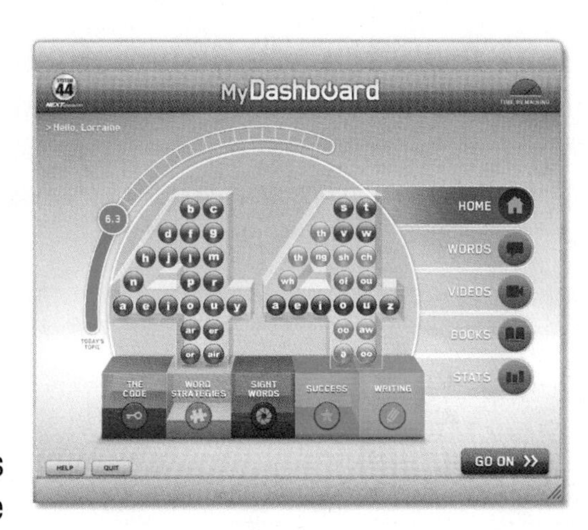

Differentiating Instruction With Modeled and Independent Reading

SRI results help match readers with appropriate texts for Modeled and Independent Reading. The *System 44* Library includes a range of high-interest, age-appropriate Paperbacks, Audiobooks, and eBooks. Each title targets decoding skills and strategies to promote comprehension while building vocabulary and content-area knowledge.

Tailor Modeled and Independent Reading to meet individual student needs by assisting students in selecting books at their reading level and interest. Then, vary the level of scaffolding and support you provide based on the text complexity. For example, provide more opportunities for book conferences and completion of written scaffolding such as QuickWrites and Graphic Organizers when students are reading more complex texts.

Differentiating Small-Group Instruction

Effective differentiated instruction is based on student performance results. *System 44* provides support and scaffolding for dynamic and flexible grouping to allow for differentiated instruction within each *44Book* Module.

44Book Grouping and Differentiating

Use the Module Planning Guide in the *44Book Teacher's Edition* to determine when to regroup students throughout a Module. Use the Teacher Dashboard to access student grouping recommendations based on performance results and review targeted instruction recommendations to address student needs.

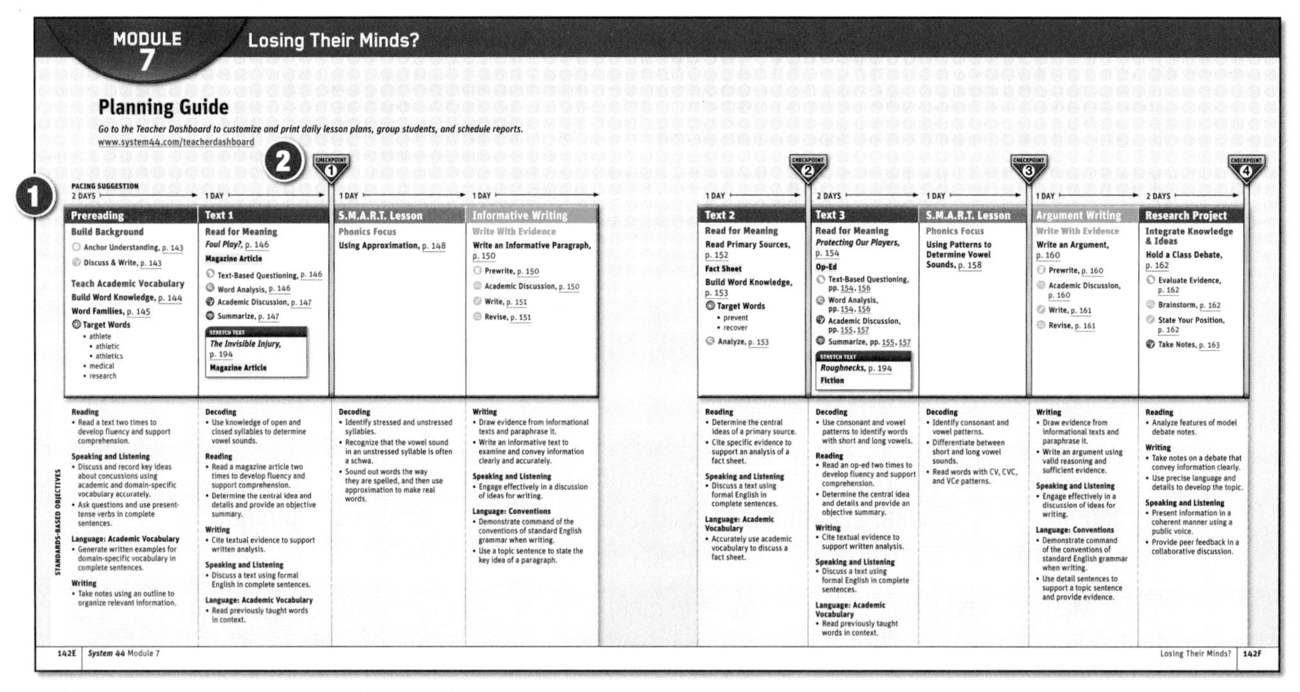

MODULE 7 Losing Their Minds?

Planning Guide

Go to the Teacher Dashboard to customize and print daily lesson plans, group students, and schedule reports.
www.system44.com/teacherdashboard

PACING SUGGESTION	2 DAYS	1 DAY	CHECKPOINT 1 — 1 DAY	1 DAY	1 DAY	CHECKPOINT 2 — 2 DAYS	1 DAY	CHECKPOINT 3 — 1 DAY	2 DAYS — CHECKPOINT 4
	Prereading	**Text 1**	**S.M.A.R.T. Lesson**	**Informative Writing**	**Text 2**	**Text 3**	**S.M.A.R.T. Lesson**	**Argument Writing**	**Research Project**
	Build Background Anchor Understanding, p. 143 Discuss & Write, p. 143 **Teach Academic Vocabulary** **Build Word Knowledge,** p. 144 **Word Families,** p. 145 **Target Words** • athlete • athletic • athletics • medical • research	**Read for Meaning** ***Foul Play?,*** p. 146 **Magazine Article** Text-Based Questioning, p. 146 Word Analysis, p. 146 Academic Discussion, p. 147 Summarize, p. 147 STRETCH TEXT ***The Invisible Injury,*** p. 194 **Magazine Article**	**Phonics Focus** **Using Approximation,** p. 148	**Write With Evidence** **Write an Informative Paragraph,** p. 150 Prewrite, p. 150 Academic Discussion, p. 150 Write, p. 151 Revise, p. 151	**Read for Meaning** **Read Primary Sources,** p. 152 **Fact Sheet** **Build Word Knowledge,** p. 153 **Target Words** • prevent • recover Analyze, p. 153	**Read for Meaning** ***Protecting Our Players,*** p. 154 **Op-Ed** Text-Based Questioning, pp. 154, 156 Word Analysis, pp. 154, 156 Academic Discussion, pp. 155, 157 Summarize, pp. 155, 157 STRETCH TEXT ***Roughnecks,*** p. 194 **Fiction**	**Phonics Focus** **Using Patterns to Determine Vowel Sounds,** p. 158	**Write With Evidence** **Write an Argument,** p. 160 Prewrite, p. 160 Academic Discussion, p. 160 Write, p. 161 Revise, p. 161	**Integrate Knowledge & Ideas** **Hold a Class Debate,** p. 162 Evaluate Evidence, p. 162 Brainstorm, p. 162 State Your Position, p. 162 Take Notes, p. 163
STANDARDS-BASED OBJECTIVES	**Reading** • Read a text two times to develop fluency and support comprehension. **Speaking and Listening** • Discuss and record key ideas about concussions using academic and domain-specific vocabulary accurately. • Ask questions and use present-tense verbs in complete sentences. **Language: Academic Vocabulary** • Generate written examples for domain-specific vocabulary in complete sentences. **Writing** • Take notes using an outline to organize relevant information.	**Decoding** • Use knowledge of open and closed syllables to determine vowel sounds. **Reading** • Read a magazine article two times to develop fluency and support comprehension. • Determine the central idea and details and provide an objective summary. **Writing** • Cite textual evidence to support written analysis. **Speaking and Listening** • Discuss a text using formal English in complete sentences. **Language: Academic Vocabulary** • Read previously taught words in context.	**Decoding** • Identify stressed and unstressed syllables. • Recognize that the vowel sound in an unstressed syllable is often a schwa. • Sound out words the way they are spelled, and then use approximation to make real words.	**Writing** • Draw evidence from informational texts and paraphrase it. • Write an informative text to examine and convey information clearly and accurately. **Speaking and Listening** • Engage effectively in a discussion of ideas for writing. **Language: Conventions** • Demonstrate command of the conventions of standard English grammar when writing. • Use a topic sentence to state the key idea of a paragraph.	**Reading** • Determine the central ideas of a primary source. • Cite specific evidence to support an analysis of a fact sheet. **Speaking and Listening** • Discuss a text using formal English in complete sentences. **Language: Academic Vocabulary** • Accurately use academic vocabulary to discuss a fact sheet.	**Decoding** • Use consonant and vowel patterns to identify words with short and long vowels. **Reading** • Read an op-ed two times to develop fluency and support comprehension. • Determine the central idea and details and provide an objective summary. **Writing** • Cite textual evidence to support written analysis. **Speaking and Listening** • Discuss a text using formal English in complete sentences. **Language: Academic Vocabulary** • Read previously taught words in context.	**Decoding** • Identify consonant and vowel patterns. • Differentiate between short and long vowel sounds. • Read words with CV, CVC, and VC*e* patterns.	**Writing** • Draw evidence from informational texts and paraphrase it. • Write an argument using valid reasoning and sufficient evidence. **Speaking and Listening** • Engage effectively in a discussion of ideas for writing. **Language: Conventions** • Demonstrate command of the conventions of standard English grammar when writing. • Use detail sentences to support a topic sentence and provide evidence.	**Reading** • Analyze features of model debate notes. **Writing** • Take notes on a debate that convey information clearly. • Use precise language and details to develop the topic. **Speaking and Listening** • Present information in a coherent manner using a public voice. • Provide peer feedback in a collaborative discussion.

142E *System 44* Module 7 | Losing Their Minds? 142F

***44Book Teacher's Edition*: Sample Planning Guide**

① *44Book* Groups

Throughout each *44Book* Module, group students based on decoding level. Provide differentiated instruction by adjusting the amount of scaffolding provided for *44Book* activities.

② CheckPoint Groups

Two days each week, regroup students based on software performance. While half of each group reads independently, target Small-Group Instruction with the other half. Stretch students with more rigorous texts or reteach phonics skills using *Resources for Differentiated Instruction*. On the next day, switch students.

Differentiating With *System 44* and *READ 180*

System 44 integrates seamlessly into *READ 180* Next Generation classrooms. If you're using this model, follow the Workshop Planning Guides in the *rBook Teacher's Edition*. The Groupinator will form *rBook* groups based on reading level and Reading CheckPoint groups based on students' performance in either *READ 180* or *System 44* software. See *READ 180 Placement, Assessment, and Reporting Guide* pages 38–51 for more information.

Navigating the Teacher Dashboard Class Page

The Teacher Dashboard streamlines and simplifies the process of differentiating instruction during Small-Group Instruction. At various points within each Module, the Groupinator creates two dynamic groups based on student performance data and provides recommendations for strategic instruction tailored to address identified student needs.

Detailed information for each class is available on the Class Page of the Teacher Dashboard. Click the **Go to Class** button on the Home Page to navigate to a Class Page.

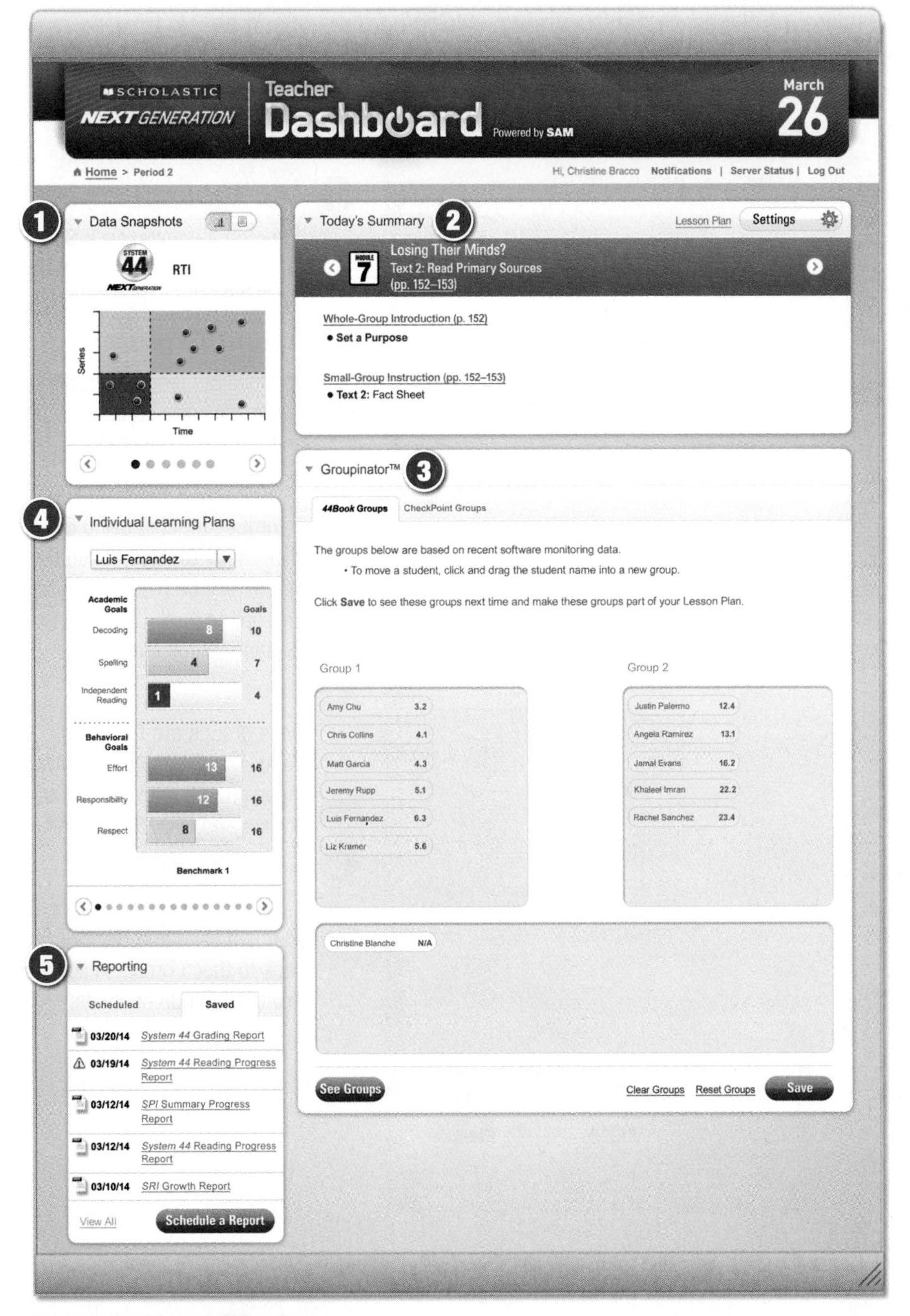

Teacher Dashboard: Class Page

1 Data Snapshots

At-a-glance views of class performance help drive instructional planning and pacing. Use the arrows to see data from each software component.

2 Today's Summary

Summaries of the day's Whole-Group Introduction and Small-Group Instruction link directly to the Interactive Teaching System. Click the left or right arrows to advance though the Module.

3 The Groupinator

Dynamic and flexible groups are created throughout a *44Book* Module, including *44Book* groups and CheckPoint groups. Review and adjust groups and link directly to accompanying lessons on the Interactive Teaching System.

4 Individual Learning Plans

Snapshots for individual students track performance toward academic and behavioral goals. Set goals in the SAM Student Digital Portfolio. Use the arrows to see data for each student.

5 Schedule Reports

Schedule the Dashboard to run SAM reports.

Grouping for *44Book* Instruction

The *44Book* provides comprehensive daily reading, vocabulary, and writing instruction. During each *44Book* lesson, students are placed into two distinct groups for Small-Group Instruction. These groups are based on decoding ability, which allows for targeted instruction to address specific areas of need.

Using the Groupinator to Manage Groups

The Groupinator on the Teacher Dashboard places students into two *44Book* groups based on SPI results. Two equal groups are organized by fluency score. Review *44Book* groups on the Class Page of the Teacher Dashboard.

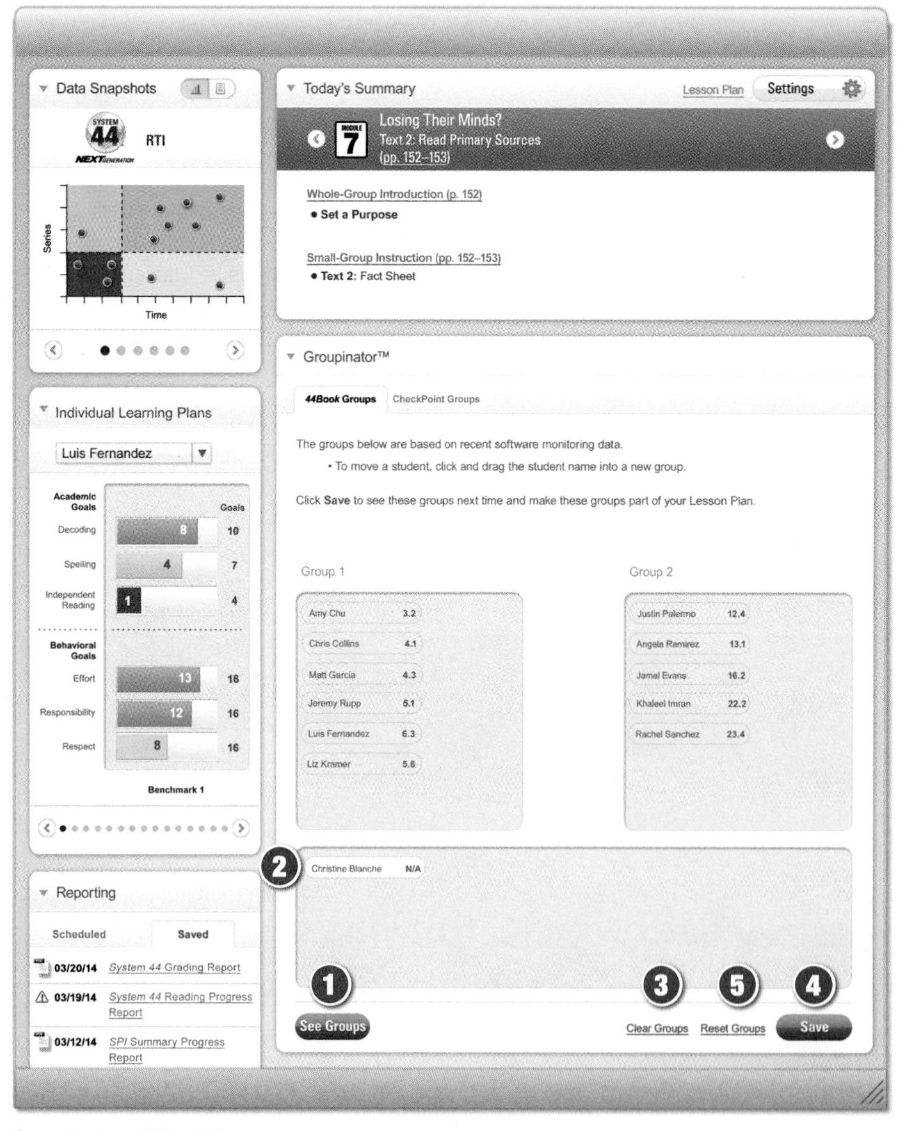

Groupinator: *44Book* Groups

1 See Groups

To group students, click **See Groups**. Refresh grouping recommendations by clicking **See Groups** again.

2 Adjust Groups

To move students into a different group, click the student's name and drag to a new group.

3 Clear Groups

To group students using other data, click **Clear Groups**. All student names will be placed into the ungrouped pool. Click and drag student names into groups.

4 Save

Once groups are final, Click **Save**. The Groupinator will retain these groups until you adjust groups and click **Save** again.

5 Reset Groups

If you have modified groups since your last save and want to revert back to those groups, click **Reset Groups** to undo changes.

Using Data to Adjust Groups

As students complete additional SPI tests, use the Groupinator to regroup students based on students' current reading levels. Click **See Groups** to automatically regroup students based on the most recent SPI results.

You may also choose to incorporate other student data into your grouping decisions. Data from the following reports may help inform grouping decisions:

- SPI Summary Progress Report (See page 82.)
- *System 44* Reading Progress Report (See page 88.)
- *System 44* Response to Intervention Report (See page 92.)

Providing Appropriate Small-Group Instructional Support

Each *44Book* lesson includes opportunities to provide varied supports to meet the needs of a variety of learners. For example, each Module includes two Stretch texts that provide access to complex, grade-level text. Use Modeled Fluent Reading to prepare all students to discuss the text. Have more advanced students reread the text with Partner Cloze and produce written responses.

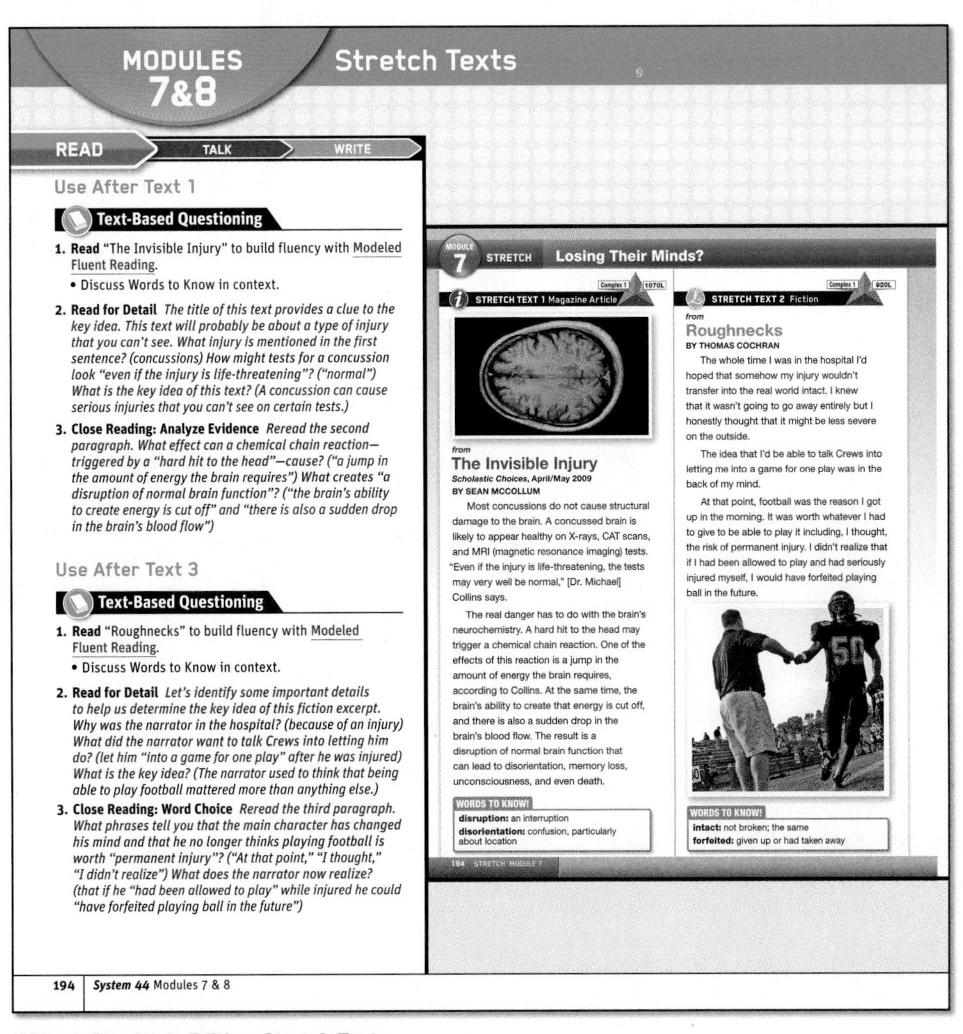

MODULES 7&8 Stretch Texts

READ TALK WRITE

Use After Text 1

Text-Based Questioning

1. **Read** "The Invisible Injury" to build fluency with Modeled Fluent Reading.
   - Discuss Words to Know in context.
2. **Read for Detail** *The title of this text provides a clue to the key idea. This text will probably be about a type of injury that you can't see. What injury is mentioned in the first sentence? (concussions) How might tests for a concussion look "even if the injury is life-threatening"? ("normal") What is the key idea of this text? (A concussion can cause serious injuries that you can't see on certain tests.)*
3. **Close Reading: Analyze Evidence** *Reread the second paragraph. What effect can a chemical chain reaction—triggered by a "hard hit to the head"—cause? ("a jump in the amount of energy the brain requires") What creates "a disruption of normal brain function"? ("the brain's ability to create energy is cut off" and "there is also a sudden drop in the brain's blood flow")*

Use After Text 3

Text-Based Questioning

1. **Read** "Roughnecks" to build fluency with Modeled Fluent Reading.
   - Discuss Words to Know in context.
2. **Read for Detail** *Let's identify some important details to help us determine the key idea of this fiction excerpt. Why was the narrator in the hospital? (because of an injury) What did the narrator want to talk Crews into letting him do? (let him "into a game for one play" after he was injured) What is the key idea? (The narrator used to think that being able to play football mattered more than anything else.)*
3. **Close Reading: Word Choice** *Reread the third paragraph. What phrases tell you that the main character has changed his mind and that he no longer thinks playing football is worth "permanent injury"? ("At that point," "I thought," "I didn't realize") What does the narrator now realize? (that if he "had been allowed to play" while injured he could "have forfeited playing ball in the future")*

MODULE 7 STRETCH **Losing Their Minds?**

STRETCH TEXT 1 Magazine Article — Complex 1 — 1070L

from
The Invisible Injury
Scholastic Choices, April/May 2009
BY SEAN MCCOLLUM

Most concussions do not cause structural damage to the brain. A concussed brain is likely to appear healthy on X-rays, CAT scans, and MRI (magnetic resonance imaging) tests. "Even if the injury is life-threatening, the tests may very well be normal," [Dr. Michael] Collins says.

The real danger has to do with the brain's neurochemistry. A hard hit to the head may trigger a chemical chain reaction. One of the effects of this reaction is a jump in the amount of energy the brain requires, according to Collins. At the same time, the brain's ability to create that energy is cut off, and there is also a sudden drop in the brain's blood flow. The result is a disruption of normal brain function that can lead to disorientation, memory loss, unconsciousness, and even death.

WORDS TO KNOW!
disruption: an interruption
disorientation: confusion, particularly about location

STRETCH TEXT 2 Fiction — Complex 1 — 920L

from
Roughnecks
BY THOMAS COCHRAN

The whole time I was in the hospital I'd hoped that somehow my injury wouldn't transfer into the real world intact. I knew that it wasn't going to go away entirely but I honestly thought that it might be less severe on the outside.

The idea that I'd be able to talk Crews into letting me into a game for one play was in the back of my mind.

At that point, football was the reason I got up in the morning. It was worth whatever I had to give to be able to play it including, I thought, the risk of permanent injury. I didn't realize that if I had been allowed to play and had seriously injured myself, I would have forfeited playing ball in the future.

WORDS TO KNOW!
intact: not broken; the same
forfeited: given up or had taken away

194 STRETCH MODULE 7

194 | *System 44* Modules 7 & 8

***44Book Teacher's Edition*: Stretch Texts**

Grouping at CheckPoints

Each *44Book* Module includes four CheckPoints in which teachers take time to regroup students for targeted differentiated instruction. The first CheckPoint of each Module appears after Text 1.

Understanding CheckPoint Groups

At each CheckPoint, the Groupinator on the Teacher Dashboard places students into two equal groups based on results from the *System 44* software. Each of the two groups is also divided into A and B groups. Students are grouped based on common areas of need, and each group is assigned a reading skill focus or independent reading.

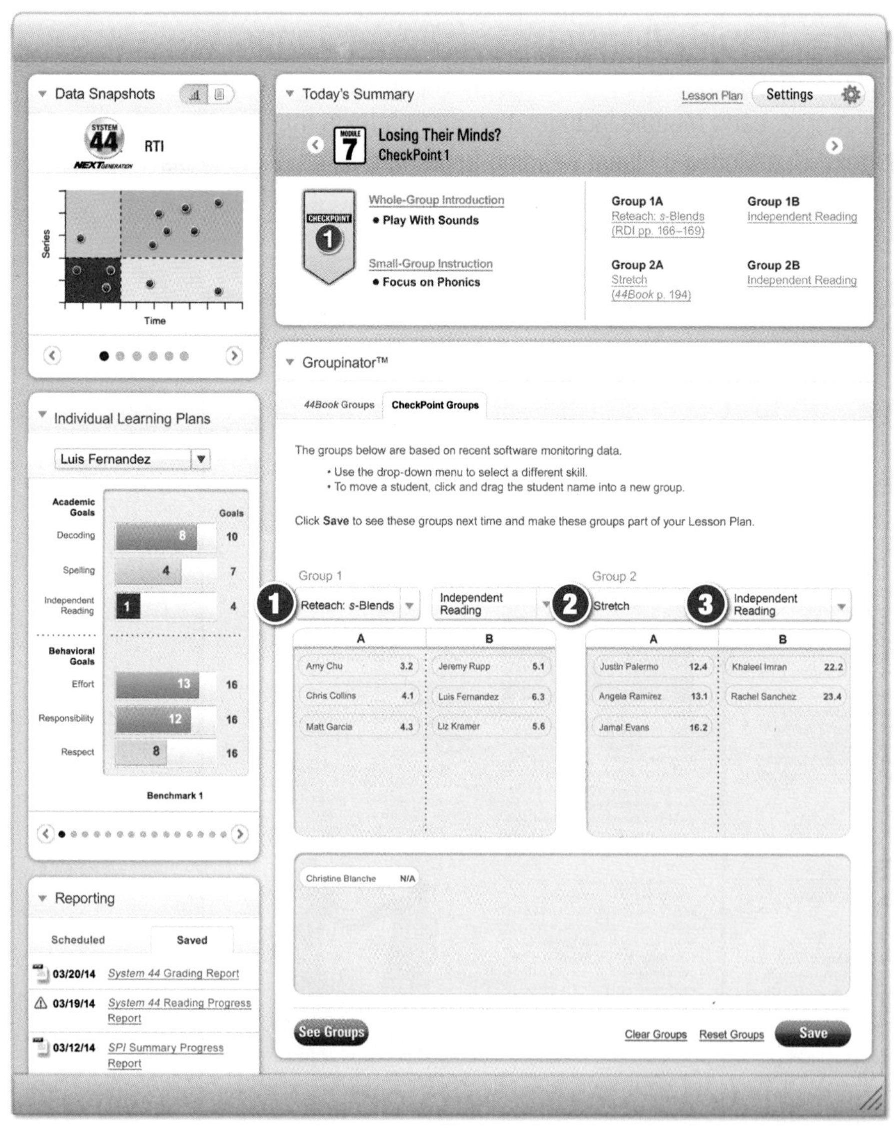

Teacher Dashboard: CheckPoint Groups

1 Reteach Groups

Students whose software results indicate they need additional support will be placed into a **Reteach** group. Use a Code, Word Strategies, or S.M.A.R.T. lesson from *Resources for Differentiated Instruction* to reteach or reinforce a phonics skill.

2 Stretch Groups

Students with strong scores on their most recent Progress Monitors may be placed into a **Stretch** group. Students in a Stretch group are assigned a more rigorous text with more independent practice. You may also provide more independent reading time for Stretch groups.

3 Independent Groups

While you are working with half of the students in each group, the other half should read independently. On the second day of the CheckPoint, you will work with this group while the other half reads independently.

The Groupinator Algorithm

The Groupinator's algorithm creates CheckPoint groups. The algorithm factors a student's current place in the Scope and Sequence and decoding skill performance to determine placement within a Stretch or Reteach group. Once each group type has been determined, a skill focus is assigned to each group. The number of Stretch or Reteach groups in each class will vary based on students' current software performance.

Using the Groupinator to Manage CheckPoint Groups

The Groupinator on the Teacher Dashboard places students into two equal CheckPoint groups based on software results. Each day of the CheckPoint, it targets a specific skill for half of the group and assigns independent reading to the other half. Review groups on the Class Page of the Teacher Dashboard.

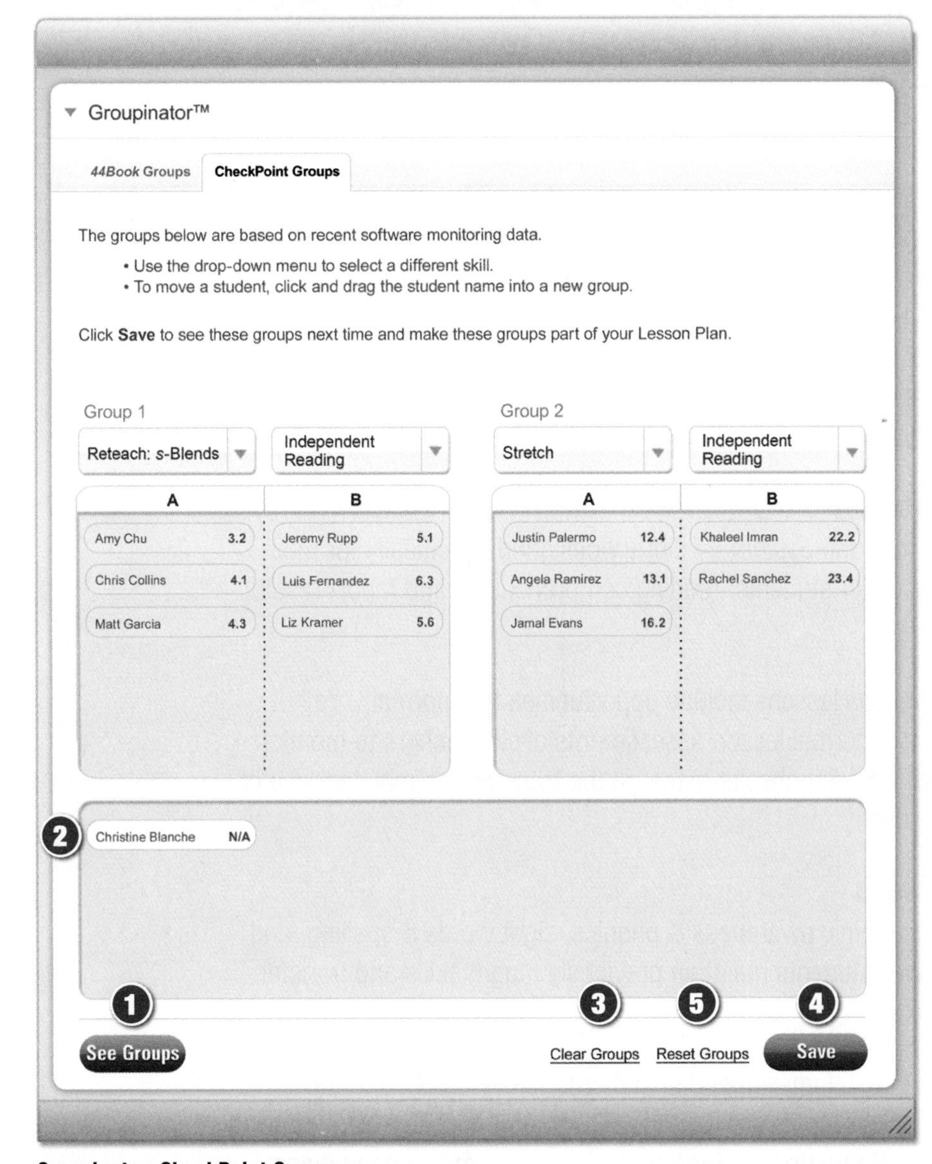

Groupinator: CheckPoint Groups

1 See Groups

To group students, click **See Groups**. Refresh grouping recommendations by clicking **See Groups** again.

2 Adjust Groups

To move students into a different group, click the student's name and drag to a new group.

3 Clear Groups

To group students using other data, click **Clear Groups**. All student names will be placed into the ungrouped pool. Click and drag student names into groups.

4 Save

Once groups are final, Click **Save**. The Groupinator will retain these groups until you adjust groups and click **Save** again.

5 Reset Groups

If you have modified groups since your last save and want to revert back to those groups, click **Reset Groups** to undo changes.

Progress Monitoring

The *System 44* software continuously collects individual student performance data. Results are used to inform both software and teacher-directed instruction. The program provides six types of progress monitoring:

Scholastic Phonics Inventory

Students take this assessment three times per year to measure baseline proficiency and monitor their progress in decoding and word recognition skills. SAM reports show results in subtest areas, overall SPI Fluency Score, and SPI Decoding Status.

Software Performance

Interactive software instruction, practice, and assessment gather data on students' accuracy and fluency with specific decoding, sight word, and word strategy skills. Results are presented in SAM reports for teacher, family, and administrator review.

Oral Reading Fluency

Students read and record instructional level passages on the software. The text in each passage targets recently taught phonics skills and academic vocabulary. Using the SAM Student Digital Portfolio, teachers can listen to and evaluate students' oral reading fluency, which is reported in the Reading Progress Report and the Student Software Performance Report (see pp. 88–89 and 96–97). In addition, see pp. 164–165 in this guide for information on administering print-based Oral Fluency Assessments (OFAs) with grade-level passages appropriate for *System 44* students.

Scholastic Reading Counts!

Students read motivating books from the *System 44* Library designed specifically for their reading level. Software quizzes monitor students' reading comprehension and report results.

Informal Assessments

Resources for Differentiated Instruction lessons include opportunities for informal, observational progress monitoring. Informal lesson assessments allow teachers to monitor mastery of lesson content. These frequent checks measure the transfer and maintenance of new skills from the software to print.

Progress Monitoring Tests

Five print assessments assess phonemic awareness & phonics, sight words & spelling, and morphology. Results show how well students maintain previously taught skills and transfer them to the reading of printed text.

These measures of progress are curriculum-embedded and criterion-referenced to the Topic and/or Series of instruction in which students are working. SAM Reports collect and organize key progress monitoring data. See **Reporting in *System 44*** (p. 68) for recommendations about when and how often to run reports.

Scholastic Phonics Inventory (SPI)

In addition to screening and placing students into *System 44*, SPI helps teachers and administrators monitor student progress at key points throughout the program. SPI contains three equivalent test forms. Each time a student logs on to take a test, the software delivers a new form.

Once you have identified students for *System 44* and placed them into the program, administer SPI at the middle and end of the school year to reassess their foundational reading skills. Use the results of these tests in conjunction with the other progress monitoring and summative assessment measures in *System 44* to:

- Monitor student response to intervention.
- Track student development of critical reading skills.
- Inform grouping and differentiate instruction.
- Evaluate student readiness to exit *System 44*.

Note: SPI should be administered **a maximum of three times per year**. More frequent testing is unlikely to show meaningful growth and may skew results by making students overly familiar with the content and format of the test. Use the following reports for more frequent progress monitoring:

- Reading Progress Report (p. 88)
- Response to Intervention Report (p. 92)
- Student Software Performance Report (p. 96)
- Student Mastery Report (p. 102)

Software Performance

The *System 44* software includes engaging and motivating opportunities for students to learn, practice, and apply skills. Each Software Topic begins with direct instruction followed by multiple activities that lead students to develop accuracy in word reading and spelling, and concludes with transfer to connected text.

Expanding Recall

The goal of *System 44* instruction is fluency and automaticity with decoding and word-recognition skills. Much of the software instruction described below uses a proven approach known as Expanding Recall to facilitate this goal. Expanding Recall helps students move newly acquired concepts and skills from working memory to long-term memory. With this instructional approach, students practice holding recently learned skills for longer and longer periods of time in working memory until these skills move to long-term memory for automatic retrieval.

The following activities use Expanding Recall to build automaticity and to measure success. You can review performance and progress with these activities in the Student Software Performance Report on SAM.

Sound Challenge Develops students' automaticity using Expanding Recall to reinforce sound-spellings in working memory. The student hears the target or review sound and quickly identifies the correct sound-spelling from a list. Results are reported as the **Sound Challenge Score** in the Student Software Performance Report.

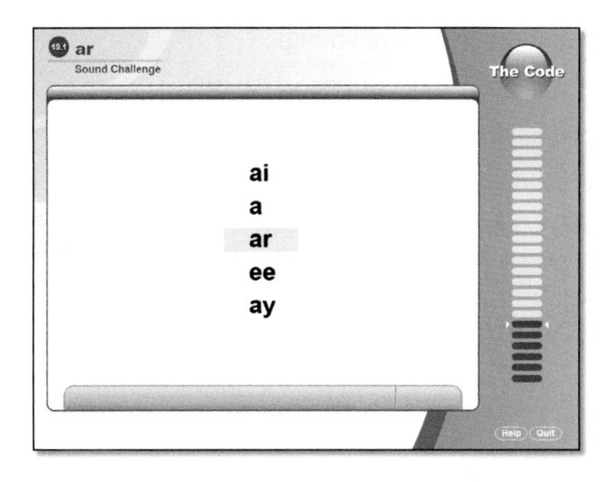

Word Challenge Develops students' automaticity in decoding words. To ensure sustained mastery, Word Challenge includes previously mastered words from past Topics. The student hears a word with the target or review spelling pattern and identifies the correct word from a list with four choices. Results are reported as the **Word Challenge Score** in the Student Software Performance Report.

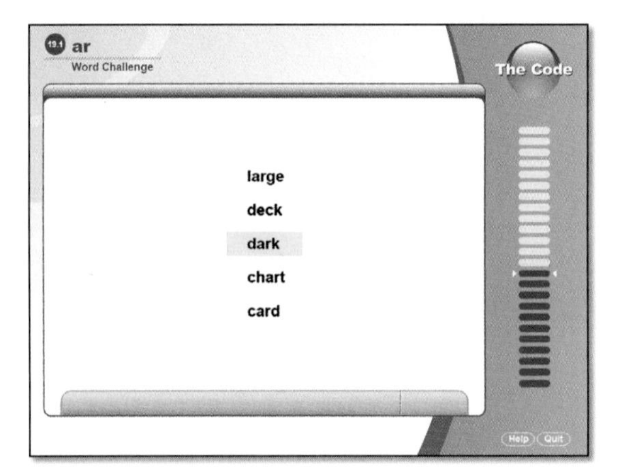

Spelling Challenge Provides independent practice to help students develop accuracy and fluency with encoding. The student hears words from the current Topic repeated at increasing speed intervals and systematically interspersed with review words from previous Topics to ensure sustained mastery. Results are reported as the **Spelling Challenge Score** in the Student Software Performance Report.

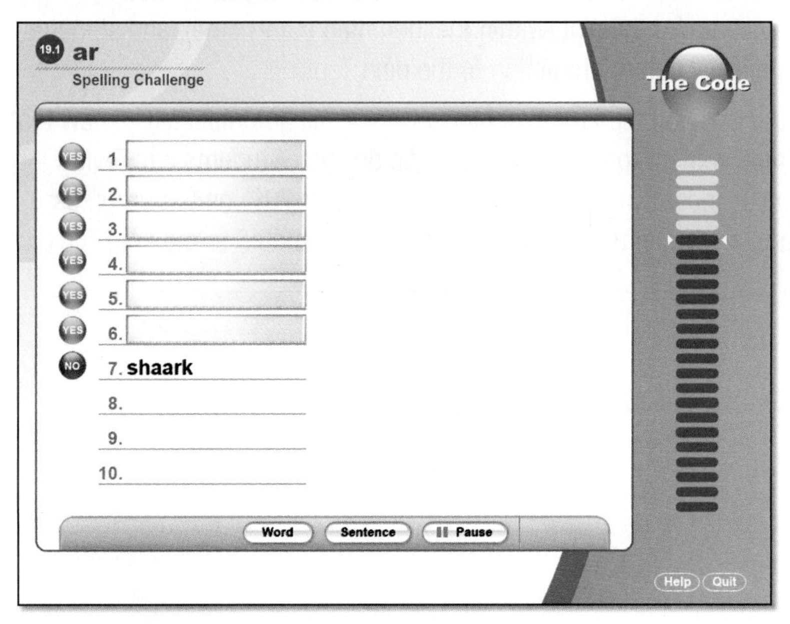

Read & Think Promotes reading for meaning and critical thinking as students read high-interest decodable text. The student reads a single decodable sentence on the screen. The computer then reads a question aloud and presents three answer choices related to that question. The student has to read for meaning to distinguish the correct choice. Results are reported as the **Read & Think Comprehension Score** in the Student Software Performance Report.

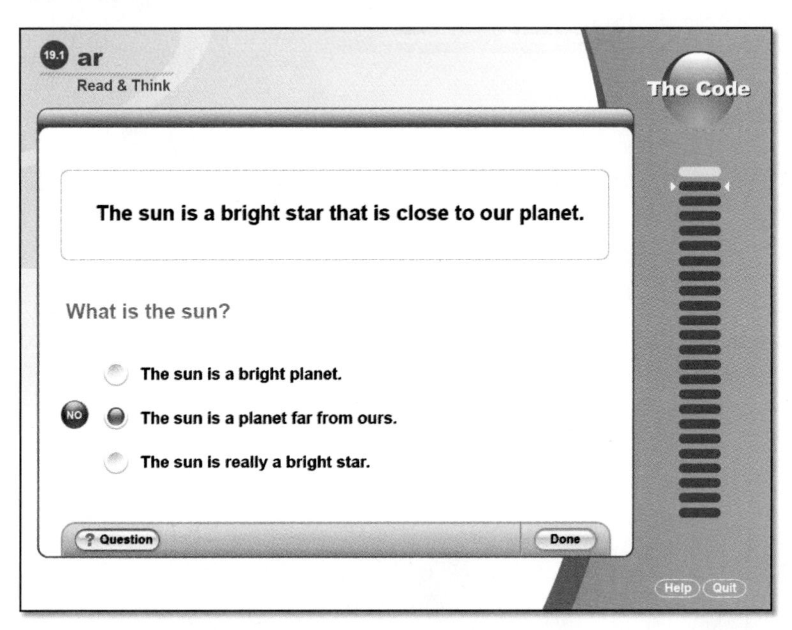

Progress Monitor

Every Topic ends with a quick Progress Monitor. This assessment resembles Word Challenge whereby the student has to identify the target word from a list of five choices. Performance indicates whether students have mastered Topic skills and content (some previously mastered words are also included to ensure skill maintenance). Mastery is defined by responses that are both accurate and fluent (within the identified cutoff time), and students need to demonstrate proficiency before promotion to the next Topic.

If students are below proficiency on the Progress Monitor, they will automatically review that Topic with new and adapted content to target their specific deficits. Students can review a Topic up to two additional times. If students do not score at least 70% on the Progress Monitor for their third software cycle, they will be provisionally promoted to the next Topic.

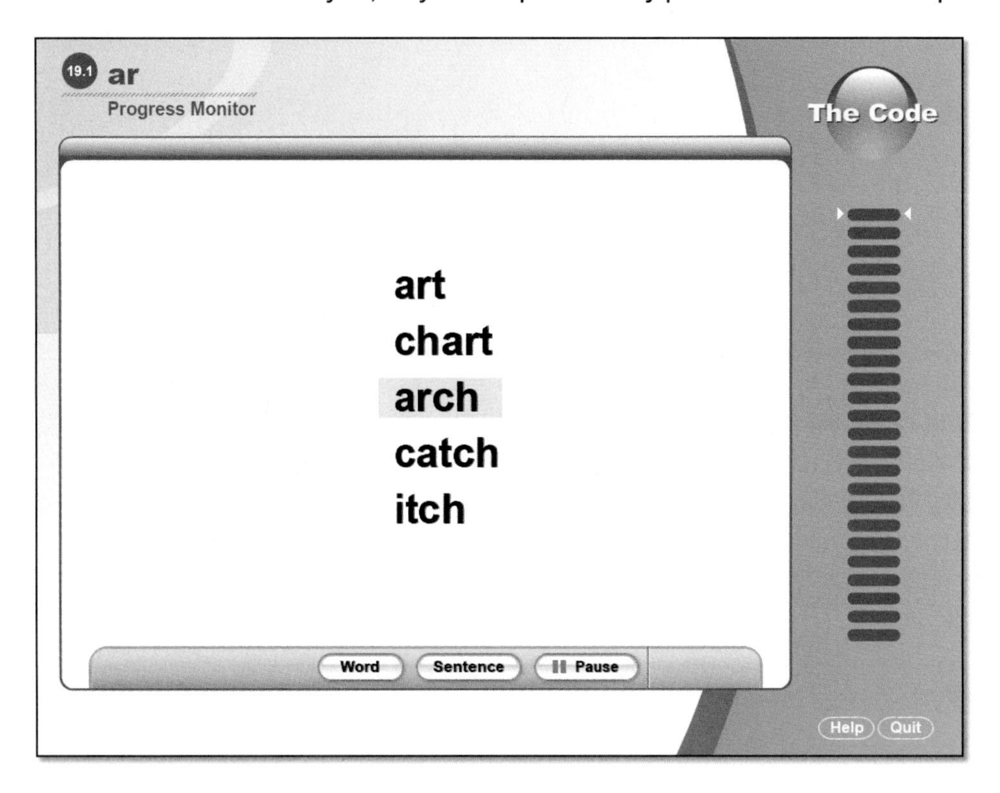

Data-Driven Placement

The goal of *System 44* is for students to learn to decode fluently and automatically so they can focus on the meaning of text. Ongoing differentiated instruction allows for students to move rapidly through the software, using instructional time efficiently, as it continues to adjust and individualize an instructional path for each student.

Fast-Track Assessments

The *System 44* software includes embedded Fast-Track assessments for data-driven placement and pacing through the program. Fast-Tracks are brief assessments (approximately 5–7 minutes) that allow students to skip individual Topics in a Series if they can demonstrate a high level of mastery in the content that is covered. At the beginning of each Series, excluding Series 1–3, 24, and 25, students have the opportunity to take a Fast-Track that assesses skill content in the Series. If students demonstrate proficiency with these skills, they move directly to the *next* Topic. The Fast-Track assessments are curriculum-embedded and launch automatically as students move through the software. Students cannot Fast-Track Topics in the Sight Words, Success, or Writing strands.

Fast-Track Structure and Content

The Fast-Track assessments include both real and nonsense word items. As with the *Scholastic Phonics Inventory*, nonsense words effectively measure the ability to decode without contextual support. By using "real words," Fast-Tracks can evaluate the reading of more sophisticated words, including those with morphological word families and multisyllable words. Students will be familiar with this format from the software instruction. Each Fast-Track assesses every skill taught within the Series.

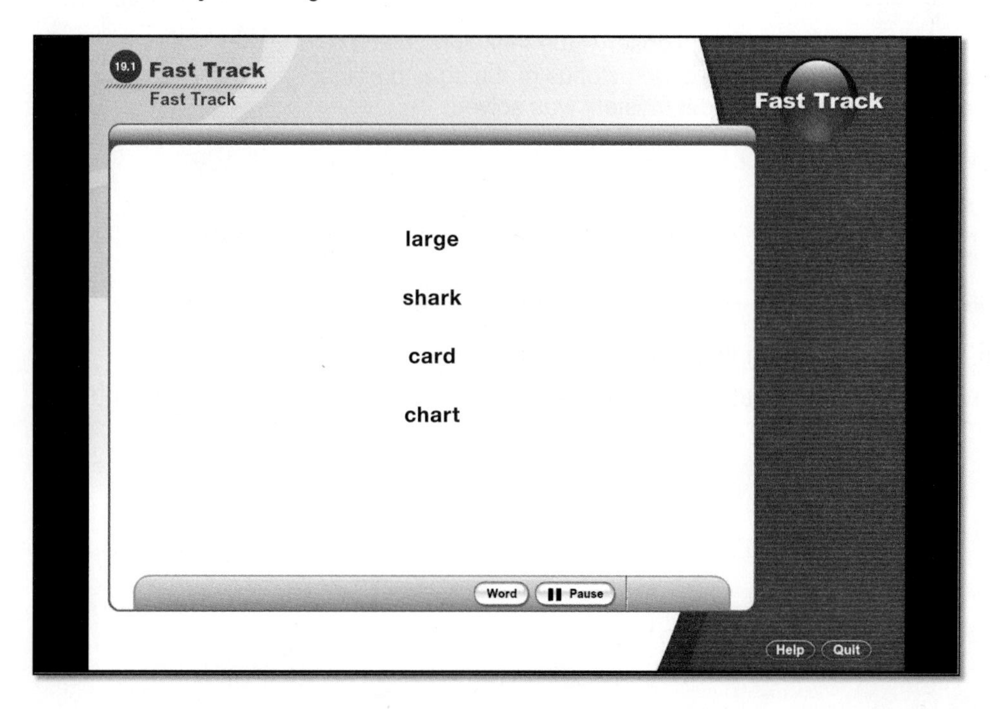

Oral Reading Fluency

Oral reading fluency is the ability to read connected text at a pace that allows for reading comprehension. Fluency is considered a key indicator of reading growth when monitored regularly. Research has shown that fluency is one of the most reliable predictors of long-term reading success.

When to Assess Oral Reading Fluency

Oral reading fluency should be monitored regularly to identify students who may require additional fluency instruction.

In the *System 44* Success Passages, students engage in repeated readings of increasingly challenging connected text with scaffolded support. These passages include multiple exemplars of recently taught phonics patterns as well as key vocabulary.

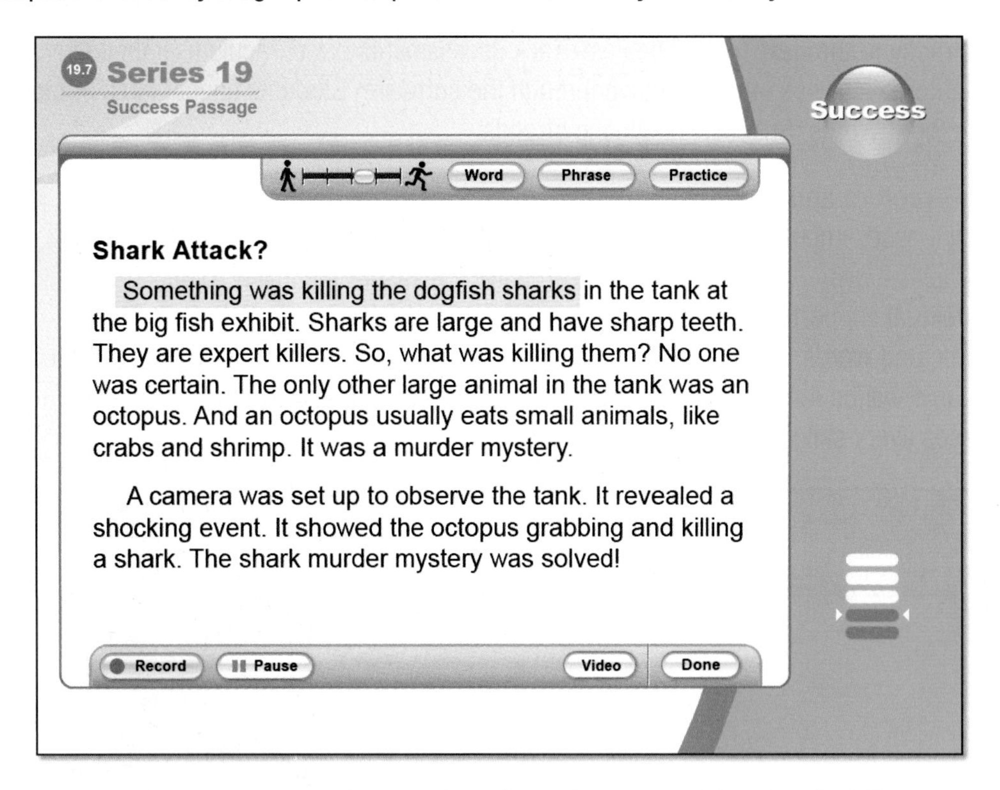

In addition, see pp. 164–165 in this guide for information on administering Oral Fluency Assessments (OFAs) with instructional level passages appropriate for *System 44* students.

Fluency Evaluation

You can monitor oral reading fluency on a regular basis by listening to students' Success Recordings. Refer to the Oral Reading Fluency Rubric below when you use the SAM Student Digital Portfolio to evaluate students' phrasing, pace, and prosody with each passage.

Oral Reading Fluency Rubric

Rating	Phrasing	Pace	Description
1. Beginning Fluency	Word-by-word.	Slow and laborious. Rate is less than 65 correct words per minute.	Reads without attention to phrasing or punctuation. Frequent repetitions, sound-outs, and multiple attempts at words.
2. Emerging Fluency	Word-by-word with some two- or three-word phrases.	Slow. Rate is 65 to 90 words per minute.	Reads with little or no expression. Repetitions and deviations from text often disrupt the flow of reading.
3. Developing Fluency	Primarily two-word phrases.	Moderately slow. Rate is 90 to 125 words per minute.	Reads with little intonation to mark ends of sentences and clauses. Word groupings are choppy and unrelated to context of sentence.
4. Proficient Fluency	Primarily three- or four-word phrases with some expression.	Beginning to be conversational but may sometimes be too slow or fast. Rate is 125 to 160 words per minute.	Reads with primarily natural phrasing with some attention to expression and few derivations from text.
5. Strong Fluency	Reads in larger meaningful phrases with attention to expression.	Almost always conversational. Rate is 160 or more words per minute.	Reads in large meaningful phrases with only occasional breaks caused by difficulties with specific words.
6. Exemplary Fluency	Reads fluently with expression.	Consistently conversational. Rate is 160 or more words per minute.	Reads with excellent phrasing and expression and a consistently smooth pace. Self-corrections are automatic.

Scholastic Reading Counts!

During independent reading small-group rotations, students will read engaging *System 44* books at their instructional level. Monitor their independent reading using *Scholastic Reading Counts!* quizzes.

System 44 Library

The *System 44* Library is a collection of 56 high-interest, age-appropriate texts for struggling elementary, middle, and high school readers. These paperbacks, audiobooks, and eBooks provide opportunities for students who are developing decoding skills to apply their knowledge to motivating, relevant texts that use the language and features of authentic fiction and nonfiction.

These books include many high-frequency words, word repetition, targeted vocabulary (both content and academic words), and natural-sounding text. As students move through progressively challenging *System 44* books, they build endurance with increasingly longer and more challenging text. Each *System 44* title is accompanied by a *Scholastic Reading Counts!* quiz.

Using *Scholastic Reading Counts!* for Progress Monitoring

Scholastic Reading Counts! is designed to help motivate and monitor independent reading progress. The program includes quizzes for each of the *System 44* Paperbacks.

Using *Scholastic Reading Counts!*, students set personal reading goals, choose books that match their interests and reading levels, and read books at their own pace. After each book, students take a *Scholastic Reading Counts!* quiz to demonstrate understanding of what they read. A student who scores below benchmark (default 70%) can take the quiz again with a different set of randomly selected questions.

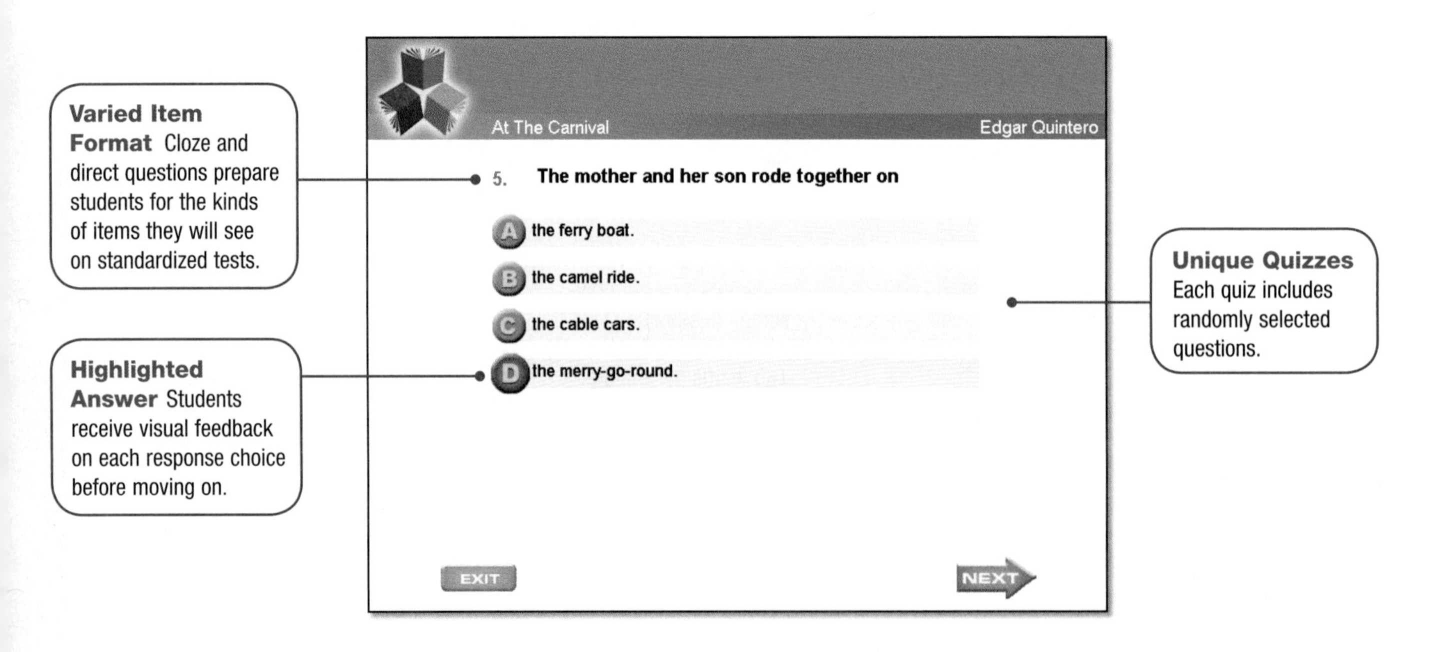

What the *Scholastic Reading Counts!* Quizzes Assess

Research reveals that reading comprehension improves significantly when students are routinely asked about what they have read. The *Scholastic Reading Counts!* quizzes enable students to demonstrate comprehension of the books they read during independent reading and practice.

How to Use the Quiz Results

As students take the *Scholastic Reading Counts!* quizzes, the Scholastic Achievement Manager (SAM) gathers and organizes data on their usage and performance. You can view this data for individuals, groups, and classes in the *Scholastic Reading Counts!* reports to:

- Monitor independent reading progress over time.
- Evaluate progress toward independent reading goals (e.g., number of books read).
- Ensure that students are reading books at the appropriate level (corresponding to their current software Series as indicated on the Self-Monitoring Chart available with **SAM Keyword:** 44 Student Chart).
- Track quiz success rates and words read.
- Identify issues students may be having with quizzes.
- Learn what books students enjoy reading.
- Measure present level of performance to set goals on the Student Goals tab of the SAM Student Digital Portfolio.
- Share students' progress with parents.
- Celebrate reading growth and achievement.

Using Book Expert to Guide Independent Reading

Targeted reading enables students to read independently, understand what they read, and build reading skills. The Book Expert in the Scholastic Achievement Manager contains information on more than 50,000 titles that are searchable by Lexile level, topic, and genre. Use the Book Expert to locate reading materials on topics that meet curriculum needs and to recommend additional books that match students' reading levels and interests. Students can access an online version of the Book Expert from home at **http://src.scholastic.com/ecatalog**.

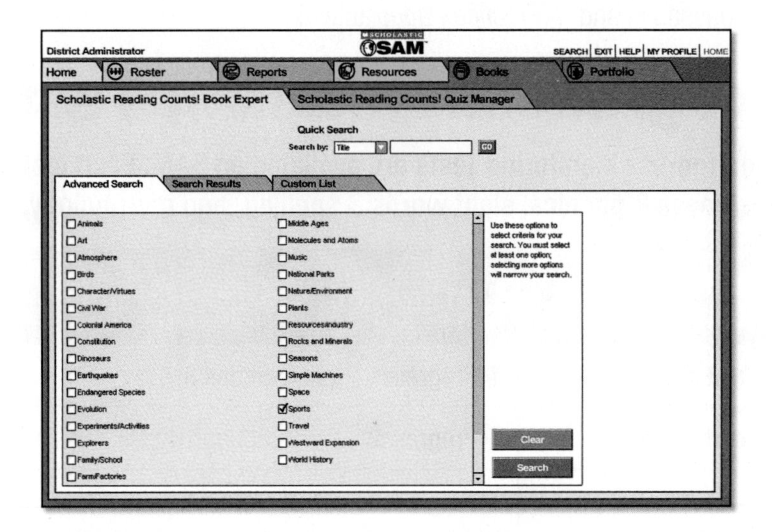

Informal Assessment

Teacher-led informal assessment is critical for monitoring students' daily progress, as well as their ability to transfer new skills from the software to print.

Every lesson in *Resources for Differentiated Instruction* concludes with an assessment. These curriculum-embedded assessments use the cloze format to build decoding and word recognition skills in the context of reading for meaning.

ASSESSMENT

Teacher-Led: Write cloze sentences on the board. Read aloud each one. On a separate sheet of paper, have students write a word from **Flip Chart 68** to complete each item. Examples:

1. Are you afraid of the ________? (dark)
2. I made you a special birthday__________. (card)
3. Those scissors are very________. (sharp)

Software Data: See the **Student Software Performance Report** for additional information on student performance on this skill (Topic 19.1).

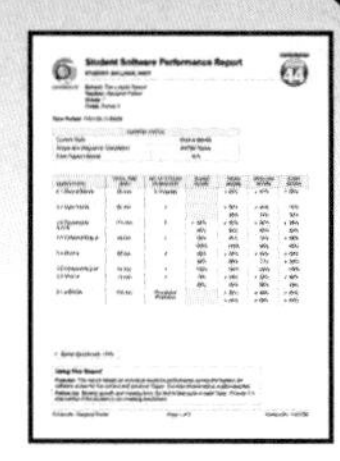

Using the Results

Regular observational assessment confirms when students are mastering and maintaining newly acquired skills. For those students who do not demonstrate mastery, consider the following action steps:

- Refer to the Student Software Performance Report for a detailed description of the student's performance on the corresponding software Topic, including: phonemic awareness, decoding, spelling, and comprehending text.
- Look for trends in performance across major skill categories (e.g., Digraphs, Short Vowels, Open Syllables, etc.) to inform small-group direct instruction and/or one-to-one intervention.
- Assign independent practice and homework from lesson-specific *Decodable Digest* passages and *44Practice Pages* activities.

Progress Monitoring Tests

Five Progress Monitoring Tests are available on SAM. Each test assesses phonemic awareness & phonics, sight words & spelling, and morphology.

Progress Monitoring Test	SAM Keyword	Administer After
Test One	44Progress1	Series 3
Test Two	44Progress2	Series 10
Test Three	44Progress3	Series 17
Test Four	44Progress4	Series 23
Test Five	44Progress5	Series 25

Summative Assessment

***System 44* includes two Summative Assessments that help monitor how well students have maintained skills and whether they can apply and transfer those skills to new contexts. The Midyear and End-of-Year Tests are:**

- Curriculum-embedded.
- Criterion-referenced to instruction in *Resources for Differentiated Instruction.*
- Designed to measure whether students have mastered and maintained the content of previously taught lessons.

Assessed Skills

Each of the Summative Assessments covers skills in these areas:

- Phonemic Awareness and Phonics
- Word Recognition and Spelling
- Vocabulary and Morphology

Summative Assessment	*Resources for Differentiated Instruction* Lessons	Phonemic Awareness and Phonics	Word Recognition and Spelling	Vocabulary and Morphology
Midyear Test	1–54	• Consonants • Short Vowels • Two- and Three-Letter Blends • Digraphs • Long Vowels	• Sight Words Sets 1–12	• Inflectional Endings • Possessives • Closed Syllables • VC*e* Syllables • Prefixes • Suffixes • Compound Words
End-of-Year Test	55–84	• Silent Consonants • Diphthongs • Vowel Teams • *r*-Controlled Vowels • Variant Vowels	• Sight Words Sets 13–21	• Prefixes • Suffixes • Roots • Vowel Team Syllables

Strategically Selected Distractors

Distractors for the test items were strategically selected to ensure that student performance accurately reflects the attainment and maintenance of the measured skill.

Distractors are real English words, decodable based on the Series covered, and similar in length to the target word.

Distractors are not homophones (*to, too, two*) when the target is read aloud, nor real words in languages other than English, and avoid potential dialect confusion (e.g., testing short *e* and short *i* together).

Item Formats

Each Summative Assessment includes 50 items. The *System 44* Scope and Sequence covers each element at least once. There are three item types:

- discrimination with image support
- word discrimination
- cloze reading activities

See sample items below.

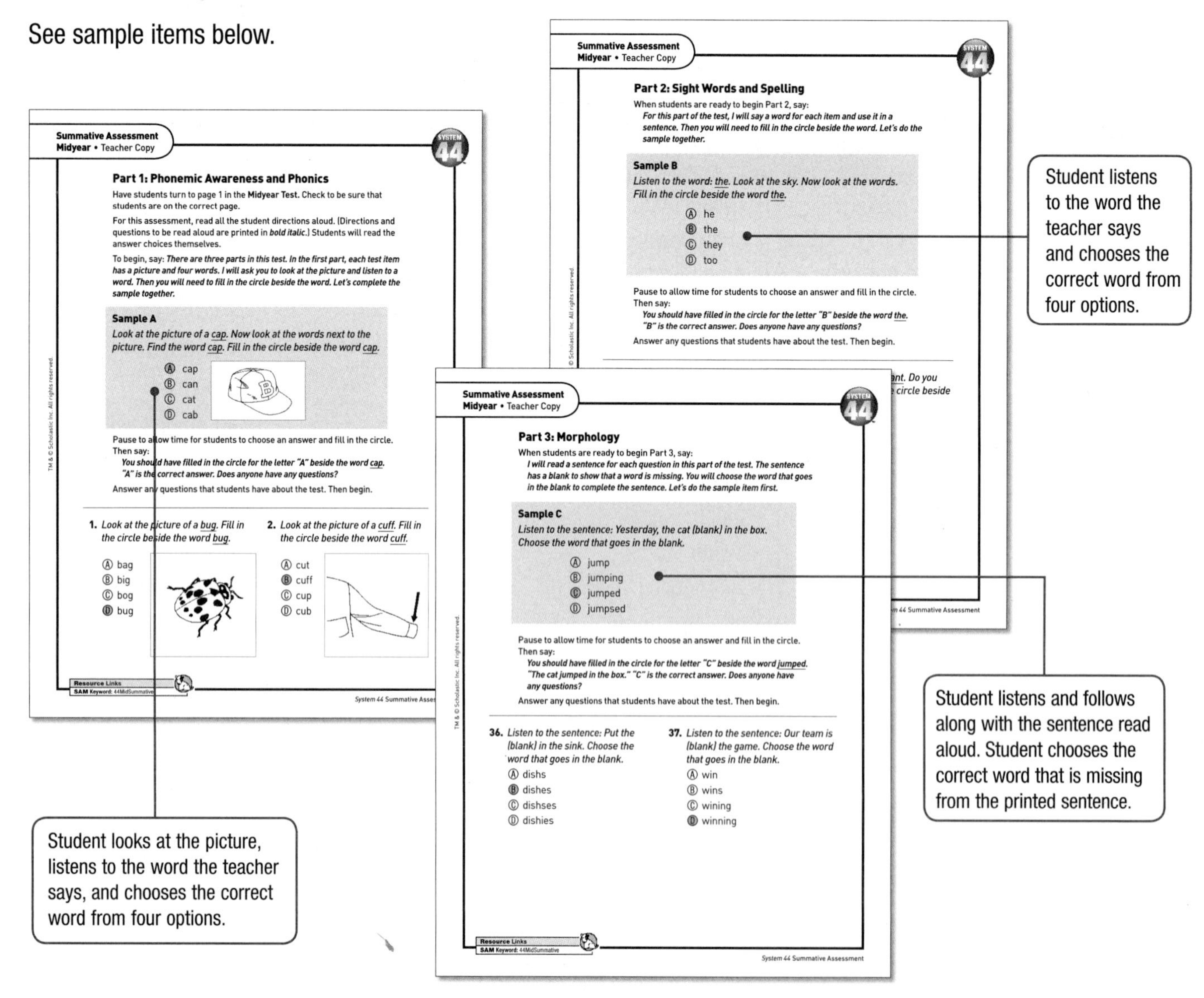

Summative Assessment
Midyear • Teacher Copy

Part 1: Phonemic Awareness and Phonics

Have students turn to page 1 in the **Midyear Test.** Check to be sure that students are on the correct page.

For this assessment, read all the student directions aloud. (Directions and questions to be read aloud are printed in ***bold italic.***) Students will read the answer choices themselves.

To begin, say: ***There are three parts in this test. In the first part, each test item has a picture and four words. I will ask you to look at the picture and listen to a word. Then you will need to fill in the circle beside the word. Let's complete the sample together.***

Sample A
Look at the picture of a cap. Now look at the words next to the picture. Find the word cap. Fill in the circle beside the word cap.
Ⓐ cap
Ⓑ can
Ⓒ cat
Ⓓ cab

Pause to allow time for students to choose an answer and fill in the circle. Then say:
You should have filled in the circle for the letter "A" beside the word cap. "A" is the correct answer. Does anyone have any questions?
Answer any questions that students have about the test. Then begin.

1. *Look at the picture of a bug. Fill in the circle beside the word bug.*
Ⓐ bag
Ⓑ big
Ⓒ bog
Ⓓ bug

2. *Look at the picture of a cuff. Fill in the circle beside the word cuff.*
Ⓐ cut
Ⓑ cuff
Ⓒ cup
Ⓓ cub

Summative Assessment
Midyear • Teacher Copy

Part 2: Sight Words and Spelling

When students are ready to begin Part 2, say:
For this part of the test, I will say a word for each item and use it in a sentence. Then you will need to fill in the circle beside the word. Let's do the sample together.

Sample B
Listen to the word: the. Look at the sky. Now look at the words. Fill in the circle beside the word the.
Ⓐ he
Ⓑ the
Ⓒ they
Ⓓ too

Pause to allow time for students to choose an answer and fill in the circle. Then say:
You should have filled in the circle for the letter "B" beside the word the. "B" is the correct answer. Does anyone have any questions?
Answer any questions that students have about the test. Then begin.

Summative Assessment
Midyear • Teacher Copy

Part 3: Morphology

When students are ready to begin Part 3, say:
I will read a sentence for each question in this part of the test. The sentence has a blank to show that a word is missing. You will choose the word that goes in the blank to complete the sentence. Let's do the sample item first.

Sample C
Listen to the sentence: Yesterday, the cat (blank) in the box. Choose the word that goes in the blank.
Ⓐ jump
Ⓑ jumping
Ⓒ jumped
Ⓓ jumpsed

Pause to allow time for students to choose an answer and fill in the circle. Then say:
You should have filled in the circle for the letter "C" beside the word jumped. "The cat jumped in the box." "C" is the correct answer. Does anyone have any questions?
Answer any questions that students have about the test. Then begin.

36. *Listen to the sentence: Put the (blank) in the sink. Choose the word that goes in the blank.*
Ⓐ dishs
Ⓑ dishes
Ⓒ dishses
Ⓓ dishies

37. *Listen to the sentence: Our team is (blank) the game. Choose the word that goes in the blank.*
Ⓐ win
Ⓑ wins
Ⓒ wining
Ⓓ winning

Resource Links
SAM Keyword: 44MidSummative

System 44 Summative Assessment

Administering Assessment

Overview

We recommend administering assessment in a standard way across schools and students, including use of the following:

- Consistent procedures to administer the test.
- Consistent scoring procedures.
- Agreed-upon interpretation guidelines.
- Identified procedures for the use of assessment outcomes to inform instruction.

Administering the *Scholastic Reading Inventory* (SRI)

The *Scholastic Reading Inventory* (SRI) test is a classroom-based assessment that can be administered on the computer and provide immediate results. Use the Scholastic Achievement Manager (SAM) to enroll students in SRI before they take a test.

When students take SRI on a computer, they will go through the following steps:

1. Log in to the program.
2. Choose topics of interest.
3. Read (or listen to) the test directions.
4. Answer the practice questions.
5. Take the test.
6. View a recommended reading list.

① **Log In** To log in, students launch the SRI application and then enter their username and password on the log-in screen.

② **Choose Book Topics** After the student logs in, SRI displays the Book Interest screen. Students can choose up to three book topics. At the end of the test, students will be able to print Recommended Reading Lists that are appropriate for their Lexile measures to guide their book selections.

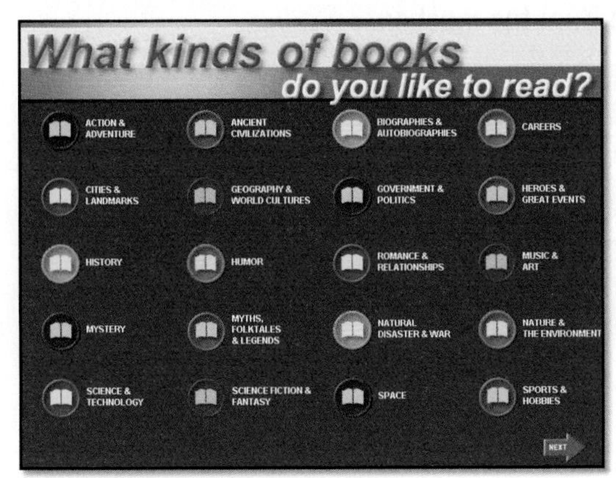

Book Interest Screen, Grades 7–12

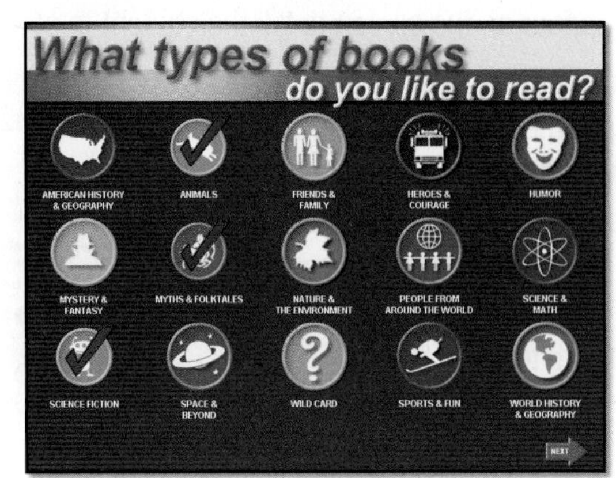

Book Interest Screen, Grades 3–6

③ **Read the Test Directions** Once a student has chosen book topics, directions appear on the computer screen that explain how to take the *Scholastic Reading Inventory* (SRI). Students can read the directions on-screen and hear them read aloud.

The *System 44 Software Manual* contains detailed instructions on how to turn off the sound option so that students don't hear the SRI directions read aloud.

Skipping a Question Students can skip up to three SRI questions without being penalized. To skip a question, the student clicks the **Skip** button.

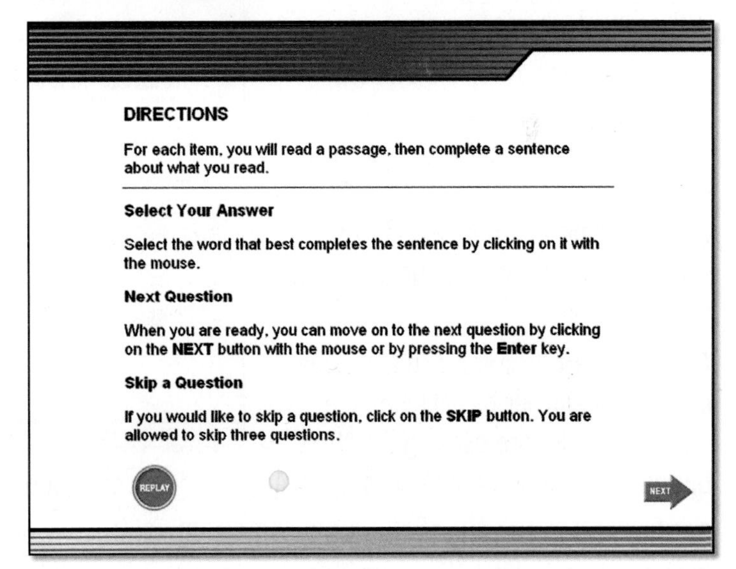

④ **Answer the Practice Questions** The purpose of the practice questions is to make sure students understand the test directions and are comfortable using the computer to take the test. Students will answer three practice questions that are formatted like those on the actual test. If a student is having difficulty with the test directions or the computer interface, a prompt will appear on the screen to tell the student to seek help from the teacher.

Targeting the Test In the Scholastic Achievement Manager, you will need to target a student as reading Above, On, Below, or Far Below grade level. This will ensure that the practice questions and first test question are at his/her appropriate level.

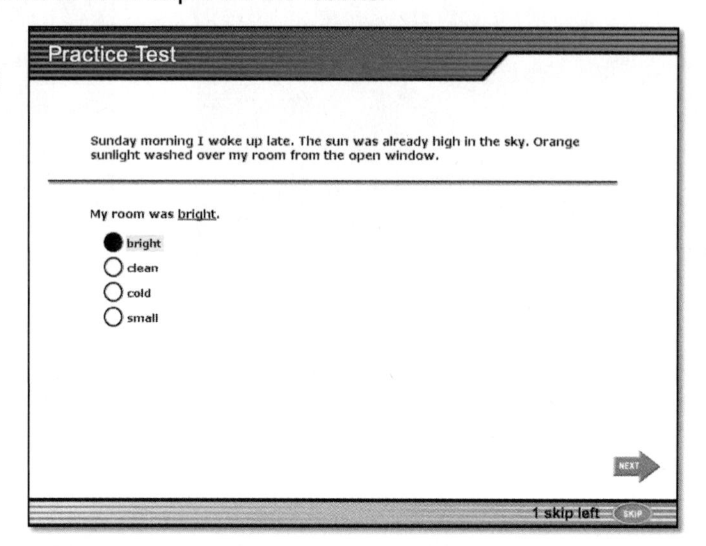

⑤ **Take the Test** A *Scholastic Reading Inventory* (SRI) test consists of brief passages from authentic fiction and nonfiction texts. After the student reads each passage, a multiple-choice question displays on the screen. The student selects an answer from four choices using the mouse and then clicks the **Next** button to go on to the next question.

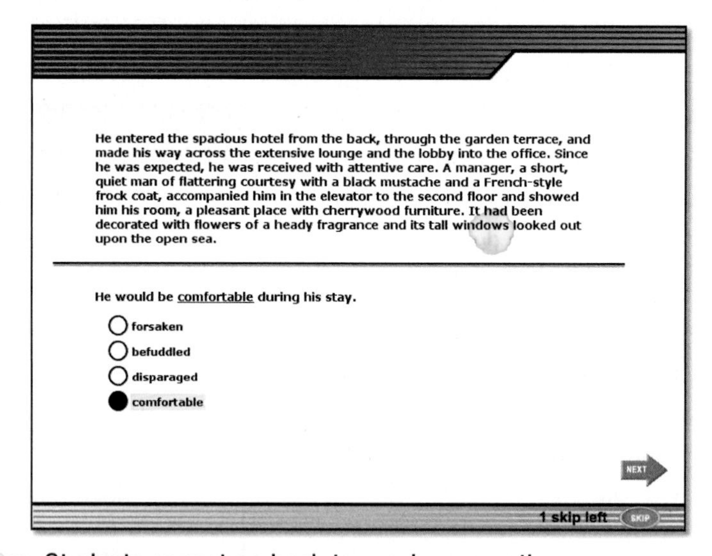

Changing an Answer Students can change an answer by clicking on a new answer before clicking the **Next** button to move on to the following screen. Students cannot go back to previous questions.

Exiting and Returning to Complete a Test Students may not have time to finish an SRI test in one sitting. If this is the case, they can save an incomplete test and return to complete it at another time. The next time they log in, SRI will automatically prompt them to continue the unfinished test.

⑥ **View a Recommended Reading List** After completing the test, each student can view a customized Recommended Reading Report. This list is based on the student's SRI results and the choices made on the Book Topic screen at the beginning of the test.

Preparing Students for an SRI Test

You want your students to provide their best effort on any assessment because you make decisions based on the data you receive. Create a supportive testing environment to help your students' performance.

Recommendations for Preparing Students to Take the SRI
1. Ensure that the testing environment is free of distractions and is conducive to testing. Whether students are testing in a computer lab or in the classroom, provide headsets so that ambient sounds do not distract students. Be sure to tell students what to do when they complete the test so that they do not distract other students. Have a plan to deal with any potential disruptions that may occur.
2. Familiarize students with the test. If you have an interactive whiteboard or projector, take a test together to show students how a computer-adaptive test works. Make sure students know that the test is not timed and they cannot go back to change any answers. Let them know that if the test is getting harder, they are doing well.
3. Discuss multiple-choice questions. In SRI, all the answers make a complete sentence, but the student has to choose the one that matches the passage and makes the most sense. Review test-taking strategies for multiple-choice questions.
4. Tell students about opportunities to skip a question. Let students know that they have three skips they can use that will not affect their test results. To skip a question, students should select the **Skip** button on the screen. The **Skip** button can only be used three times. Once a student has skipped three questions, the **Skip** button will not be available.
5. Students may need to take breaks. SRI is not timed. Monitor students for test fatigue and demonstrate how to save the test when you are modeling the test for them. If you believe your students cannot manage the entire assessment at once, schedule the test over multiple days. You will get more accurate results and improve motivation if students are not overwhelmed.

Administering the *Scholastic Phonics Inventory* (SPI)

The *Scholastic Phonics Inventory* (SPI) is a computer-based test of basic letter recognition, decoding, and sight word knowledge. For information on how it works, validity, and results, refer to the section *Scholastic Phonics Inventory* (pp. 26–33) in this guide.

Use the Scholastic Achievement Manager (SAM) to enroll students in the SPI.

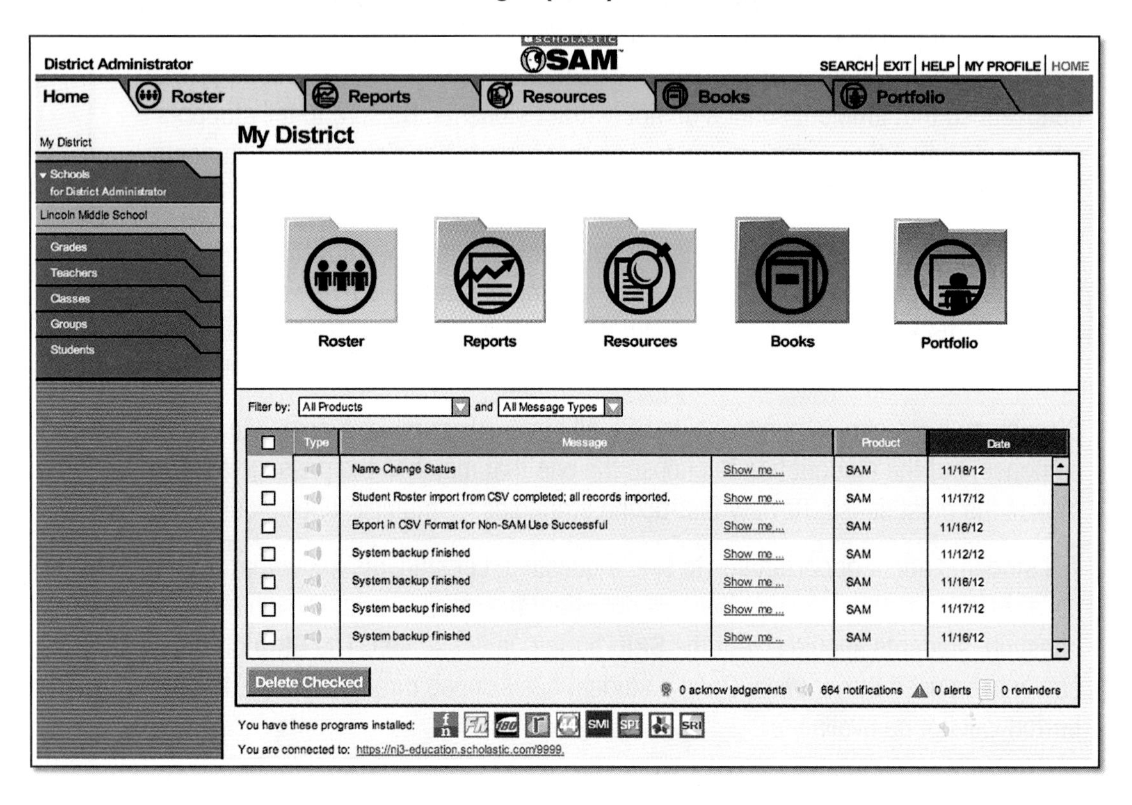

Steps to Administering the SPI

① **Log In** To log in, students launch the SPI application, enter their username and password on the log-in screen, and then click the **Go On** button to begin.

② **Take the Assessment** Students will follow the audio directions to begin the first section of the SPI, which contains 11 practice items. During all sections of the assessment, students can access the **Pause**, **Play**, and **Replay** buttons.

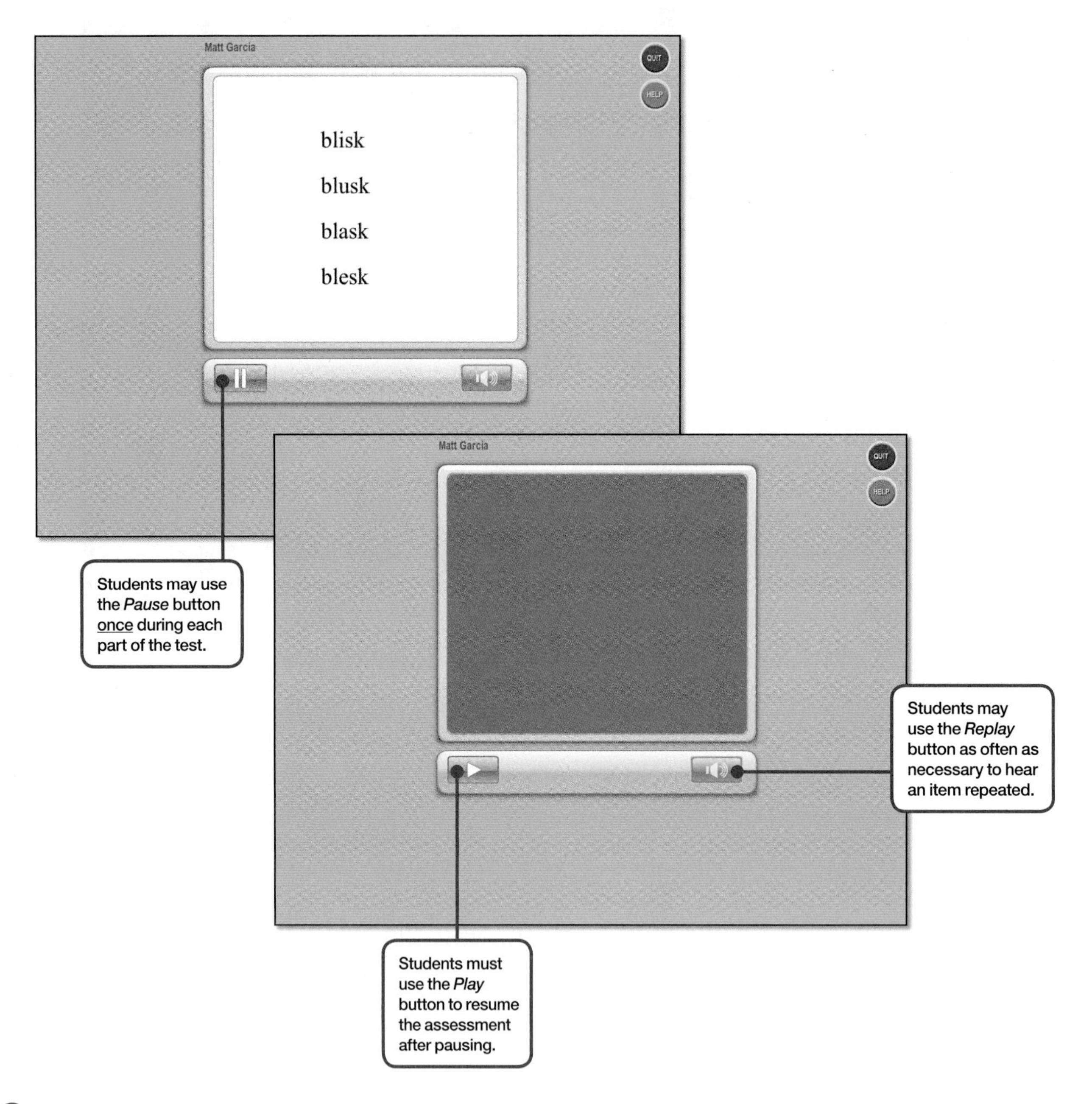

③ **Exit the SPI** Once a student answers the last SPI question, he or she will be asked to click the **Go On** button to complete the test and exit. (The **Go On** button is also used to advance students to the next section of the assessment; e.g., after Letter Names and before Sight Words).

Preparing Students for the SPI

Screening and diagnostic placement with the SPI ensures that only those students who require intensive phonics intervention receive *System 44* instruction. Creating a supportive testing environment will help students perform to the best of their abilities on the SPI. For subsequent progress monitoring SPI tests, emphasize that the purpose is to find out how well students are reading.

Recommendations for Preparing Students to Take the SPI
1. Test the headphones for volume at each computer station prior to administering the test.
2. Ensure that the classroom environment is quiet and free of distractions during testing. It is essential for students to clearly hear audio prompts.
3. Make sure each student knows his or her password.
4. Situate students so they can pay attention and focus. Be strategic about where students sit.
5. Remind students that the SPI is a test designed to measure their reading skills and plan an instructional program that is just right for them. When students take the SPI at the middle and end of the school year, remind them that it will show how much progress they have made. Therefore, students should try their best to show what they know.
6. Explain to students that the SPI uses some nonsense words—words that have no meaning—because these words help measure decoding skills.
7. Ask students to raise their hand if questions or concerns arise during testing. They should be sure to press the **Pause** button to stop the test.
8. Tell students that while they should try to answer as quickly as possible, answering correctly is important.
9. Finally, teachers should closely monitor the administration of the SPI . Although the test is intended for independent administration, teachers should be present and aware of what is happening at all times to prevent confusion and distractions.

Administering Progress Monitoring Tests and Summative Assessments

System 44 Progress Monitoring Tests can be administered at five points in the curriculum: Test 1 after completing Lesson 23 in *Resources for Differentiated Instruction* or Series 3 in the software, Test 2 after completing Lesson 45 or Series 10, Test 3 after completing Lesson 64 or Series 17, Test 4 after completing Lesson 82 or Series 23, and Test 5 after completing Series 25.

System 44 Summative Assessments can be administered at two points in the curriculum: midyear (or after completing Lesson 54 in *Resources for Differentiated Instruction* or Series 13 in the software) and at the end of the year (or after completing Lesson 84 or Series 25).

Students complete these assessments at their desks. They are designed for efficient class administration and quick scoring and analysis of results.

Accessing the Assessments

The assessments are downloadable resources on the Scholastic Achievement Manager. To access the Progress Monitoring Tests, use **SAM Keywords:** 44Progress1, 44Progress2, 44Progress3, 44Progress4, and 44Progress5. To access the Summative Assessments, use **SAM Keyword:** 44MidSummative to access the Midyear Test and **SAM Keyword:** 44EndSummative to access the End-of-Year Test. Downloads include both the student and teacher versions of each assessment, as well as the Scoring Sheets and Answer Keys.

See the *System 44 Software Manual: Using Resources in SAM* for a detailed description of how to locate the Summative Assessments.

Planning for the Assessments

To administer an assessment, you will need to identify the students to be assessed, prepare the testing materials, and schedule appropriate testing time.

Identifying Students

To identify groups of students who are ready for testing, keep track of when students complete Series 3, 10, 13, 17, 23, and 25 in the software. Then administer the appropriate assessment.

Preparing Materials

Print the Teacher Copy and the Student Copy for the assessment. Make a copy of the student version for each student to be tested. Staple the pages of each student's test together to prevent the need for students to write their names on each page.

Item Format

Each Progress Monitoring Test contains 30 items organized into three sections: Phonemic Awareness and Phonics, Sight Words and Spelling, and Morphology. Each Summative Assessment contains 50 items organized into three sections: Phonemic Awareness and Phonics, Word Recognition and Spelling, and Vocabulary and Morphology.

Each test includes three types of items: discrimination with image support, word discrimination, and cloze sentences. Sample items are included for every item format to ensure students understand the directions and how to respond. Total testing time for each Progress Monitoring Test is about 10–15 minutes, and total testing time for each Summative Assessment is about 15–20 minutes. You may wish to give students a short break after each section.

Administering the Assessment

Follow the steps below when administering an assessment to a group of students:

1. Remind students to write their names at the top of the test.
2. Tell students that they will be answering 30 or 50 questions. Each question has four possible answer choices. Students should carefully listen to each question read aloud and then choose the best answer to the question. There is only one correct answer.
3. Read the first sample item. Have students mark their answers by filling in the circle beside the answer of their choice. Remind students to mark their answers clearly and fully.
4. Show students the correct answer choice for the sample item. If students want to change an answer, they should erase the darkened circle completely or draw an X through the answer and fill in their final choice.
5. Ask students if they have any questions before moving on.
6. Proceed with the test by reading each question stem and having students mark their answers. Pause for 10–15 seconds after each question to allow time for students to think and respond. Then move to the next question.
7. If students have not yet marked an answer within the time limit, instruct them that they need to move on to the next question.
8. Remember to pronounce all test words as clearly as possible with correct articulation.
9. When you come to the end of a section, allow students to take a short (two-minute) break.
10. Proceed through each section of the assessment as outlined above.

The Teacher Copy of the assessments includes detailed scripting, which can be read verbatim to ensure a standardized administration of these tests.

Scoring and Interpreting Results

Score the Progress Monitoring Tests and Summative Assessments to evaluate maintained and applied learning. Follow the steps below to score and interpret the assessments.

1. Print the Answer Key for the particular test you administered. The Answer Key provides the correct answer and the target decoding or word recognition skill for each item.
2. Locate and print the Progress Monitoring Test or Summative Assessment Score Sheet in SAM. Make a copy for each student. Use the Answer Key to mark each correct answer by circling the item number on the Score Sheet. Mark each incorrect answer by drawing an **X** through the item number.
3. After marking all of a student's answers, count the number of items answered correctly in each section and on the total test. Write this number in the box labeled "Number Correct"—for each section and for the total test.
4. Determine Percentage Scores (%) by dividing the number correct by the total number of items in each section and multiplying by 100. Do the same for the entire test. For Progress Monitoring Tests, determine how many items out of 30 were correct and multiply that value by 100. For Summative Assessments, determine how many items out of 50 were correct and multiply that value by 100.
5. Remember to determine Percentage Scores for each section *and* the entire assessment. Both scores are necessary to determine if a student passed the assessment.

Using the Results

Students who pass a Progress Monitoring Test or Summative Assessment demonstrate strong transfer and applied learning from the program. They should continue with *System 44* software and small-group instruction following program recommendations.

To pass an assessment, students should meet the following criteria:

- Score at least 75% in each section of the test
- Score at least 80% on the total test

Students who do *not* pass the assessments require teacher-directed follow-up. Consider the following:

- Review incorrect answers in each section of the test to determine specific skill weaknesses.
- Look for poor performance skill trends (e.g., long vowels, closed syllables).
- Look for poor performance-item-type trends (e.g., word discrimination vs. cloze sentences).
- Review and reteach skills that have not been maintained through:
  - Small-group instruction using *Resources for Differentiated Instruction*
  - One-to-one intervention during independent practice
  - Homework with targeted SAM resources

Preparing Students for Print Assessments

As with the software-based assessments, it is important to create a supportive testing environment that will promote optimum student performance.

Preparing Students to Take a Progress Monitoring or Summative Assessment
1. Ensure that the classroom environment is quiet and free of distractions during testing. Students will need to hear you read the question stems aloud and to follow along as you read.
2. Situate students so they can pay attention and focus. Be strategic about which students you allow to sit together.
3. Make sure each student has a sharpened pencil or pen.
4. Remind students that the test is designed to measure what students have been learning in *System 44*.
5. Remind students that some questions may be more difficult than others. They should try to answer all questions the best they can.
6. Ask that students raise a hand if they have questions or concerns during testing.
7. Suggest periodic break times after each section for students to stand up and stretch if they choose.

Reporting in *System 44*

Scholastic Reading Inventory (SRI) Reports

Scholastic Reading Counts! (SRC!) Reports

System 44 Reports Overview

Each time students log in to the *System 44* software, the Scholastic Achievement Manager (SAM) captures information on their software usage and progress in key skill areas. You can access this information for individual students, groups, or an entire class through the *System 44* reports.

Specifically, you can use *System 44* reports to:

- Assess phonemic awareness, decoding, spelling, and comprehension skills.
- Plan targeted activities for small-group instruction.
- Group and regroup students to target specific skills.
- Provide individualized feedback to motivate students.
- Assign grades based on performance in the entire *System 44* instructional model.
- Update families and caregivers on their child's progress with *System 44*.
- Determine when a student is prepared to exit *System 44*.

System 44 Reports

The following table describes how you can use *System 44* reports with individuals and groups of students.

If You Want to . . .	Run This Report
. . . determine initial placement into the *System 44* instruction	SPI Screening and Placement Report (p. 80)
. . . monitor class performance and changes in decoding status	SPI Summary Progress Report (p. 82)
. . . review an individual student's progress on SPI over time	SPI Student Progress Report (p. 84)
. . . identify students who are not meeting usage or cumulative performance expectations	*System 44* Reading Progress Report (p. 88)
. . . compare each student's response to the Median RTI	*System 44* Response to Intervention Report (p. 92)
. . . find cumulative information helpful for grading	*System 44* Grading Report (p. 94)
. . . review an individual student's strengths and weaknesses across the software zones for each Topic	*System 44* Student Software Performance Report (p. 96)
. . . identify Topics that each student has Fast-Tracked	*System 44* Student Software Performance Report (p. 96)
. . . correlate students' instructional time on the software with their mastery of Topics in each instructional category	*System 44* Student Mastery Report (p. 102)
. . . introduce families and caregivers to *System 44*	*System 44* Family Letter (p. 104)
. . . update families and caregivers on their children's progress	*System 44* Family Report (p. 106)
. . . analyze growth between two SRI tests	SRI Growth Report (p. 108)
. . . group and regroup students according to Lexile measure	SRI Intervention Grouping Report (p. 114)
. . . track how many *SRC!* quizzes students have passed	*SRC!* Books Read Report (p. 138)
. . . identify students who may be struggling with *SRC!* quizzes	*SRC!* Quiz Alert (p. 146)
. . . monitor student participation and progress in *SRC!*	*SRC!* Reading Progress Report (p. 148)

Meeting Teachers' Reporting Needs

As students use the *System 44* software, the Scholastic Achievement Manager (SAM) gathers data about program usage and performance. SAM reports enable you to monitor progress and plan instruction. SAM reports are available for the following components:

- *Scholastic Phonics Inventory* (SPI)
- *System 44* software
- *Scholastic Reading Inventory* (SRI)
- *Scholastic Reading Counts!* (*SRC!*)

Using Reports Data

SAM includes several types of reports to meet assessment and reporting needs. The following table briefly describes each of them.

Report Type	Use These Reports to . . .
Diagnostic	identify skills individual students are struggling with
Progress Monitoring	monitor students' achievement and progress
Instructional Planning	target teacher-led instruction to meet students' needs
School-to-Home	share progress information with families and caregivers
Alerts	address problems students may be having
Acknowledgments	recognize student successes

SAM reports are designed for flexible use. You can specify a time period for data. Data are also exportable to other applications. Reports viewed on the computer contain links to targeted instructional resources available through SAM. The *System 44 Software Manual* includes detailed instructions for how to export data and access SAM resources.

Sharing Reports

You may wish to print reports to share with students, families, or your principal. Reviewing report data can motivate students to be accountable and invested in their progress. School-to-Home reports update families and caregivers about a child's progress and involve them in their child's continued success. Reports also demonstrate a program's usage and impact for school and district-level administrators.

Purposeful Reporting

The following table describes specific purposes and benefits of the SPI and *System 44* reports.

SAM	Report	Purpose	Benefit
Diagnostic	1. SPI Screening and Placement Report	• Initial placement into Series 1 (Consonants and Short Vowels), Series 4 (Blends and Digraphs), or *READ 180*	• Results provide baseline decoding and word recognition performance data • Meets requirements for diagnostic screening assessment and multiple points of entry
	2. *System 44* Student Software Performance Report	• Provides detailed feedback on an individual student's strengths and weaknesses within the software zones • Identifies Fast-Tracked Topics • Monitors number of cycles to mastery and provisional promotion	• Analyzes how a student performs with a phonics element under different conditions: phonemic awareness, decoding, spelling, and reading connected text • Reports on the transfer and application of new skills • Links directly to SAM resources for further instruction
Progress Monitoring	3. SPI Summary Progress Report	• Shows changes in students' performance and progress on SPI over time	• Results show which students are making progress and which students may need more support • Helps determine when students are ready to exit *System 44*
	4. SPI Student Progress Report	• Provides detailed feedback on an individual student's strengths and weaknesses	• Provides information for customizing instruction • Helps determine when students are ready to exit *System 44*
	5. *System 44* Reading Progress Report	• Use every six weeks as a progress monitoring measure • Provides teachers with a view of all students' status, usage, and cumulative performance	• Provides a quick summary of all important *System 44* indicators • Identifies students exhibiting low or unusual usage and performance trends
	6. *System 44* Response to Intervention Report	• Graphically presents students' mastery of the *System 44* intervention over time • Displays Median RTI information as benchmark comparison with peers	• Meets RTI requirements for data-driven progress monitoring • Monitors students whose progress may be too slow and/or below the class average

SAM	Report	Purpose	Benefit
	7. *System 44* Individual Learning Plan Report	• Monitor students' progress toward individual academic and behavioral goals • Identifies students who are meeting, exceeding, or falling short of their goals	• Supports students' Individual Education Programs • Enables data-driven progress monitoring
	8. *System 44* Grading Report	• Tracks students' progress and achievements • Includes information from each part of the Instructional Model	• Helps teachers grade students • Monitors students whose progress is above or below the class average
	9. *System 44* Student Mastery Report	• Graphs an individual student's mastery of the six instructional categories (Consonants, Vowels, Sight Words, Word Parts, Syllables, and Success)	• Correlates students' instructional time on the software with their mastery of Topics in each category • Reports students' software rate of completion by minutes/Topic
	10. *System 44* Student Learning Plan Report	• Shows an individual student's progress toward individual academic and behavioral goals • Includes benchmarks to determine whether students are on track	• Supports students' Individual Education Programs • Provides data for conferences with families and other educators
School-to-Home	11. SPI Introductory Family Letter and Follow-Up Family Letter	• Informs families of their child's upcoming SPI test • Informs families of their child's decoding status • Provides suggestions for reading at home	• Facilitates the school-to-home connection • Helps families prepare students for SPI assessment • Contributes to family-teacher conferences
	12. *System 44* Family Letter and Family Report	• Informs families of their child's participation in the *System 44* program • Informs families of their child's usage and progress • Links to family resources	• Facilitates the school-to-home connection • Provides families with examples of student progress and success • Contributes to family-teacher conferences

System 44 Reports Timeline

The following timeline provides examples of how to use reports data throughout the school year to inform individual instruction, group students, and communicate with families about progress in *System 44*.

After 1 to 2 Weeks

After students have taken their first *Scholastic Reading Inventory* (SRI) test:

- Run the **SRI Intervention Grouping Report** to review Lexile measures.

Before students take the *Scholastic Phonics Inventory* (SPI):

- Print the **SPI Introductory Family Letter (SAM Keyword: SPI Letter 1)** and send home with students to inform families of their child's upcoming SPI test.

After students have taken the SPI:

- Run the **SPI Screening and Placement Report** to review Decoding Diagnoses.
- Print the **SPI Follow-Up Family Letter (SAM Keyword: SPI Letter 2)** and send home with students to inform families of their child's decoding status.

After students have been identified for *System 44*:

- Print the ***System 44* Family Letter (SAM Keyword: 44 Family)** and send home with students to inform families of their child's placement in *System 44*.

After 1 Month

After students have been using the software for a minimum of four weeks:

- Use the ***System 44* Student Software Performance Report** to begin evaluating strengths and weaknesses in phonemic awareness, decoding, spelling, and comprehension. Run it up to once per week to see whether students require more than one cycle to master any Topics.
- Run the ***System 44* Reading Progress Report** as a class or group-level progress monitoring measure. Review current status, usage, and cumulative performance for each student. Ensure that all students have the opportunity to be on the software for 25 minutes a day.

After 2 Months

After students have been using the software for approximately eight weeks:

- Run the ***System 44* Response to Intervention Report** to determine how each student is performing against the Median RTI for group, class, or school.
- Run the ***System 44* Student Mastery Report** to monitor each student's mastery over time for each of the instructional categories. Review the graph with students to encourage and motivate them.

Using *System 44* Reports

You can find more information on the *System 44* reports in *Resources for Differentiated Instruction:*

- Review how regularly running reports can meet the needs of **special education** students and help with **IEPs** on pp. 492-493.
- Read what research says about the importance of **data-driven decision making** on pp. 508-509.

After 3 Months

After students have been using the software for 12–16 weeks:

- Send the ***System 44* Family Report** home with each student to explain what students are working on and how they are progressing.

After students have taken the SPI again at the middle of the school year:

- Run the **SPI Summary Progress Report** to review changes in students' decoding statuses.
- Run the **SPI Student Progress Report** to review students' individual progress with letter names, sight words, and nonsense words.

After 6 Months

After students are two-thirds through the school year:

- Run the ***System 44* Reading Progress Report** to ensure students are receiving adequate time on the software and are meeting performance expectations.
- Run the ***System 44* Student Software Performance Report** to review students' individual diagnostic needs for any additional instruction and practice.

After 9 Months

When students are nearing the end of the school year:

- Run the ***System 44* Student Mastery Report** to determine where students are in the scope and sequence and what remains for them to master.
- Run the ***System 44* Response to Intervention Report** for an overview of how all students are responding to *System 44* in comparison to the Median RTI.
- Send a final ***System 44* Family Report** home with students so that families can review progress and celebrate student reading success with *System 44*.

After students have taken the SPI again at the end of the school year:

- Run the **SPI Summary Progress Report** to evaluate students' progress.
- Run the **SPI Student Progress Report** to review detailed information about individual student performance on each SPI subtest.

Managing Reports on the Teacher Dashboard

The Teacher Dashboard can simplify the reports analysis process. Review the aggregated SAM data on the Teacher Dashboard. Use the Teacher Dashboard Reports Scheduler to schedule SAM reports to be sent to your email inbox.

Scheduling SAM Reports

Analyze SAM reports regularly. Use your school calendar, your testing calendar, and your *44Book* Planning Guides to determine the most appropriate times to schedule each report.

In addition, review aggregated data on the Teacher Dashboard. These Data Snapshots provide an overview of student participation in each component of the software. Identify any areas of concern and schedule accompanying SAM reports to analyze.

Use the Report Scheduler to run the following reports:

- SPI Summary Progress Report
- *System 44* Reading Progress Report
- *System 44* Grading Report
- SRI Growth Report
- *SRC!* Reading Progress Report

Launch the Report Scheduler

1. Log in to the Teacher Dashboard anytime to schedule a SAM Report.
2. Review the Data Snapshots for each class. Review results to determine which reports to review.
3. From the Teacher Dashboard Home Page or Class Page, click **Schedule a Report** to launch the Report Scheduler.

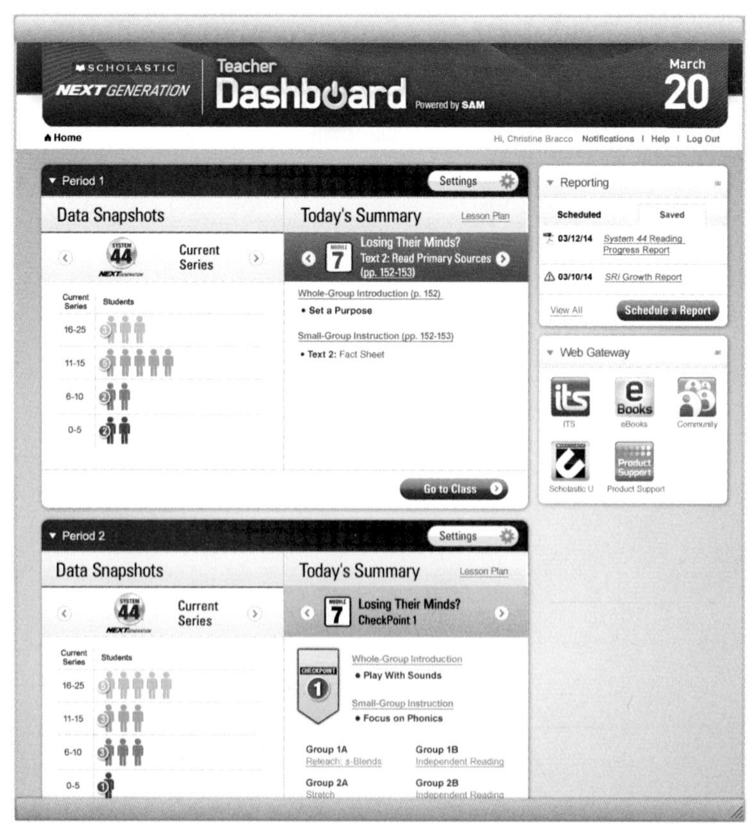

Teacher Dashboard: Home Page

Using the Teacher Dashboard Report Scheduler

The Report Scheduler on the Teacher Dashboard contains many of the same features and functions as reports settings found in SAM. Use these settings to schedule a report.

Schedule a Report

1. **Who:** Select a class.
2. **What:** Select a program and a report.
3. **Time Period:** Select whether to run the report for the last two weeks, the grading period, or the school year. The selected time period is dependent on the date you schedule the report to be run.
4. **When:** Select the date to run the report.
5. **Confirm:** Review your selection. Click **DONE** to schedule the report.

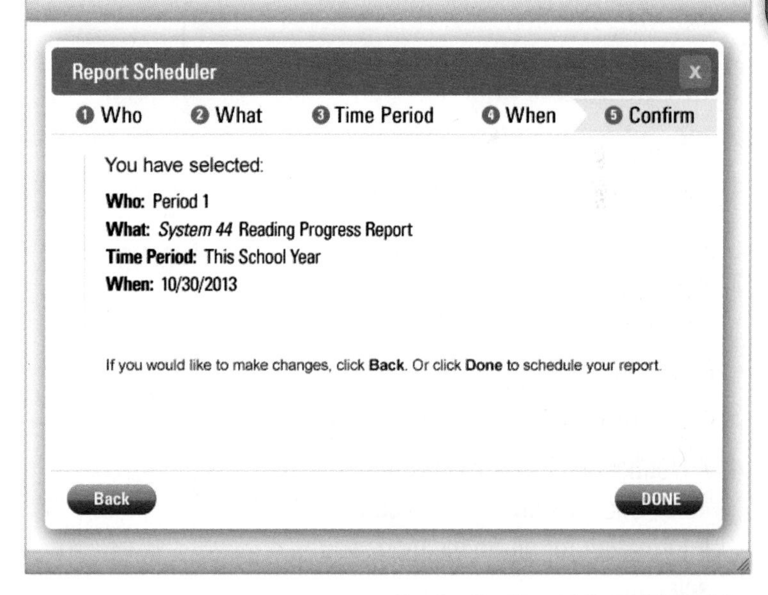

Teacher Dashboard: Report Scheduler

Review a Report

When the report is ready, you will receive an email notification. The report will be available in the Report Scheduler as a PDF. Use the Reporting in *System 44* section of this guide to complete an analysis of student results. Use that analysis to make instructional decisions and redirect student focus where necessary.

Teacher Dashboard Notifications

The Teacher Dashboard simplifies the reports analysis process. Use the Teacher Dashboard to manage weekly Notification digests. Review the Notifications and use the information to determine which SAM reports to schedule for further analysis.

Launch the Notifications Wizard

Log in to the Teacher Dashboard anytime to set or modify Notifications settings. From the Teacher Dashboard Home Page, click **Notifications** to launch the Notifications Wizard.

You will receive a digest each week that lists any students who fit any Notification alert criteria. All Notifications will appear in one digest. You may change your Notifications options at any time.

Teacher Dashboard: Home Page

Manage Notifications

1. Click the **Notifications** link on the Home Page of the Teacher Dashboard.
2. Place a check mark next to any Notifications you wish to receive. Uncheck any you do not wish to receive.
3. Click **Save** to schedule the Notifications.
4. A Notification email will be sent to your inbox once a week and will contain information for all Notifications you selected.
5. Return to this screen to adjust Notifications options at any time.

Teacher Dashboard: Notifications Wizard

Notifications Options

You can choose to receive one or more of the Notifications listed below. By default, the Teacher Dashboard will send weekly email alerts to inform you of any student performance results fitting specific criteria during the previous week. You may choose to opt out or change your Notifications settings at any time.

Receive This Notification	When	Follow-Up Reports
	***System 44* Software**	
Low Weekly Software Usage	A student logged in for less than 3 sessions the previous week.	*System 44* Reading Progress Report *System 44* Response to Intervention Report
Series Completion	A student completed a Series in the previous week.	*System 44* Reading Progress Report *System 44* Student Software Performance Report
Cycles to Mastery	A student began a second or third cycle through a Topic in the previous week.	*System 44* Student Software Performance Report

Screening and Placement Report

Purpose

This report details the performance of a class or group of students on the SPI placement test.

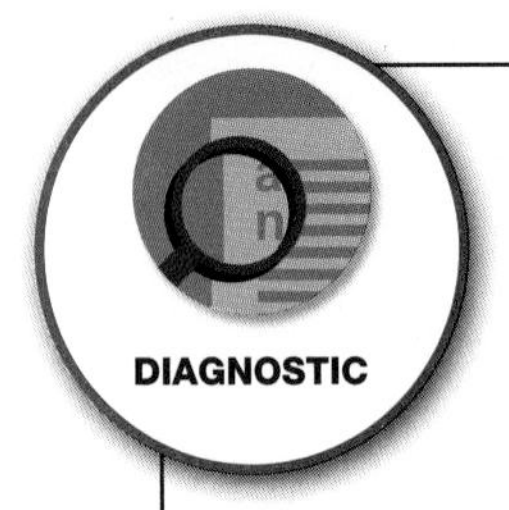

Screening and Placement Report

CLASS: PERIOD 2

School: Cesar Chavez Middle School
Teacher: Mercedes Cole
Grade: 7

Time Period: 08/24/11 – 02/02/12 ❶

STUDENT	❷ DATE OF SPI PLACEMENT TEST	❸ % ACCURATE AND FLUENT ON SPI SUBTESTS					❹ SPI FLUENCY SCORE	❺ SPI DECODING STATUS	❻ SRI SCORE (LEXILE®)
		LETTER NAMES ACCURACY	SIGHT WORDS ACCURACY	SIGHT WORDS FLUENCY	NONSENSE WORDS ACCURACY	NONSENSE WORDS FLUENCY			
Anderson, Darrell	09/04/11	100%	80%	13%	60%	17%	9	Beginning Decoder	BR
Benson, Kate	09/07/11	100%	90%	40%	77%	27%	20	Developing Decoder	350
Donato, Aimee	09/04/11	100%	80%	37%	70%	13%	15	Developing Decoder	220
Gonzalez, Lydia	09/04/11	55%	10%	N/A	7%	N/A	5*	Pre-Decoder	BR
Huang, Hsin-Yi	09/04/11	100%	80%	13%	80%	17%	9	Beginning Decoder	150
Lee, Andrea	09/08/11	100%	97%	80%	90%	77%	47	Advancing Decoder	450
Mamdani, Aliyah	09/07/11	100%	70%	13%	80%	43%	17	Developing Decoder	280
Molina, Robert	09/04/11	100%	83%	37%	83%	23%	18	Developing Decoder	330
Price, Jamal	09/07/11	100%	63%	27%	57%	20%	14	Developing Decoder	250
Rubio, Alejandro	09/04/11	100%	90%	33%	80%	37%	21	Developing Decoder	360
Sanders, Renee	09/22/11	91%	63%	13%	53%	13%	8	Beginning Decoder	BR
Turner, Aiden	09/10/11	73%	20%	7%	10%	3%	3	Pre-Decoder	BR
Young, Kevin	09/04/11	100%	80%	17%	67%	17%	10	Beginning Decoder	200

SPI FLUENCY SCORE	DECODING STATUS	RECOMMENDED INSTRUCTION AND PLACEMENT
0–10	Pre-Decoder	Phonemic awareness, letter names, letter-sound correspondence
0–10	Beginning Decoder	Foundational Phonics
11–22	Developing Decoder	Targeted phonics remediation
23–60	Advancing Decoder	Vocabulary, comprehension, fluency

* Student received accommodations during this test administration.

Using This Report

Purpose: This report details the performance of a class or group of students on the SPI placement test.

Follow-Up: Use SPI results and other evaluation data to place each student into an appropriate intervention. If you are using Scholastic programs, Pre- and Beginning Decoders are recommended for Series 1 of *System 44*, Developing Decoders are recommended for Series 4 of *System 44*, and Advancing Decoders are recommended for *READ 180*.

How It Helps

I use SPI results and other evaluation data to place students into appropriate intervention.

Understand the Data

1 Time Period
This report displays the results of each student's first SPI test within the current school year.

2 Date of SPI Placement Test
The date of each student's first SPI test.

3 Percent Accurate and Fluent on SPI Subtests
The percentage of items in each subtest answered correctly (accuracy) and within the given time limit (fluency). Only accuracy is assessed for the Letter Names subtest.

4 SPI Fluency Score
The total number of fluent responses in the Sight Words and Nonsense Words subtests, out of 60 items. Note: If accuracy-only scoring has been selected for a student who requires accommodations, this is the total number of accurate responses in these subtests.

5 SPI Decoding Status
A criterion-referenced indicator of each student's foundational reading skills. For a full description of each Decoding Status, see page 33.

- **Pre-Decoder:** A student with little or no knowledge of letter names or letter-sound correspondences. This student will place into Series 1 of the *System 44* software.
- **Beginning Decoder:** A student who can identify letter names but cannot decode fluently. This student will place into Series 1 of the *System 44* software.
- **Developing Decoder:** A student who can fluently decode words with consonants and short vowels but cannot fluently decode more complex words. This student will place into Series 4 of the *System 44* software.
- **Advancing Decoder:** A student who can decode with adequate fluency. This student will place into *READ 180* if the program is available.

6 SRI Score (Lexile)
Each student's most recent score on the *Scholastic Reading Inventory* if available in SAM.

Use the Data

Who: Teachers, Administrators (Teacher, Class, or Group report)

When: After the initial administration of SPI

How: Apply the information from this report in the following ways:

Diagnose Reading Abilities

- Determine if a decoding problem is impacting reading comprehension.

Place Students

- Screen students into the *System 44* program.
- Provide differentiated placement for students within the *System 44* instruction. Fast-Track assessments will continue to customize student placement and movement through the software.

Review Related Reports

- *System 44* Student Software Performance Report (p. 96)
- SRI Intervention Grouping Report (p. 114)

Data in Action

Phonemic Awareness Students who are assessed as Pre- or Beginning Decoders may need direct, teacher-led instruction in Phonemic Awareness and Alphabet Recognition. Further evaluate these students' foundational literacy skills with the Phonemic Awareness, Alphabet Recognition, and Print Concepts assessments described in *Resources for Differentiated Instruction*.

Summary Progress Report

Purpose

This report shows changes in performance and progress on SPI over time.

Summary Progress Report

CLASS: PERIOD 2

School: Cesar Chavez Middle School
Teacher: Mercedes Cole
Grade: 7

Time Period: 08/24/11 – 05/31/12 

	LAST THREE TESTS IN SELECTED TIME PERIOD								
	TEST 1			TEST 2			TEST 3		
STUDENT	❷ TEST DATE	❸ SPI FLUENCY SCORE	❹ SPI DECODING STATUS	TEST DATE	SPI FLUENCY SCORE	SPI DECODING STATUS	TEST DATE	SPI FLUENCY SCORE	SPI DECODING STATUS
Anderson, Darrell	09/04/11	9	Beginning	01/12/12	14	Developing	05/27/12	23	Advancing
Benson, Kate	09/07/11	20	Developing	01/13/12	27	Advancing	05/25/12	34	Advancing
Donato, Aimee	09/04/11	15	Developing	01/13/12	21	Developing	05/27/12	29	Advancing
Gonzalez, Lydia	09/04/11	5*	Pre-	01/12/12	23*	Beginning	05/25/12	16*	Developing
Huang, Hsin-Yi	09/04/11	9	Beginning	01/12/12	15	Developing	05/25/12	23	Advancing
Lee, Andrea	09/08/11	47	Advancing	N/A	N/A	N/A	N/A	N/A	N/A
Mamdani, Aliyah	09/07/11	17	Developing	01/12/12	24	Advancing	05/25/12	33	Advancing
Molina, Robert	09/04/11	18	Developing	01/15/12	27	Advancing	05/27/12	36	Advancing
Price, Jamal	09/07/11	14	Developing	01/12/12	22	Developing	05/25/12	30	Advancing
Rubio, Alejandro	09/04/11	21	Developing	01/12/12	28	Advancing	05/25/12	40	Advancing
Sanders, Renee	09/22/11	8	Beginning	01/12/12	12	Developing	05/25/12	21	Developing
Turner, Aiden	09/10/11	3	Pre-	01/13/12	10	Beginning	05/28/12	20	Developing
Young, Kevin	09/04/11	10	Beginning	01/12/12	17	Developing	05/21/12	31	Advancing

SPI FLUENCY SCORE	DECODING STATUS	RECOMMENDED INSTRUCTION
0–10	Pre-Decoder	Phonemic awareness, letter names, letter-sound correspondence
0–10	Beginning Decoder	Foundational Phonics
11–22	Developing Decoder	Targeted phonics remediation
23–60	Advancing Decoder	Vocabulary, comprehension, fluency

* Student received accommodations during this test administration.

Using This Report

Purpose: This report shows changes in performance and progress on SPI over time for a class or group of students.

Follow-Up: Use SPI results and other evaluation data to monitor student response to intervention and inform grouping.

How It Helps

I use this report to monitor student response to intervention and to form groups for Small-Group Instruction.

Understand the Data

1 Time Period
This report displays the results of up to three SPI tests within the selected time period.

2 Test Date
The date of each SPI test administration.

3 SPI Fluency Score
The total number of fluent responses in the Sight Words and Nonsense Words subtests, out of 60 items. Note: If accuracy-only scoring has been selected for a student who requires accommodations, this is the total number of *accurate* responses in these subtests.

4 SPI Decoding Status
A criterion-referenced indicator of each student's foundational reading skills. For a full description of each Decoding Status, see page 33.

- **Pre-Decoder:** A student with little or no knowledge of letter names or letter-sound correspondences.
- **Beginning Decoder:** A student who can identify letter names but cannot decode fluently.
- **Developing Decoder:** A student who can fluently decode words with consonants and short vowels but cannot fluently decode more complex words.
- **Advancing Decoder:** A student who can decode with adequate fluency.

Use the Data

Who: Teachers and Administrators (Teacher, Class, or Group report)

When: After each subsequent administration of SPI

How: Apply the information from this report in the following ways:

Monitor Progress

- Assess growth over time for your class or groups of students.
- Evaluate the effectiveness of instruction.

Establish Groups

- Inform grouping for differentiated instruction. The Teacher Dashboard's Groupinator will recommend new *44Book* groups each time students take a SPI test. Use the Groupinator to adjust groups.

Review Related Reports

- *System 44* Reading Progress Report (p. 90)
- *System 44* Response to Intervention Report (p. 92)

Data in Action

Monitoring Progress SPI contains three equivalent test forms and students automatically receive a new form each time they take SPI. Administer SPI a maximum of three times per year to avoid skewed results from students becoming overly familiar with the test.

Student Progress Report

Purpose

This report shows detailed performance data and progress on SPI over time for an individual student.

Student Progress Report

STUDENT: YOUNG, KEVIN

SCHOLASTIC SPI PHONICS INVENTORY

School: Cesar Chavez Middle School
Teacher: Mercedes Cole
Grade: 7
Class: Period 2

Time Period: 08/24/11 – 05/28/12 ❶

Current SRI Score (Lexile®): 450
Test Date: 05/25/11

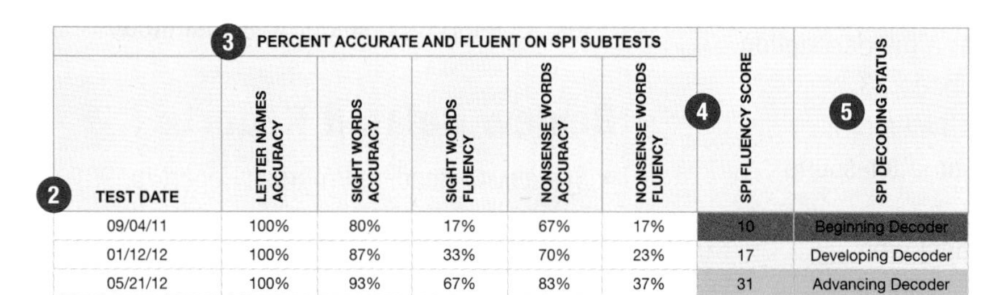

❷ TEST DATE	❸ PERCENT ACCURATE AND FLUENT ON SPI SUBTESTS: LETTER NAMES ACCURACY	SIGHT WORDS ACCURACY	SIGHT WORDS FLUENCY	NONSENSE WORDS ACCURACY	NONSENSE WORDS FLUENCY	❹ SPI FLUENCY SCORE	❺ SPI DECODING STATUS
09/04/11	100%	80%	17%	67%	17%	10	Beginning Decoder
01/12/12	100%	87%	33%	70%	23%	17	Developing Decoder
05/21/12	100%	93%	67%	83%	37%	31	Advancing Decoder

SPI FLUENCY SCORE	DECODING STATUS	RECOMMENDED INSTRUCTION
0–10	Pre-Decoder	Phonemic awareness, letter names, letter-sound correspondence
0–10	Beginning Decoder	Foundational Phonics
11–22	Developing Decoder	Targeted phonics remediation
23–60	Advancing Decoder	Vocabulary, comprehension, fluency

Using This Report

Purpose: This report shows detailed performance data and progress on SPI over time for an individual student.

Follow-Up: Use SPI results and other evaluation data to monitor student progress and customize instructional plans.

How It Helps

This report helps me monitor student progress and customize instructional plans.

Understand the Data

❶ Time Period
This report displays the results of all SPI tests taken by a student within the selected time period.

❷ Test Date
The date of each SPI test administration.

❸ Percent Accurate and Fluent on SPI Subtests
The percentage of items in each subtest answered correctly (accuracy) and within the given time limit (fluency). Only accuracy is assessed for the Letter Names subtest.

❹ SPI Fluency Score
The total number of fluent responses in the Sight Words and Nonsense Words subtests, out of 60 items. Note: If accuracy-only scoring has been selected for a student who requires accommodations, this is the total number of *accurate* responses in these subtests.

❺ SPI Decoding Status
A criterion-referenced indicator of each student's foundational reading skills. For a full description of each Decoding Status, see page 33.

- **Pre-Decoder:** A student with little or no knowledge of letter names or letter-sound correspondences.
- **Beginning Decoder:** A student who can identify letter names but cannot decode fluently.
- **Developing Decoder:** A student who can fluently decode words with consonants and short vowels but cannot fluently decode more complex words.
- **Advancing Decoder:** A student who can decode with adequate fluency.

Use the Data

Who: Teachers and Administrators (Student report)

When: After each administration of SPI

How: Apply the information from this report in the following ways:

Review Test Results

- Monitor student development of foundational reading skills.
- Assess student response to intervention.

Share Results

- Share performance results with students and families.
- At IEP meetings, share results with support specialists.

Review Related Reports

- *System 44* Student Software Performance Report (p. 96)
- *System 44* Student Mastery Report (p. 102)

Data in Action

Student Conferences Share data reports with students to make them accountable for their reading achievement. Celebrate their successes and identify areas where they need more practice. Work together to set reasonable goals.

SPI Reports

Introductory Family Letter

Print this letter (**SAM Keyword:** **SPI Letter 1**) and make copies for each student. The resource contains both an English and a Spanish version of the letter.

Purpose

Send this letter home before administering SPI to inform families that their child will take an SPI test. This fosters the school-to-home connection and allows them to support their child's efforts.

STUDENT:

School:
Teacher:

Dear Parent or Caregiver:

On ____________________, your child will complete the *Scholastic Phonics Inventory* (SPI), a test of basic reading skills. SPI will determine whether your child would benefit from instruction in foundational reading skills to support his or her reading comprehension. The results of the test will help us design an instructional program that matches your child's needs.

SPI is a brief test that is usually completed in about ten minutes. Students take the test independently on a computer. SPI measures whether students can identify individual letters and words accurately and quickly. These skills are essential building blocks for reading development.

Please make sure that your child comes to school ready to take SPI on the day of the test. Remind your child that the purpose of the test is to design an instructional path to support his or her reading achievement.

Once testing is complete, I will send home a letter with your child's results. In the meantime, please feel free to contact me with any questions.

Thank you for your support.

Sincerely,

How It Helps

I send the Introductory Family Letter home at the beginning of the year to let families know that their children will be taking SPI.

Follow-Up Family Letter

Print this letter (**SAM Keyword:** SPI Letter 2) and make copies for each student. Use the SPI Screening and Placement Report (p. 80) or SPI Summary Progress Report (p. 82) to complete the test results. The resource contains both an English and a Spanish version of the letter.

Purpose

This letter provides a student's SPI test results and suggestions for building reading skills at home.

STUDENT:

School:
Teacher:

Date:

Dear Parent or Caregiver:

Your child has completed the *Scholastic Phonics Inventory* (SPI), a test of basic reading skills. SPI measures whether students can identify letters and words accurately and quickly. These skills are essential to reading development because they support comprehension.

SPI results identify a student's level of foundational reading skills as one of the following:

- **Pre-Decoder** A student who has little or no familiarity with letters or the sounds they stand for.
- **Beginning Decoder** A student who can identify letters but cannot sound out or read words fluently (i.e., accurately and quickly).
- **Developing Decoder** A student who can sound out and read some words fluently but not others.
- **Advancing Decoder** A student who can sound out and read words fluently.

Below are the results of your child's test.

Test Date:
Decoding Status:
Comments:

I am using the results of this test to provide your child with instruction in the skills he or she needs to become a proficient reader.

Here are some ways you can support your child's reading development at home:

- **The Daily Read** Make reading a daily activity by reading to or with your child for 20 minutes each day.
- **Fast and Fun Reads** Use magazines, newspapers, comic books, recipes, TV schedules, travel guides, and road signs as reading opportunities—wherever you are and whatever you and your child are doing.
- **The Movie or the Book** Rent videos or DVDs on topics that interest your child. Help your child find books on similar topics.
- **Read and Ride** Listen to books on tape or CD while traveling by car, or bri personal player with headphones for your child to listen to books on a bus plane.
- **Read and Chat** Talk with your child about what he or she is reading. Ask c about the characters and events in the story.

Please feel free to contact me with any questions. Thank you for your support.

Sincerely,

How It Helps

I send the Follow-Up Family Letter home after each test to update families on their children's reading progress.

Reading Progress Report | Best Practice Report

Purpose

Run this report every six weeks as a progress monitor of all students' status, usage, and cumulative performance in *System 44*.

Reading Progress Report

CLASS: PERIOD 3

School: The Lincoln School
Teacher: Margaret Parker
Grade: 7

Time Period: 08/15/13 - 11/30/13 ❶

STUDENT	STATUS				USAGE		CUMULATIVE PERFORMANCE					
	CURRENT TOPIC	TOPIC NAME	SCOPE & SEQUENCE COMPLETED	NO. OF TOPICS COMPLETED /160	❷ MEDIAN SESSION TIME (MIN.)	❸ TOTAL TIME (MIN.)	❹ WORDS READ	❺ DECODING ACCURACY SCORE	❻ DECODING FLUENCY SCORE	❼ SPELLING SCORE	❽ COMPREHENSION SCORE	❾ ORAL READING FLUENCY RECORDING SCORE (OUT OF 6)
Anderson, Michael	2.3	Consonants ***h, k***	7%	11	▸ 10	310	2,205	▸ 68%	▸ 65%	▸ 60%	▸ 69%	2
Benson, Carol	7.4	***sh, ch, -tch***	29%	46	▸ 12	552	12,529	75%	▸ 65%	75%	76%	2
Charles, Riko	10.1	Long a ***(a_e)***	39%	63	18	1,134	23,790	95%	▸ 67%	▸ 60%	88%	5
Donata, Amy	4.2	Double Consonants	16%	26	20	520	10,688	88%	85%	77%	80%	3
Dunley, Sarah	8.2	Digraph Review	31%	50	15	750	20,869	90%	88%	89%	90%	4
Ellison, Roland	3.1	***s***-Blends	11%	17	15	408	7,547	85%	80%	78%	78%	5
Gonzalez, Lydia	8.5	More on Ending ***-ed***	33%	53	18	954	22,371	92%	90%	90%	87%	5
Huang, Hsin-Yi	9.2	Unstressed Closed Syllables ***(i, o, u)***	36%	57	17	969	24,333	85%	82%	88%	91%	5
Lee, Andrea	3.3	Consonants ***j, w***	11%	18	▸ 12	216	7,355	80%	▸ 68%	▸ 68%	72%	2
Lowell, Sarah	6.4	More ***s***-Blends	25%	40	15	600	16,725	72%	70%	70%	70%	4

▸ Indicates below benchmark usage or performance expectations

Using This Report

Purpose: Run this report every six weeks for a progress monitoring overview of all students' status, usage, and cumulative performance.

Follow-Up: Use this report to identify students who may be struggling with a particular Topic and/or not using the software adequately. Review this report when using the System 44 Grading Worksheet in the SARG.

How It Helps

I use this report to identify students who are struggling or need to spend more time on the software.

Understanding the Data

1 Time Period
Run for This School Year to review comprehensive performance results. Customize time period settings to analyze student progress within shorter time periods.

2 Median Session Time (Minutes)
Median minutes spent per session per day (updated each time a student logs on and off). The red flag indicates that Median Session Time is less than 15 minutes. A low number may indicate infrequent software use or logging off before the end of the rotation.

3 Total Time (Minutes)
Cumulative minutes students have spent on the *System 44* software. This does not include time spent on in-progress Topics or on the student home page.

4 Words Read
Cumulative number of words read to date. This report also credits a student for words read in books in the *System 44* Library for which the student successfully completed a *Scholastic Reading Counts!* quiz.

5 Decoding Accuracy Score
Average percentage of target words scored as accurate on the Progress Monitor.

6 Decoding Fluency Score
Average percentage of target words scored as fluent on the Progress Monitor. (A score of fluent indicates a response that is both accurate and within the cut-off time.)

7 Spelling Score
Average percentage of target spelling words scored as fluent on the Spelling Challenge.

8 Comprehension Score
Average percentage of questions answered correctly on the first attempt at Read & Think.

9 Oral Reading Fluency Recording Score (Out of 6)
Average fluency score based on evaluation of all scored Success Passages.

Use the Data

Who: Teachers and Administrators (Teacher, Class, or Group report)

When: Every six weeks

How: Apply the information from this report in the following ways:

Monitor Software Participation

- Monitor cumulative usage and performance for your class or groups of students.
- Identify students who are consistently not meeting usage or performance expectations. If multiple students' median session time is low, use a timer to ensure that each rotation is timed appropriately.

Review Performance Results

- If average performance scores are low, review software usage tips with students. Remind students that their first answers are recorded.

Review Related Reports

- *System 44* Response to Intervention Report (p. 92)
- *System 44* Grading Report (p. 94)
- *System 44* Student Mastery Report (p. 102)

Data in Action

Accuracy and Fluency This report differentiates between decoding accuracy and decoding fluency. If your students are acquiring new decoding skills but struggling with decoding fluency, provide additional timed practice using the Flip Chart and SAM resources.

Analyze the Results | Reading Progress Report

Students should be able to complete each Series in one or two weeks with strong results in each zone.

DATA STORY

Student: Michael Anderson
Current Topic: 2.3
Topics Completed: 11
Median Session Time: 10 minutes

Identify students like Michael who struggle with software usage.

Reading Progress Report
CLASS: PERIOD 3

PROGRESS MONITORING
School: The Lincoln School
Teacher: Margaret Parker
Grade: 7

SYSTEM 44 NEXT GENERATION

Time Period: 08/15/13 - 11/30/13

STUDENT	STATUS				USAGE		CUMULATIVE PERFORMANCE					
	CURRENT TOPIC	TOPIC NAME	SCOPE & SEQUENCE COMPLETED	NO. OF TOPICS COMPLETED /160	MEDIAN SESSION TIME (MIN.)	TOTAL TIME (MIN.)	WORDS READ	DECODING ACCURACY SCORE	DECODING FLUENCY SCORE	SPELLING SCORE	COMPREHENSION SCORE	ORAL READING FLUENCY RECORDING SCORE (OUT OF 6)
Anderson, Michael	2.3	Consonants ***h, k***	7%	11	►10	310	2,205	►68%	►65%	►60%	►69%	2
Benson, Carol	7.4	***sh, ch, -tch***	29%	46	►12	552	12,529	75%	►65%	75%	76%	2
Charles, Riko	10.1	Long a ***(a_e)***	39%	63	18	1,134	23,790	95%	►67%	►60%	88%	5
Donata, Amy	4.2	Double Consonants	16%	26	20	520	10,688	88%	85%	77%	80%	3
Dunley, Sarah	8.2	Digraph Review	31%	50	15	750	20,869	90%	88%	89%	90%	4
Ellison, Roland	3.1	***s***-Blends	11%	17	15	408	7,547	85%	80%	78%	78%	5
Gonzalez, Lydia	8.5	More on Ending ***-ed***	33%	53	18	954	22,371	92%	90%	90%	87%	5
Huang, Hsin-Yi	9.2	Unstressed Closed Syllables ***(i, o, u)***	36%	57	17	969	24,333	85%	82%	88%	91%	5
Lee, Andrea	3.3	Consonants ***j, w***	11%	18	►12	216	7,355	80%	►68%	►68%	72%	2
Lowell, Sarah	6.4	More ***s***-Blends	25%	40	15	600	16,725	72%	70%	70%	70%	4

► Indicates below benchmark usage or performance expectations

Enlargement: Reading Progress Report

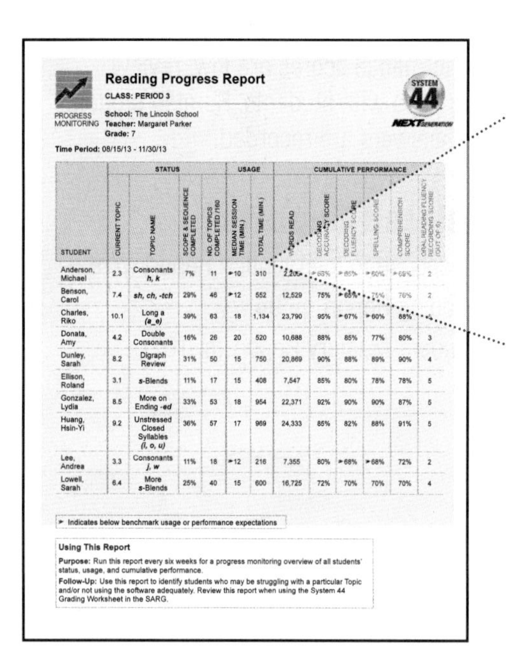

Reading Progress Report
CLASS: PERIOD 3
School: The Lincoln School
Teacher: Margaret Parker
Grade: 7
Time Period: 08/15/13 - 11/30/13
► Indicates below benchmark usage or performance expectations

Using This Report

Purpose: Run this report every six weeks for a progress monitoring overview of all students' status, usage, and cumulative performance.

Follow-Up: Use this report to identify students who may be struggling with a particular Topic and/or not using the software adequately. Review this report when using the System 44 Grading Worksheet in the SARG.

Data Point	Data Analysis	NEXT STEPS
1 Michael has only completed 11 Topics while the class median is 43 Topics completed.	Michael has been in this class since the beginning of the year. He isn't progressing through Topics as quickly as he should.	Review results on the *System 44* Student Software Performance Report to determine the cause for low Topic completion.
2 Michael is spending less than 15 minutes per day on the software.	Most of the class is maintaining appropriate session times. Michael is likely off-task during this rotation.	Have students track daily progress on a Software Log and review the log during Small-Group Instruction.
3 Michael's performance in each zone is weak.	Michael is struggling in all areas of the software. He struggles most with spelling.	Provide one-to-one intervention using *Resources for Differentiated Instruction.*

BEST PRACTICES

DATA STORY

Student: Hsin-Yi Huang
Current Topic: 9.2
Topics Completed: 57
Median Session Time: 17 minutes

Identify students like Hsin-Yi who are progressing in the System 44 *software.*

Reading Progress Report

CLASS: PERIOD 3

PROGRESS MONITORING

School: The Lincoln School
Teacher: Margaret Parker
Grade: 7

SYSTEM 44 NEXT GENERATION

Time Period: 08/15/13 - 11/30/13

STUDENT	STATUS				USAGE (1)		CUMULATIVE PERFORMANCE (2)				(3)	
	CURRENT TOPIC	TOPIC NAME	SCOPE & SEQUENCE COMPLETED	NO. OF TOPICS COMPLETED /160	MEDIAN SESSION TIME (MIN.)	TOTAL TIME (MIN.)	WORDS READ	DECODING ACCURACY SCORE	DECODING FLUENCY SCORE	SPELLING SCORE	COMPREHENSION SCORE	ORAL READING FLUENCY RECORDING SCORE (OUT OF 6)
Anderson, Michael	2.3	Consonants *h, k*	7%	11	► 10	310	2,205	► 68%	► 65%	► 60%	► 69%	2
Benson, Carol	7.4	*sh, ch, -tch*	29%	46	► 12	552	12,529	75%	► 65%	75%	76%	2
Charles, Riko	10.1	Long a *(a_e)*	39%	63	18	1,134	23,790	95%	► 67%	► 60%	88%	5
Donata, Amy	4.2	Double Consonants	16%	26	20	520	10,688	88%	85%	77%	80%	3
Dunley, Sarah	8.2	Digraph Review	31%	50	15	750	20,869	90%	88%	89%	90%	4
Ellison, Roland	3.1	*s*-Blends	11%	17	15	408	7,547	85%	80%	78%	78%	5
Gonzalez, Lydia	8.5	More on Ending *-ed*	33%	53	18	954	22,371	92%	90%	90%	87%	5
Huang, Hsin-Yi	9.2	Unstressed Closed Syllables *(i, o, u)*	36%	57	17	969	24,333	85%	82%	88%	91%	5
Lee, Andrea	3.3	Consonants *j, w*	11%	18	► 12	216	7,355	80%	► 68%	► 68%	72%	2
Lowell, Sarah	6.4	More *s*-Blends	25%	40	15	600	16,725	72%	70%	70%	70%	4

► Indicates below benchmark usage or performance expectations

Enlargement: Reading Progress Report

Using This Report

Purpose: Run this report every six weeks for a progress monitoring overview of all students' status, usage, and cumulative performance.

Follow-Up: Use this report to identify students who may be struggling with a particular Topic and/or not using the software adequately. Review this report when using the System 44 Grading Worksheet in the SARG.

Data Point	Data Analysis	NEXT STEPS
(1) Hsin-Yi has completed 57 Topics.	Hsin-Yi is completing software at a quick pace. She may be Fast-Tracking.	Review results on the *System 44* Response to Intervention Report to see how many Topics Hsin-Yi has Fast-Tracked.
(2) Hsin-Yi has read 24,333 words, which is the highest in the class.	Hsin-Yi has probably read many books from the *System 44* Library and passed the *SRC!* quizzes.	Celebrate words read with graphs or certificates.
(3) Hsin-Yi's performance in each zone is strong, especially in comprehension.	High results confirm that Hsin-Yi may be ready for more challenge.	Challenge Hsin-Yi to read Stretch Texts more independently.

Response to Intervention Report

Purpose

Use this report to monitor and compare your students' responses to the *System 44* intervention over time. Use the Median RTI as a benchmark for each student's progress relative to his/her peers.

Response to Intervention Report

CLASS: PERIOD 3

School: Cesar Chavez Middle School
Teacher: Mercedes Cole
Grade: 7

09/06/11 – 05/15/12 ❶

STUDENT	DATE STARTED SYSTEM 44	TOTAL TIME (MIN.)	❷ NO. OF SESSIONS	❸ MASTERY TO DATE (OUT OF 25 SERIES)	NO. OF TOPICS MASTERED	❹ NO. OF TOPICS FAST TRACKED	❺ MIN./ TOPIC
Anderson, Darrell	09/15/11	1,305	130	15	102	57	15
Benson, Kate	09/15/11	1,365	125	14	97	0	14
Donato, Aimee	10/03/11	945	100	9	63	8	17
Gonzalez, Lydia	09/26/11	1,095	112	11	78	33	24
Huang, Hsin-Yi	09/09/11	1,170	155	17	115	24	13
Lee, Andrea	09/09/11	1,305	142	16	112	36	17
Mamdani, Aliyah	10/03/11	26	3	0	2	0	13
Molina, Robert	09/09/11	1,056	120	12	86	18	18
Price, Jamal	09/15/11	1,163	124	13	90	20	17
Rubio, Alejandro	09/09/11	1,230	126	15	106	29	16
Sanders, Renee	09/09/11	1,288	128	16	109	28	16
Turner, Aiden	10/03/11	1,047	105	9	64	0	16
Young, Kevin	09/09/11	1,350	134	17	114	42	19
❻ **MEDIAN RTI**		**1,170**	**125**	**14**	**97**	**24**	**16**

- This series was skipped due to initial placement.
- This series includes at least one topic that was Fast Tracked.
- This series was completed by the student.
- This series has not been completed.

Using This Report

Purpose: Use this report to monitor and compare your students' response to the System 44 intervention over time. Use the Median RTI as a benchmark for each student's progress and mastery relative to the average in your class.

Follow-Up: Be aware of any students whose progress may be slow or whose learning trajectory is consistently below the class average. Consider adjusting teacher-led instruction and independent practice for students who are not moving at an adequate pace through the program.

How It Helps

This report identifies students whose progress is slow, who aren't spending enough time on the software, or whose mastery is consistently below the Median RTI.

Understand the Data

1 Time Period
This report is based on cumulative usage and mastery to the date it is run.

2 Number of Sessions
Cumulative number of days the student logged on to the software.

3 Mastery to Date
Total number of instructional Series mastered to date (out of 25 Series). Green boxes represent Series that were skipped due to initial placement, and gray boxes represent Series in which at least one Topic was Fast-Tracked.

4 Number of Topics Fast-Tracked
Total number of Topics a student Fast-Tracked. (Note: When students pass a Fast-Track assessment, they skip the following Topic of instruction.)

5 Minutes/Topic
Average number of minutes it takes to complete a Topic. Does not include Fast-Tracked Topics.

6 Median RTI
Represents the median usage and mastery for the class or group of students reported.

Use the Data

Who: Teachers (Teacher, Class, or Group report)

When: Every six weeks

How: Apply the information from this report in the following ways:

Monitor Student Progress

- Correlate students' software usage with their mastery to date. Topics Fast-Tracked will impact mastery because every Fast-Tracked Topic is considered mastered in zero minutes.
- Note the total number of Topics Fast-Tracked.
- Compare each student's response to the Median RTI.

Conference With Students

- Follow up directly with students whose software usage or progress is below the Median RTI. Help students set and track goals for daily software use.

Review Related Reports

- *System 44* Reading Progress Report (p. 88)
- *System 44* Student Software Performance Report (p. 96)
- *System 44* Student Mastery Report (p. 102)

Data in Action

Median RTI Response to Intervention is a teaching framework that recommends regular progress monitoring and a comparison of students to a determined benchmark. Use the Median RTI to compare each student against his or her peers for both usage and mastery. If students are below the Median RTI, review their software usage, Rate of Completion (see p. 102), and number of Topics Fast-Tracked.

Grading Report

Purpose

This report shows information gathered from *System 44* software, *Scholastic Reading Counts!*, and SAM Student Digital Portfolio.

Grading Report

CLASS: PERIOD 3

School: The Lincoln School
Teacher: Margaret Parker
Grade: 7

Time Period: 12/01/11 — 02/02/12 ❶

	SYSTEM 44 PROGRESS MONITORING					SRC!	CLASS ASSIGNMENTS	
	❷	❸	❹	❺	❻	❼	❽	❾
STUDENT	TOPIC PROGRESS MONITOR SCORE	SPELLING SCORE	COMPRE-HENSION SCORE	ORAL READING FLUENCY RECORDING SCORE (OUT OF 6)	WRITING SCORE (OUT OF 4)	SRC! QUIZ AVERAGE (NO. OF BOOKS)	AVERAGE SCORE	FINAL GRADE
Anderson, Darrell	86%	85%	86%	2	1	78% (4)	90%	
Benson, Kate	95%	95%	95%	2	3	83% (5)	75%	
Donato, Aimee	80%	80%	80%	N/A	N/A	85% (4)	N/A	
Gonzalez, Lydia	79%	74%	79%	3	—	43% (4)	92%	
Huang, Hsin-Yi	74%	91%	74%	6	2	92% (5)	95%	
Lee, Andrea	68%	88%	76%	5	2	58% (4)	78%	
Mamdani, Aliyah	79%	77%	72%	2	—	90% (3)	85%	
Molina, Robert	94%	87%	71%	3	4	89% (7)	93%	
Price, Jamal	88%	92%	69%	1	2	88% (5)	75%	
Rubio, Alejandro	65%	72%	79%	4	2	78% (5)	N/A	
Sanders, Renee	71%	69%	82%	5	3	72% (7)	88%	
Turner, Aiden	82%	77%	83%	4	4	81% (5)	N/A	
AVERAGE	80%	82%	79%	—	—	78%	85%	

* Only letter grades were entered in SAM Student Digital Portfolio

USING THIS REPORT

Purpose: This report shows information gathered during each part of the System 44 Next Generation Instructional Model to help you determine student grades.

Follow-Up: Communicate grades with students and families.

ENTERING INFORMATION

If "N/A" appears for a studer data has not been entered. Fluency and Writing, evalua using rubrics in SAM Studer For Class Assignments, ent SAM Digital Portfolio.

How It Helps

I use this report as a starting point when determining student grades. It contains useful summaries of student performance.

Understand the Data

1. **Time Period**
   Default time period setting of This Grading Period displays student results during the current grading period. For best results, ensure grading periods are properly established in SAM.

2. **Topic Progress Monitor Score**
   Average Progress Monitor score for all cycles in all Topics in the time period.

3. **Spelling Score**
   Percent of target spelling words scored as fluent on the first attempt at Spelling Challenge in the Spelling Zone.

4. **Comprehension Score**
   Percent of questions answered correctly on the first attempt at Read & Think in the Fluency Zone.

5. **Oral Reading Fluency Recording Score (Out of 6)**
   Score entered in SAM Student Digital Portfolio for most recently completed Success Zone fluency recording.

6. **Writing Score (Out of 4)**
   Score entered in SAM Student Digital Portfolio for most recently published Writing response.

7. ***SRC!* Quiz Average (Number of Books)**
   Average score on all *Scholastic Reading Counts!* quizzes taken. Number in parentheses indicates total *SRC!* quizzes attempted during the selected time period.

8. **Class Assignments**
   Use the Grading Tool in the SAM Student Digital Portfolio to add grades for *44Book* work, QuickWrites and Graphic Organizers, participation, etc.

9. **Final Grade**
   This column is intentionally blank. After printing the report, determine and write in grades based on the data.

Use the Data

Who: Teachers (Teacher, Class, or Group report)

When: At the end of each grading period

How: Apply the information in this report in the following ways:

Determine Grades

- Use the data from this report as a starting point for assessing performance in the *System 44* software, Modeled and Independent Reading, and Whole- and Small-Group Instruction.
- Include other factors when determining final student grades. See Assigning Student Grades on page 162 for more information.

Review Software Usage

- Students with low scores in any of the *System 44* software zones may be struggling with appropriate software usage. Review software usage tips with students each grading period.
- Students with low *SRC!* quiz averages may be struggling with comprehension of texts in the Modeled and Independent Reading Rotation or struggling with taking quizzes. Conference with students and review written work such as daily reading logs or Graphic Organizers to determine what support to provide.

Review Related Reports

- *System 44* Reading Progress Report (p. 88)
- *SRC!* Reading Progress Report (p. 148)

Data in Action

Grading in *System 44* Consider students' complete progress and performance in the *System 44* classroom. Balance grades from each part of the Instructional Model—Whole-Group Introduction, Small-Group Instruction, Modeled and Independent Reading, and Instructional Software.

Student Software Performance Report | Best Practice Report

Purpose

This report details an individual student's performance in the *System 44* software.

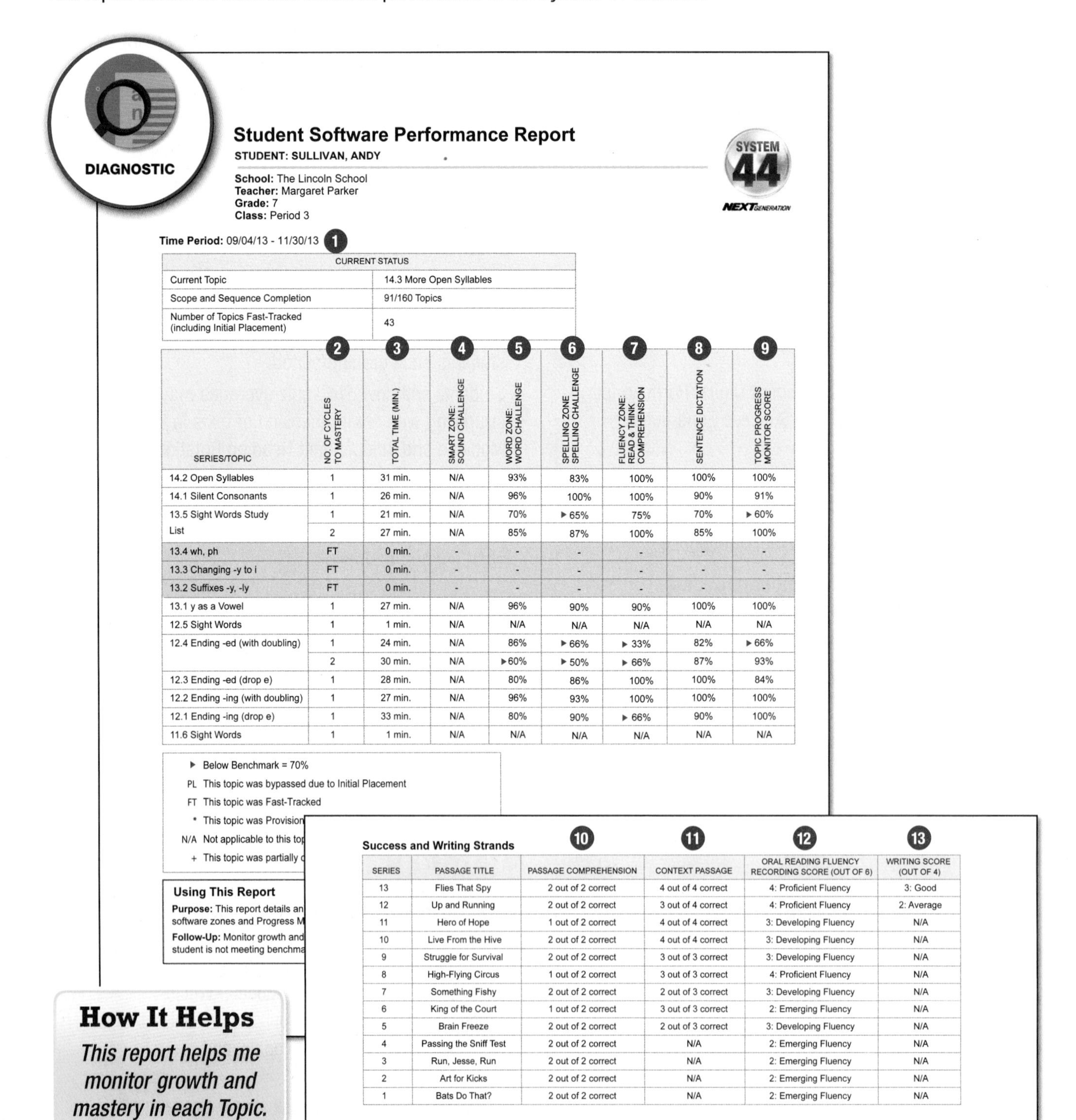

DIAGNOSTIC

Student Software Performance Report

STUDENT: SULLIVAN, ANDY

School: The Lincoln School
Teacher: Margaret Parker
Grade: 7
Class: Period 3

SYSTEM 44 NEXT GENERATION

Time Period: 09/04/13 - 11/30/13 (1)

CURRENT STATUS	
Current Topic	14.3 More Open Syllables
Scope and Sequence Completion	91/160 Topics
Number of Topics Fast-Tracked (including Initial Placement)	43

SERIES/TOPIC	(2) NO. OF CYCLES TO MASTERY	(3) TOTAL TIME (MIN.)	(4) SMART ZONE: SOUND CHALLENGE	(5) WORD ZONE: WORD CHALLENGE	(6) SPELLING ZONE SPELLING CHALLENGE	(7) FLUENCY ZONE: READ & THINK COMPREHENSION	(8) SENTENCE DICTATION	(9) TOPIC PROGRESS MONITOR SCORE
14.2 Open Syllables	1	31 min.	N/A	93%	83%	100%	100%	100%
14.1 Silent Consonants	1	26 min.	N/A	96%	100%	100%	90%	91%
13.5 Sight Words Study List	1	21 min.	N/A	70%	▶ 65%	75%	70%	▶ 60%
	2	27 min.	N/A	85%	87%	100%	85%	100%
13.4 wh, ph	FT	0 min.	-	-	-	-	-	-
13.3 Changing -y to i	FT	0 min.	-	-	-	-	-	-
13.2 Suffixes -y, -ly	FT	0 min.	-	-	-	-	-	-
13.1 y as a Vowel	1	27 min.	N/A	96%	90%	90%	100%	100%
12.5 Sight Words	1	1 min.	N/A	N/A	N/A	N/A	N/A	N/A
12.4 Ending -ed (with doubling)	1	24 min.	N/A	86%	▶ 66%	▶ 33%	82%	▶ 66%
	2	30 min.	N/A	▶60%	▶ 50%	▶ 66%	87%	93%
12.3 Ending -ed (drop e)	1	28 min.	N/A	80%	86%	100%	100%	84%
12.2 Ending -ing (with doubling)	1	27 min.	N/A	96%	93%	100%	100%	100%
12.1 Ending -ing (drop e)	1	33 min.	N/A	80%	90%	▶ 66%	90%	100%
11.6 Sight Words	1	1 min.	N/A	N/A	N/A	N/A	N/A	N/A

▶ Below Benchmark = 70%
PL This topic was bypassed due to Initial Placement
FT This topic was Fast-Tracked
* This topic was Provision
N/A Not applicable to this top
+ This topic was partially c

Using This Report
Purpose: This report details an
software zones and Progress M
Follow-Up: Monitor growth and
student is not meeting benchma

Success and Writing Strands

SERIES	PASSAGE TITLE	(10) PASSAGE COMPREHENSION	(11) CONTEXT PASSAGE	(12) ORAL READING FLUENCY RECORDING SCORE (OUT OF 6)	(13) WRITING SCORE (OUT OF 4)
13	Flies That Spy	2 out of 2 correct	4 out of 4 correct	4: Proficient Fluency	3: Good
12	Up and Running	2 out of 2 correct	3 out of 4 correct	4: Proficient Fluency	2: Average
11	Hero of Hope	1 out of 2 correct	4 out of 4 correct	3: Developing Fluency	N/A
10	Live From the Hive	2 out of 2 correct	4 out of 4 correct	3: Developing Fluency	N/A
9	Struggle for Survival	2 out of 2 correct	3 out of 3 correct	3: Developing Fluency	N/A
8	High-Flying Circus	1 out of 2 correct	3 out of 3 correct	4: Proficient Fluency	N/A
7	Something Fishy	2 out of 2 correct	2 out of 3 correct	3: Developing Fluency	N/A
6	King of the Court	1 out of 2 correct	3 out of 3 correct	2: Emerging Fluency	N/A
5	Brain Freeze	2 out of 2 correct	2 out of 3 correct	3: Developing Fluency	N/A
4	Passing the Sniff Test	2 out of 2 correct	N/A	2: Emerging Fluency	N/A
3	Run, Jesse, Run	2 out of 2 correct	N/A	2: Emerging Fluency	N/A
2	Art for Kicks	2 out of 2 correct	N/A	2: Emerging Fluency	N/A
1	Bats Do That?	2 out of 2 correct	N/A	2: Emerging Fluency	N/A

How It Helps

This report helps me monitor growth and mastery in each Topic.

Understand the Data

1 Time Period
This report is based on students' work during the selected time period.

2 Number of Cycles to Mastery
Number of complete passes through the Topic's activities in an instructional strand. (Provisional Promotion: Software moves student to the next Topic after three cycles regardless of mastery.)

3 Total Time (Minutes)
Total number of minutes on the software to complete a Topic.

4 Smart Zone: Sound Challenge
Percent of target sound-spellings scored as fluent on the first attempt at Sound Challenge.

5 Word Zone: Word Challenge
Percent of target words scored as fluent on the first attempt at Word Challenge.

6 Spelling Zone: Spelling Challenge
Percent of target spelling words scored as fluent on the first attempt at Spelling Challenge. "N/A" indicates that a student spelled all words correctly in the spelling check-up to bypass the Spelling Challenge.

7 Fluency Zone: Read & Think Comprehension
Percent of questions answered correctly on the first attempt at Read & Think.

8 Sentence Dictation
Percent of words typed correctly on the first attempt at Dictation.

9 Topic Progress Monitor Score
Percent of words scored as fluent in the Progress Monitor.

10 Passage Comprehension
Number of caption items answered correctly on the first attempt at the Comprehension activity.

11 Context Passage
Number of questions answered correctly on the first attempt at the Context Passage.

12 Oral Reading Fluency Recording Score (Out of 6)
Fluency score based on teacher evaluation of a Success Passage recording for a Series.

13 Writing Score (Out of 4)
Writing score based on teacher evaluation of a written summary for a Series.

Use the Data

Who: Teachers (Student report)

When: Up to once per week

How: Apply the information from this report in the following ways:

Monitor Participation

- Monitor skill growth from the first to last cycle in each software zone. Note improvement in scores and rate of completion.
- Diagnose performance patterns that indicate relative strengths vs. weaknesses in phonemic awareness, decoding, spelling, and/or comprehension.
- Identify students who required three cycles in a Topic to target with small-group or one-to-one intervention. Use *Resources for Differentiated Instruction* lessons and SAM resources to reinforce the Topic and provide additional practice.

Share Results

- Celebrate software progress—completed Series and zone scores.
- Conference with students to determine causes for low scores or repeated cycles to mastery. Reteach appropriate software usage procedures at the beginning of each grading period.
- Share results at family-teacher conferences.

Review Related Reports

- *System 44* Individual Learning Plan Report (p. 100)
- *System 44* Student Mastery Report (p. 102)

Data in Action

Topic Progress Monitor Scores If students score below 70% on Code and Words Strategies Topics, they will automatically review the Topic up to two additional times. If students score below 100% on Sight Words Topics, they will automatically review the Topic up to two additional times. Sight Words Topic Progress Monitor scores below 70% are not flagged.

Analyze the Results | Student Software Performance Report

The software's individualized support allows students to earn consistently strong results in each zone.

DATA STORY

Student: Andy Sullivan
Current Topic: 14.3
Topics Fast-Tracked: 43

Andy is making good progress in the System 44 *software. Recognize achievements while targeting any weaknesses.*

Student Software Performance Report

STUDENT: SULLIVAN, ANDY

DIAGNOSTIC

School: The Lincoln School
Teacher: Margaret Parker
Grade: 7
Class: Period 3

SYSTEM 44 NEXT GENERATION

Time Period: 09/04/13 - 11/30/13

CURRENT STATUS	
Current Topic	14.3 More Open Syllables
Scope and Sequence Completion	91/160 Topics
Number of Topics Fast-Tracked (including Initial Placement)	43

SERIES/TOPIC	NO. OF CYCLES TO MASTERY	TOTAL TIME (MIN.) ❶	SMART ZONE: SOUND CHALLENGE	WORD ZONE: WORD CHALLENGE	SPELLING ZONE SPELLING CHALLENGE	FLUENCY ZONE: READ & THINK COMPREHENSION	SENTENCE DICTATION	TOPIC PROGRESS MONITOR SCORE
14.2 Open Syllables	1	31 min.	N/A	93%	83%	100%	100%	100%
14.1 Silent Consonants	1	26 min.	N/A	96%	100%	100%	90%	91%
13.5 Sight Words Study List	1	21 min.	N/A	70%	▸ 65%	75%	70%	▸ 60%
❷	2	27 min.	N/A	85%	87%	100%	85%	100%
13.4 wh, ph	FT	0 min.	-	-	-	-	-	-
13.3 Changing -y to i	FT	0 min.	-	-	-	-	-	-
13.2 Suffixes -y, -ly	FT	0 min.	-	-	-	-	-	-
13.1 y as a Vowel	1	27 min.	N/A	96%	90%	90%	100%	100%
12.5 Sight Words	1	1 min.	N/A	N/A	N/A	N/A	N/A	N/A
12.4 Ending -ed (with doubling)	1	24 min.	N/A	86%	▸ 66% ❸	▸ 33%	82%	▸ 66%
	2	30 min.	N/A	▸ 60%	▸ 50%	▸ 66%	87%	93%
12.3 Ending -ed (drop e)	1	28 min.	N/A	80%	86%	100%	100%	84%
12.2 Ending -ing (with doubling)	1	27 min.	N/A	96%	93%	100%	100%	100%
12.1 Ending -ing (drop e)	1	33 min.	N/A	80%	90%	▸ 66%	90%	100%
11.6 Sight Words	1	1 min.	N/A	N/A	N/A	N/A	N/A	N/A

▸ Below Benchmark = 70%
PL This topic was bypassed due to Initial Placement
FT This topic was Fast-Tracked
* This topic was Provisionally Promoted
N/A Not applicable to this topic
\+ This topic was partially completed in Time Period date range

Enlargement: Student Software Performance Report

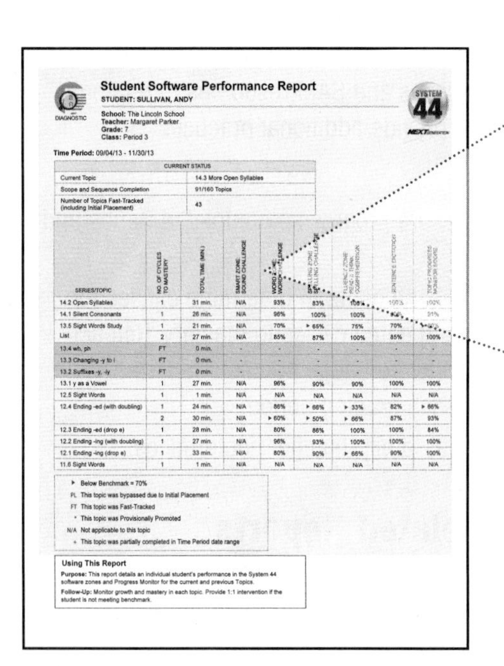

Using This Report

Purpose: This report details an individual student's performance in the System 44 software zones and Progress Monitor for the current and previous Topics.

Follow-Up: Monitor growth and mastery in each topic. Provide 1:1 intervention if the student is not meeting benchmark.

Data Point	Data Analysis	NEXT STEPS
❶ Andy is completing Topics steadily.	Andy has been in this class since the beginning of the year. He is progressing through Topics about as quickly as he should.	Use the *System 44* Family Report to share progress with families.
❷ Andy has repeated two Topics recently. He needed two cycles to master Topics 13.5 and 12.4.	The software is identifying weaknesses in Andy's decoding skills.	When students repeat Topics, teach corresponding lessons from *Resources for Differentiated Instruction* during Small-Group Instruction.
❸ Andy's Fluency Zone: Read & Think Comprehension scores are sometimes low.	Struggles with fluency could be preventing Andy from comprehending texts.	Use Oral Fluency Assessments to determine students' fluency abilities.

DATA STORY

Student: Michael Anderson
Current Topic: 2.3
Topics Fast-Tracked: 0

Michael is struggling with software usage. Identify indicators of student challenges and provide appropriate support.

Student Software Performance Report

DIAGNOSTIC

STUDENT: ANDERSON, MICHAEL

School: The Lincoln School
Teacher: Margaret Parker
Grade: 7
Class: Period 3

SYSTEM 44 NEXT GENERATION

Time Period: 09/04/13 - 11/30/13

CURRENT STATUS	
Current Topic	2.3 Consonants h, k
Scope and Sequence Completion	10/160 Topics
Number of Topics Fast-Tracked (including Initial Placement)	0

SERIES/TOPIC	NO. OF CYCLES TO MASTERY	TOTAL TIME (MIN.)	SMART ZONE: SOUND CHALLENGE	WORD ZONE: WORD CHALLENGE	SPELLING ZONE SPELLING CHALLENGE (2)	FLUENCY ZONE: READ & THINK COMPREHENSION	SENTENCE DICTATION	TOPIC PROGRESS MONITOR SCORE
2.3 Consonants h, k	1	24 min.	76%	▸ 67%	▸ 63%	▸ 57%	-	▸ 66%
	2+	3 min.	-	-	-	-	-	-
(3) 2.2 Consonants d, f	1	22 min.	82%	76%	70%	75%	-	80%
2.1 Short i	1	28 min.	▸ 63%	▸ 66%	▸ 68%	72%	-	71%
(1) 1.7 Ending -s	1	27 min.	N/A	▸ 56%	▸ 69%	▸ 66%	-	▸ 47%
	2	23 min.	N/A	▸ 62%	72%	▸ 57%	-	▸ 52%
	3*	25 min.	N/A	73%	70%	70%	-	▸ 66%
1.6 Sight Words Study List	1	21 min.	N/A	81%	▸ 65%	85%	-	70%
1.5 Consonants b, r	1	24 min.	77%	77%	70%	▸ 68%	-	85%
1.4 Consonants p, c	1	19 min.	72%	75%	▸ 60%	▸ 65%	-	76%
1.3 Short a	1	24 min.	▸ 62%	▸ 68%	▸ 57%	72%	-	▸ 60%
	2	22 min.	70%	75%	▸ 68%	▸ 66%	-	71%
1.2 Consonants t, n	1	20 min.	82%	80%	73%	70%	-	78%
1.1 Consonants m, s	1	28 min.	78%	72%	▸ 63%	▸ 57%	-	72%

▸ Below Benchmark = 70%
PL This topic was bypassed due to Initial Placement
FT This topic was Fast-Tracked
* This topic was Provisionally Promoted
N/A Not applicable to this topic
+ This topic was partially completed in Time Period date range

Enlargement: Student Software Performance Report

Using This Report

Purpose: This report details an individual student's performance in the System 44 software zones and Progress Monitor for the current and previous Topics.

Follow-Up: Monitor growth and mastery in each topic. Provide 1:1 intervention if the student is not meeting benchmark.

Data Point	Data Analysis	NEXT STEPS
(1) Michael was Provisionally Promoted from Topic 1.7 after he failed the Progress Monitor three times.	Michael's Progress Monitor scores improved with each cycle, but he still did not achieve 70%.	Provide one-to-one intervention with corresponding lessons from *Resources for Differentiated Instruction.*
(2) Michael's spelling score is consistently low.	The software shows that Michael struggles in the Spelling Zone.	Build students' encoding abilities with dictation practice during Small-Group Instruction.
(3) Michael recently did well on Topic 2.2.	Michael met the benchmark score of 70% in each zone.	Find successes to celebrate for every student and share results with families.

Individual Learning Plan Report

Purpose

This report details an individual student's progress toward the academic and behavioral goals set by teachers in an individual learning plan.

Individual Learning Plan Report

STUDENT: LEE, ANDREA

School: The Lincoln School
Teacher: Margaret Parker
Grade: 7
Class: Period 3

Time Period: 08/20/13 – 09/06/13 ❶

CURRENT STATUS AND USAGE	
SPI Decoding Status	Developing Decoder
Current Topic	1.7 Ending ***-s***
Total Time (Min.)	106 min.

CURRENT BENCHMARK PERIOD 08/20/13 – 10/25/13				
ACADEMIC GOALS	ASSESSMENT	❷ BENCHMARK GOAL	❸ CURRENT PROGRESS	❹ PROGRESS TO GOAL
Decoding	Progress Monitor	10 Topics	4 Topics	**40%**
Spelling	Spelling Challenge	7 Challenges	2 Challenges	**29%**
Independent Reading	*SRC!* quizzes	6 books	1 book	**17%**

BEHAVIORAL GOALS	❺ OVERALL GOAL	WHOLE GROUP POINTS	SMALL GROUP POINTS	INDEPENDENT READING POINTS	SOFTWARE	❻ TOTAL POINTS
Effort	16	2	3	4	3	**12**
Responsibility	16	2	2	2	2	**8**
Respect	16	4	4	4	4	**16**

USING THIS REPORT

Purpose: Use this report to track a student's progress toward his or her individual learning plan goals and adjust goals as needed.

Follow-Up: Conference with students and families about progress.

ACADEMIC GOALS

The decoding goal is measured in Topics completed with a Progress Monitor score of at least 70%. The spelling goal is measured in Spelling Challenges completed with a score of at least 70%. The independent reading goal is measured in SRC! quizzes completed with a score of at least 70%.

How It Helps

I use this report to see whether students are on track to meet their goals for the benchmark period.

Understand the Data

1 Time Period
Default time period setting of This Grading Period displays student results for the current benchmark period. For best results, ensure grading periods are properly established in SAM.

2 Benchmark Goal
The academic goals set in the SAM Student Digital Portfolio.

3 Current Progress
For decoding, the number of Topics a student has completed with a Progress Monitor score of at least 70%. For spelling, the number of Spelling Challenges a student has completed with a score of at least 70%. For independent reading, the number of *SRC!* quizzes a student has completed with a score of at least 70%.

4 Progress to Goal
The student's current progress toward each academic goal. Green indicates that progress meets or exceeds expected completion based on how many days of the benchmark period have passed. Yellow indicates progress within 5% of expected completion. Red indicates progress that is more than 5% below expected completion.

5 Overall Goal
Each behavioral goal is 16 points, based on a maximum of four points in each part of the Instructional Model. The points for Whole Group, Small Group, Independent Reading, and Software are the most recent scores entered in SAM Digital Portfolio.

6 Total Points
The total points a student earned for each behavioral goal. Scores of 12–16 are green, 5–11 are yellow, and 0–4 are red.

Use the Data

Who: Teachers (Student report)

When: At least once each grading period

How: Apply the information in this report in the following ways:

Monitor Progress

- Use the data from this report to determine whether students are on track to meet the goals of their individual learning plans.
- Conference with students to celebrate progress that is on track to meet their goals. If students are not on track, explain what they need to accomplish before the end of the benchmark period and work together to create a plan.

Share Results

- Discuss results with support specialists at IEP meetings.
- Share results at family-teacher conferences.

Review Related Reports

- *System 44* Student Software Performance Report (p. 96)
- *System 44* Student Mastery Report (p. 102)

Data in Action

Behavioral Goals Behavioral goal scores show the most recent scores entered in the SAM Student Digital Portfolio. Students may earn up to four points for each part of the *System 44* Instructional Model. If "N/A" appears, it indicates that data has not been entered.

Student Mastery Report

Purpose

This report details an individual student's response to the *System 44* instruction.

Student Mastery Report

STUDENT: SULLIVAN, ANDY

School: The Lincoln School
Teacher: Margaret Parker
Grade: 7
Class: Period 3

Time Period: 09/05/08 - 01/10/09 ①

② **Date Started System 44:** 09/05/08
Rate of Completion: 25 Minutes/Topic

THE SYSTEM	DATE STARTED	TOTAL TIME (MIN.) ③	TOPICS MASTERED/160 ④	PERCENT MASTERED ⑤
Consonants	09/05/08	525	34/34	100%
Vowels	09/08/08	234	13/29	45%
Sight Words	09/12/08	240	15/21	71%
Word Parts	09/13/08	225	15/28	54%
Syllables	10/02/08	240	12/23	52%
Success	09/14/08	270	12/25	48%
⑥ **Total Scope & Sequence**	**09/05/08**	**1,734**	**101/160**	**63%**

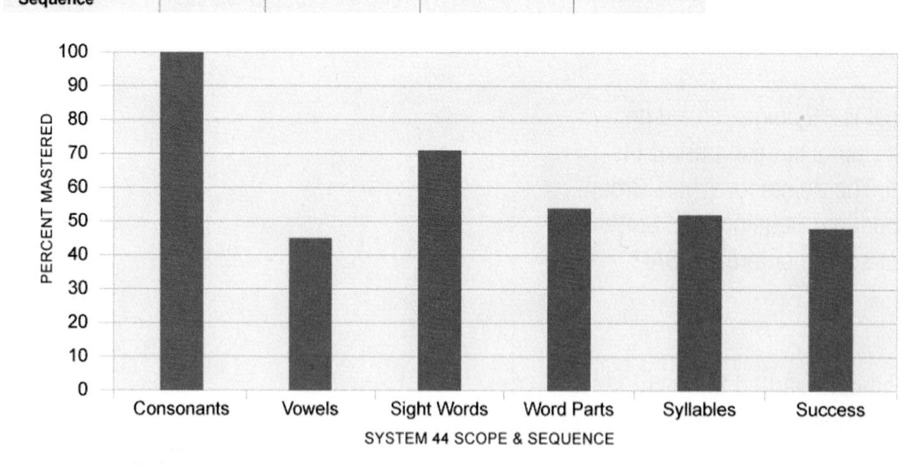

Using This Report

Purpose: This report details an individual student's response to the System 44 instruction. Use this report to evaluate a student's progress over time through the software Scope and Sequence.

Follow-Up: Correlate students' instructional time on the software with their mastery of Topics in the instructional categories. Provide remediation in areas of slow progress.

How It Helps

I use this report to evaluate a student's progress through the software scope and sequence over time.

Understand the Data

1 Time Period
This report is based on a student's work during the selected time period.

2 Rate of Completion
The average number of minutes it takes a student to complete a Topic.

3 Total Time (Minutes)
Minutes on the software in each instructional category.

4 Topics Mastered/160
Number of Topics mastered out of the total in each instructional category. (Note: Any Topics for which students have been provisionally promoted after three cycles of instruction are included in this value.)

5 Percent Mastered
Percent of Topics mastered in each instructional category.

6 Total Scope & Sequence
Instructional time, Topics mastered, and percent mastered for the entire scope and sequence.

Use the Data

Who: Teachers (Student report)

When: Every four to six weeks

How: Apply the information from this report in the following ways:

Monitor Student Progress

- Monitor students' Rate of Completion and compare it to their peers.
- Correlate software time with progress and mastery in each instructional category.

Share Results

- Note when an instructional category is mastered and the time it took to reach mastery.
- Motivate students by sharing their progress and skill growth with them.

Review Related Reports

- *System 44* Response to Intervention Report (p. 92)
- *System 44* Student Software Performance Report (p. 96)

Data in Action

Scope & Sequence Mastery Refer to the graph in this report for a quick snapshot of how each student is progressing through the software scope and sequence. Note how much the student has mastered of each instructional category.

Family Letter

Purpose

This letter can be sent home to inform families of their child's enrollment in the *System 44* program.

SCHOOL-TO-HOME

STUDENT:

School:

Teacher:

SYSTEM 44 NEXT GENERATION

Date:

Dear Parent or Caregiver:

________________________ was enrolled in a decoding intervention program called *System 44* on __________. This program is divided into 160 Topics of instruction that will provide your child with the foundations to be a good reader. *System 44* teaches students to decode so that they can focus on understanding text.

This report shows results of the assessments that were used to identify your child as a good candidate for *System 44.* You will receive regular reports throughout the year about your child's progress.

Assessment	*Results*
❶ **SRI* Test Score**	
❷ **SPI ** Decoding Diagnosis and Date**	

* *Scholastic Reading Inventory (SRI) is a comprehension test that monitors students' reading levels and matches them to text.*

** *Scholastic Phonics Inventory (SPI) is a decoding and word recognition screening assessment.*

❸ You can support your child's reading at home by:

- Visiting the *System 44* website (**www.scholastic.com/system44**) to learn more about the program.
- Visiting **www.scholastic.com/system44/familyportal** for additional suggestions to motivate your child to read and learn.
- Taking every opportunity to read with your child.

Thank you for supporting your child's work in *System 44.*

Sincerely,

How It Helps

This report is available in seven languages: Spanish, Vietnamese, Cantonese, Haitian Creole, Filipino, Hmong, and English.

Understand the Data

1 SRI Test Score
Student's Lexile score based on initial SRI performance.

2 SPI Decoding Diagnosis and Date
Student's SPI decoding diagnosis and the date the test was given. (Note: The SPI identifies Pre-, Beginning, Developing, and Advancing Decoders.)

3 Suggestions
Immediately involve families with resources to learn more about *System 44* and to support their child at home.

Use the Data

Who: Teachers, Students, Families (Student report)

When: Print this letter (**SAM Keyword: 44 Family**) once students have been enrolled in *System 44*.

How: Apply the information from this report in the following ways:

Prepare the Family Letter

- Write the student's name and the date he or she was enrolled in *System 44*.
- Print the SPI Screening and Placement Report.
- Locate the SRI Test Score and record that information under the Results column.
- Locate the SPI Test Date and record that information under the Results column.
- Locate the Decoding Diagnosis and record the diagnosis next to the SPI Test Date.
- Sign your name at the bottom.

Offer Further Explanation

- Take time during Back-To-School Night or during family-teacher conferences to review this information with family members.

Review Related Reports

- SPI Introductory Family Letter (p. 86)
- *System 44* Family Report (p. 106)
- SRI Parent Report (p. 135)
- *SRC!* Parent Report I (p. 158)

Data in Action

Share Information With Families Involve families as early as possible in their child's participation in *System 44*. Be prepared to answer any questions about how and why their child was placed in the program. Refer to the SPI Screening and Placement Report to explain their child's decoding diagnosis. Encourage regular communication between you, the family, and the student. Ask families for insight into their child's interests and goals.

Family Report

Purpose

This letter can be sent home to families as an update on their child's progress with *System 44.*

SYSTEM 44 NEXT GENERATION

STUDENT: SULLIVAN, ANDY

School: The Lincoln School
Teacher: Margaret Parker
Grade: 7
Class: Period 3

February 10, 2009

Dear Parent or Caregiver,

Andy began using a decoding intervention program called *System 44*, on September 12, 2008.
This program is divided into 160 Topics that will provide your child with the foundations to be a good reader.
The goal of *System 44* is to get students decoding well so that they can focus on understanding text.
We will provide you with regular updates on how Andy is progressing.

Here's how Andy is doing:

	PROGRESS INDICATOR	STATUS	
1	SRI* Test Score and Date	150 Lexiles® (09/05/08)	
2	Total Instruction Mastered	114/160 Topics	
3	***System 44* Instruction**	**Start Date**	**Topics Completed**
	Consonants	09/12/08	34 out of 34
	Vowels	09/22/08	18 out of 29
	Syllables	10/11/08	14 out of 23
	Word Parts	10/07/08	16 out of 28
	Sight Words	09/20/08	17 out of 21
	Success	09/21/08	15 out of 25
	Total Number of System 44 Books Read	8	
	Most Recent System 44 Book Read	Killer Croc	

* Scholastic Reading Inventory (SRI) is a comprehension test that monitors students' reading levels and matches them to text.

4 You can support Andy's reading at home by:

- Visiting the *System 44* website regularly **(www.scholastic.com/system44)** to learn about the program.
- Visiting **www.scholastic.com/familymatters/read** for additional suggestions to motivate your child to read and learn.
- Taking every opportunity to read with your child.

Thank you for supporting Andy's work in *System 44*.

Sincerely,

How It Helps

I use this report to discuss student progress during family-teacher conferences.

Understand the Data

1 SRI Test Score and Date
Student's Lexile measure based on SRI performance and the date the test was given.

2 Total Instruction Mastered
Total number of Topics (out of 160) that the student has mastered.

3 *System 44* Instruction
The *System 44* Scope and Sequence is structured into six instructional categories: consonants, vowels, syllables, word parts, sight words, and success.

4 Suggestions
Resources to help families learn more about *System 44* and how to support their child's reading progress at home.

Use the Data

Who: Teachers, Students, Families (Student report)

When: Every six to nine weeks

How: Apply the information from this report in the following ways:

Offer Further Explanation

- Explain students' data and progress to families during family-teacher conferences.

Check In Periodically

- Contact families from time to time to offer support and find out about any home reading routines they have found to be successful.

Review Related Reports

- SPI Follow-Up Family Letter (p. 87)
- *System 44* Student Software Performance Report (p. 96)
- SRI Parent Report (p. 135)
- *SRC!* Parent Report II (p. 159)

Data in Action

Motivating Students The information in this report can be motivational to students. Review this report, along with the *System 44* Student Mastery Report, with students periodically to highlight progress and provide encouragement.

Growth Report | Best Practice Report

Purpose

This report measures student Lexile growth between two SRI tests within a selected time period.

Growth Report

CLASS: Schirmer 3

School: Lincoln Middle School
Teacher: Margaret Schirmer
Grade: 7

Time Period: 08/24/11 – 02/02/12 

STUDENT	GRADE	FIRST TEST IN SELECTED TIME PERIOD LEXILE®	DATE	LAST TEST IN SELECTED TIME PERIOD LEXILE®	DATE	GROWTH IN LEXILE®*
Chu, Amy	7	443	09/01/11	834	01/26/12	391
Krynski, Theo	7	984	09/04/11	1120	01/25/12	136
Collins, Chris	7	784	09/04/11	868	01/26/12	84
Ramirez, Gabriella	7	661	09/02/11	743	01/28/12	82
Bracco, Christine	7	643	08/31/11	709	01/27/12	66
Evans, Jamal	7	665	08/31/11	719	01/25/12	54
Fernandez, Luis	7	200	08/31/11	242	01/25/12	42
Palermo, Justin	7	400	09/12/11	438	01/27/12	38
Rupp, Jeremy	7	691	09/02/11	727	01/27/12	36
Kramer, Liz	7	775	09/02/11	809	01/26/12	34
Sanchez, Rachel	7	783	09/02/11	792	01/25/12	9
Imran, Khaleel	7	710	08/31/11	719	01/25/12	9
Garcia, Matt	7	550	09/01/11	N/A	N/A	N/A
Felix, Tonya	7	6 BR (20)	09/01/11	BR (10)	01/25/12	(-10)
Cooper, Tiffany	7	880	09/02/11	781	01/25/12	(-99)

* Scale for bar chart is based on highest Lexile® growth within selected time period.

Using This Report

Purpose: To identify the growth each student is making, check the dates of the two tests for an individual student. On average, students are expected to grow approximately 75-100 Lexiles per year.

Follow-Up: Provide opportunities to challenge students who show significant progress. Provide appropriate levels of intervention and support to students who are showing little growth. If zero or negative Lexile growth is recorded, check to see if students' test experience is problematic in some way and retest accordingly.

How It Helps

I use this report to track my students' reading gains. I share these results with my school administrators.

Understand the Data

1 Time Period
Run for This School Year to review year-to-date reading progress from the first test administration to the most recent test. Customize time periods to review results between any two SRI test dates.

2 First Test in Selected Time Period
Lexile score and test date for the first SRI test administered within selected time period.

3 Last Test in Selected Time Period (Lexile)
Lexile score from most recent SRI test within selected time period. N/A indicates a second test was not completed within selected time period.

4 Last Test in Selected Time Period (Date)
Most recent SRI test date within selected time period. N/A indicates a second test was not completed within selected time period.

5 Growth in Lexile
Lexile increase from the first test to the last test within selected time period. Report is sorted by overall growth and graphs are scaled to student with largest growth. Declines in Lexile between two tests are indicated in parentheses.

6 BR
A Lexile score of "BR" indicates a Beginning Reader. Students who score BR have an SRI score of less than 100 Lexile points.

Use the Data

Who: Teachers, Administrators (Teacher, Class, or Group report)

When: After each SRI administration

How: Apply the information from this report in the following ways:

Monitor Growth

- If students have taken the SRI more than twice, analyze the Growth Report for different testing administrations. For example, run the report to track growth between test 1 and test 3, test 1 and test 2, or test 2 and test 3.
- Celebrate growth. Discuss growth rates and progress toward goal. Print student reports to share during conferences.
- Share results with administrators. Print this report to keep your school administration updated on your students' reading progress.

Target Support

- Target additional support to students who are not showing strong gains or students whose current SRI scores are below grade level expectations.
- Review results for students whose scores declined. Analyze individual SRI Student Test Printouts and conference with students to determine the cause for the decline in score. Discuss appropriate interventions with your school administration.

Review Related Reports

- SRI Growth Goals Report (p. 112)
- SRI Intervention Grouping Report (p. 114)
- SRI Targeted Reading Report (p. 120)
- SRI Student Progress Report (p. 128)

Data in Action

Expected Growth A student's expected annual growth depends on grade level and initial Lexile score. Expected growth for students reading at the 25th percentile is 140L for grades 3–5, 70L for grades 6–8, and 50L for grades 9–11.

Analyze the Results | Growth Report

Establish individual growth expectations to help students strive for reading performance targets.

DATA STORY

Student: Tiffany Cooper
Current Lexile: 781
SRI Growth: -99

Identify students like Tiffany who struggle with SRI performance. Determine potential cause and appropriate follow-up support.

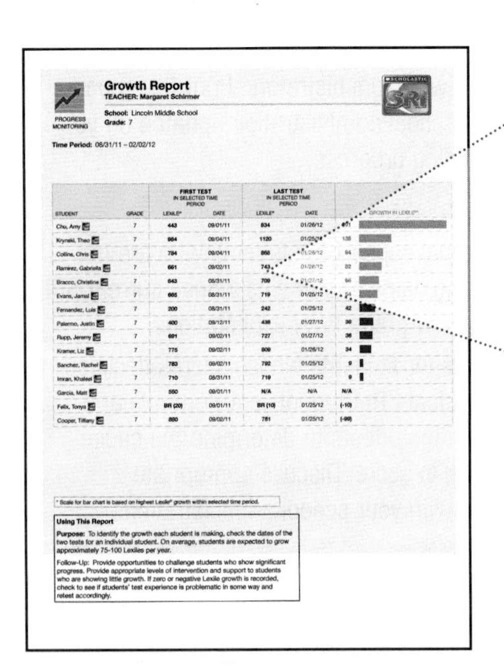

Growth Report
TEACHER: Margaret Schirmer

PROGRESS MONITORING

School: Lincoln Middle School
Grade: 7

Time Period: 08/31/11 – 02/02/12

STUDENT	GRADE	FIRST TEST IN SELECTED TIME PERIOD: LEXILE®	FIRST TEST: DATE	LAST TEST IN SELECTED TIME PERIOD: LEXILE®	LAST TEST: DATE	❶ GROWTH IN LEXILE®*
Chu, Amy	7	443	09/01/11	834	01/26/12	391
Krynski, Theo	7	984	09/04/11	1120	01/25/12	136
Collins, Chris	7	784	09/04/11	868	01/26/12	84
Ramirez, Gabriella	7	661	09/02/11	743	01/28/12	82
Bracco, Christine	7	643	08/31/11	709	01/27/12	66
Evans, Jamal	7	665	08/31/11	719	01/25/12	54
Fernandez, Luis	7	200	08/31/11	242	01/25/12	42
Palermo, Justin	7	400	09/12/11	438	01/27/12	38
Rupp, Jeremy	7	691	09/02/11	727	01/27/12	36
Kramer, Liz	7	775	09/02/11	809	01/26/12	34
Sanchez, Rachel	7	783	09/02/11	792	01/25/12	9
Imran, Khaleel	7	710	08/31/11	719	01/25/12	9
Garcia, Matt	7	550	09/01/11	N/A	N/A	N/A
Felix, Tonya	7	BR (20)	09/01/11	BR (10)	01/25/12	(-10)
Cooper, Tiffany	7	❷ 880	09/02/11	781	01/25/12	(-99) ❸

* Scale for bar chart is based on highest Lexile® growth within selected time period.

Using This Report

Purpose: To identify the growth each student is making, check the dates of the two tests for an individual student. On average, students are expected to grow approximately 75-100 Lexiles per year.

Follow-Up: Provide opportunities to challenge students who show significant progress. Provide appropriate levels of intervention and support to students who are showing little growth. If zero or negative Lexile growth is recorded, check to see if students' test experience is problematic in some way and retest accordingly.

Growth Report
TEACHER: Margaret Schirmer

PROGRESS MONITORING

School: Lincoln Middle School
Grade: 7

Time Period: 08/31/11 – 02/02/12

STUDENT	GRADE	FIRST TEST IN SELECTED TIME PERIOD: LEXILE®	FIRST TEST: DATE	LAST TEST IN SELECTED TIME PERIOD: LEXILE®	LAST TEST: DATE	❶ GROWTH IN LEXILE®*
Chu, Amy	7	443	09/01/11	834	01/26/12	391
Krynski, Theo	7	984	09/04/11	1120	01/25/12	136
Collins, Chris	7	784	09/04/11	868	01/26/12	84
Ramirez, Gabriella	7	661	09/02/11	743	01/28/12	82
Bracco, Christine	7	643	08/31/11	709	01/27/12	66
Evans, Jamal	7	665	08/31/11	719	01/25/12	54
Fernandez, Luis	7	200	08/31/11	242	01/25/12	42
Palermo, Justin	7	400	09/12/11	438	01/27/12	38
Rupp, Jeremy	7	691	09/02/11	727	01/27/12	36
Kramer, Liz	7	775	09/02/11	809	01/26/12	34
Sanchez, Rachel	7	783	09/02/11	792	01/25/12	9
Imran, Khaleel	7	710	08/31/11	719	01/25/12	9
Garcia, Matt	7	550	09/01/11	N/A	N/A	N/A
Felix, Tonya	7	BR (20)	09/01/11	BR (10)	01/25/12	(-10)
Cooper, Tiffany	7	❷ 880	09/02/11	781	01/25/12	(-99) ❸

* Scale for bar chart is based on highest Lexile® growth within selected time period.

Using This Report

Purpose: To identify the growth each student is making, check the dates of the two tests for an individual student. On average, students are expected to grow approximately 75-100 Lexiles per year.

Enlargement: Growth Report

	Data Point	Data Analysis	NEXT STEPS
❶	Most of the class made some growth between September and January test administrations.	Many students in the class are on target to reach grade level proficiency by the end of this school year.	Share current results and discuss exit criteria with school administration.
❷	Tiffany's fall Lexile score is an 880, and she is currently in 7th grade.	Tiffany's fall results indicate that she needs to make at least a 25-point Lexile gain to reach proficiency by the end of the year.	Use initial results and grade level to set realistic growth expectations for each student.
❸	Tiffany's January test results indicate a large drop in score from her September results.	Small dips in score may occur as the SRI adapts to the student's reading level, but a drop of more than 60 points indicates a larger problem.	Review individual student performance on the SRI Test Printout and conference with the student to determine cause for score decline.

Review Additional Data

Cross-reference the SRI Student Test Printout to analyze specific test results.

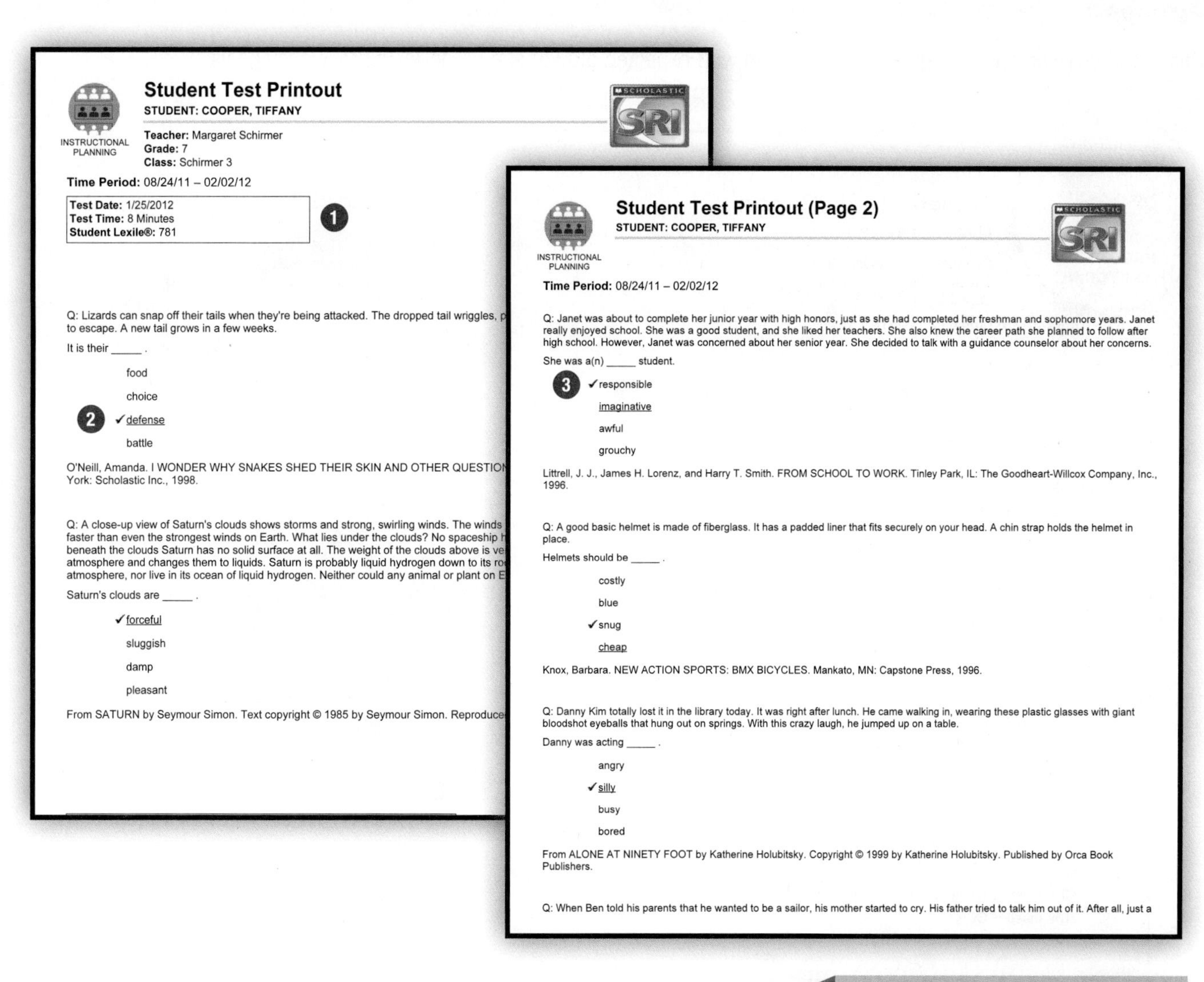

Student Test Printout
STUDENT: COOPER, TIFFANY

INSTRUCTIONAL PLANNING

Teacher: Margaret Schirmer
Grade: 7
Class: Schirmer 3

Time Period: 08/24/11 – 02/02/12

Test Date: 1/25/2012
Test Time: 8 Minutes
Student Lexile®: 781

❶

Q: Lizards can snap off their tails when they're being attacked. The dropped tail wriggles, p
to escape. A new tail grows in a few weeks.

It is their _____ .

food
choice
❷ ✓defense
battle

O'Neill, Amanda. I WONDER WHY SNAKES SHED THEIR SKIN AND OTHER QUESTIO
York: Scholastic Inc., 1998.

Q: A close-up view of Saturn's clouds shows storms and strong, swirling winds. The winds
faster than even the strongest winds on Earth. What lies under the clouds? No spaceship h
beneath the clouds Saturn has no solid surface at all. The weight of the clouds above is ve
atmosphere and changes them to liquids. Saturn is probably liquid hydrogen down to its ro
atmosphere, nor live in its ocean of liquid hydrogen. Neither could any animal or plant on E

Saturn's clouds are _____ .

✓forceful
sluggish
damp
pleasant

From SATURN by Seymour Simon. Text copyright © 1985 by Seymour Simon. Reproduce

Student Test Printout (Page 2)
STUDENT: COOPER, TIFFANY

INSTRUCTIONAL PLANNING

Time Period: 08/24/11 – 02/02/12

Q: Janet was about to complete her junior year with high honors, just as she had completed her freshman and sophomore years. Janet really enjoyed school. She was a good student, and she liked her teachers. She also knew the career path she planned to follow after high school. However, Janet was concerned about her senior year. She decided to talk with a guidance counselor about her concerns.

She was a(n) _____ student.

❸ ✓responsible
imaginative
awful
grouchy

Littrell, J. J., James H. Lorenz, and Harry T. Smith. FROM SCHOOL TO WORK. Tinley Park, IL: The Goodheart-Willcox Company, Inc., 1996.

Q: A good basic helmet is made of fiberglass. It has a padded liner that fits securely on your head. A chin strap holds the helmet in place.

Helmets should be _____ .

costly
blue
✓snug
cheap

Knox, Barbara. NEW ACTION SPORTS: BMX BICYCLES. Mankato, MN: Capstone Press, 1996.

Q: Danny Kim totally lost it in the library today. It was right after lunch. He came walking in, wearing these plastic glasses with giant bloodshot eyeballs that hung out on springs. With this crazy laugh, he jumped up on a table.

Danny was acting _____ .

angry
✓silly
busy
bored

From ALONE AT NINETY FOOT by Katherine Holubitsky. Copyright © 1999 by Katherine Holubitsky. Published by Orca Book Publishers.

Q: When Ben told his parents that he wanted to be a sailor, his mother started to cry. His father tried to talk him out of it. After all, just a

Data Point	Data Analysis	NEXT STEPS
❶ Tiffany only took 8 minutes to complete her test.	Although the total time it takes to complete a test varies by student, it should typically take about 20 minutes.	Discuss the nature of the test with students prior to beginning the test. Conference about previous results and goals for the current test.
❷ Tiffany answered the first couple of questions correctly.	At first Tiffany's responses indicate that she is properly prepared for the test.	Ensure that all students are mentally and emotionally prepared for the test and that the environment is conducive for testing.
❸ Tiffany began answering multiple questions incorrectly in a row, starting with the 4th question.	Tiffany's performance declined quickly. During a conference, Tiffany shared that another student began bothering her during the test.	When students' scores decline more than 60 points, you may wish to remove the score and allow the student to retest.

Growth Goals Report

Purpose

This report compares Fall to Spring Lexile growth with expected growth and grade-level proficiency goals.

Growth Goals Report

CLASS: SCHIRMER 3

School: Lincoln Middle School
Teacher: Margaret Schirmer
Grade: 7

Time Period: 09/03/12 – 06/07/13 ❶

STUDENT	❷ ACTUAL FALL SRI LEXILE MEASURE	❸ EXPECTED SPRING LEXILE	❹ ACTUAL SPRING SRI LEXILE	❺ EXPECTED FALL TO SPRING GROWTH	❻ ACTUAL FALL TO SPRING GROWTH	❼ BASIC PROFICIENCY GOALS (25TH PERCENTILE)	❽ GRADE LEVEL PROFICIENCY GOALS (50TH PERCENTILE)	❾ COLLEGE AND CAREER READINESS GOALS (75TH PERCENTILE)
Bracco, Christine	600	681	650	81	50	780	955	1,095
Chu, Amy	1,080	1,118	1,130	38	50	780	955	1,095
Collins, Chris	720	784	783	64	63	780	955	1,095
Cooper, Maya	450	568	656	118	206	780	955	1,095
Cooper, Tiffany	650	723	747	73	97	780	955	1,095
Evans, Jamal	999	1,042	1,043	43	44	780	955	1,095
Felix, Tonya	1,100	1,390	1,405	290	305	780	955	1,095
Garcia, Matt	856	908	939	52	83	780	955	1,095
Imran, Khaleel	757	817	1,000	60	243	780	955	1,095
Kramer, Liz	450	568	756	118	306	780	955	1,095

❿ 80% meeting Expected Growth Goal
60% meeting Basic Goal
40% meeting Grade Level Proficiency Goal
20% meeting CCR Goal

Using This Report

Purpose: The purpose of this report is to help teachers set individual growth goals for students that are based on a series of benchmarks which includes: Expected Growth, the 25th and the 50th percentile rank, and College and Career Readiness goals by grade level. Expected growth is defined as the amount of Lexile growth students achieve under typical instructional conditions. Growth varies by grade level and reading achievement, with younger and/or less proficient readers demonstrating greater growth.

Follow-Up: This report helps teachers accelerate students to higher and more rigorous reading levels by setting obtainable goals over time. When students are not on track to achieving goals, teachers will know the exact level of Lexile a student needs to grow and can intensify services.

How It Helps

I use this report to set individual growth goals for students.

Understand the Data

❶ **Time Period**
Run for This School Year to review year-to-date reading progress from the first test administration to the most recent test.

❷ **Actual Fall SRI Lexile Measure**
Lexile score for the first SRI test administered within the selected time period.

❸ **Expected Spring Lexile**
The expected score under typical conditions based on grade level and reading achievement.

❹ **Actual Spring SRI Lexile**
Lexile score for the most recent SRI test administered within the selected time period.

❺ **Expected Fall to Spring Growth**
The amount of Lexile growth under typical instructional conditions.

❻ **Actual Fall to Spring Growth**
Lexile increase from the first test to the last test within the selected time period. Declines in Lexile between the tests are indicated in parentheses and should be interpreted as no growth.

❼ **Basic Proficiency Goals (25th Percentile)**
The Lexile measure for the 25th percentile of students in the same grade. Red indicates students who are not meeting this goal, and green indicates students who are meeting it.

❽ **Grade Level Proficiency Goals (50th Percentile)**
The Lexile measure for the 50th percentile of students in the same grade. Red indicates students who are not meeting this goal, and green indicates students who are meeting it.

❾ **College and Career Readiness Goals (75th Percentile)**
The Lexile measure for the 75th percentile of students in the same grade. Red indicates students who are not meeting this goal, and green indicates students who are meeting it.

❿ **Percent Meeting Goals**
Percent of students meeting goals for expected growth, basic proficiency, grade-level proficiency, and college and career readiness.

Use the Data

Who: Teachers, Administrators (Teacher, Class, or Group report)

When: After the last SRI administration of the school year

How: Apply the information in this report in the following ways:

Set Growth Goals

- Use information to inform planning. Discuss expected growth rates and progress toward goals. Print student reports to share during conferences.
- Share results with administrators. Print this report to keep your school administration updated on your students' reading progress.

Target Support

- Target additional support to students who are not meeting expected growth goals or proficiency goals.
- Review results for students whose scores declined. Discuss appropriate interventions with your school administration.

Review Related Reports

- SRI Growth Report (p. 108)
- SRI Intervention Grouping Report (p. 114)
- SRI Student Progress Report (p. 128)

Data in Action

Conferencing With Students Begin by celebrating positive aspects of classroom performance. Use current student results and benchmark data to help students understand their progress and articulate their goals for success. Have students write their goals in the My Achievements section of their *44Books*.

Intervention Grouping Report | Best Practice Report

Purpose

This report groups students based on SRI performance standards.

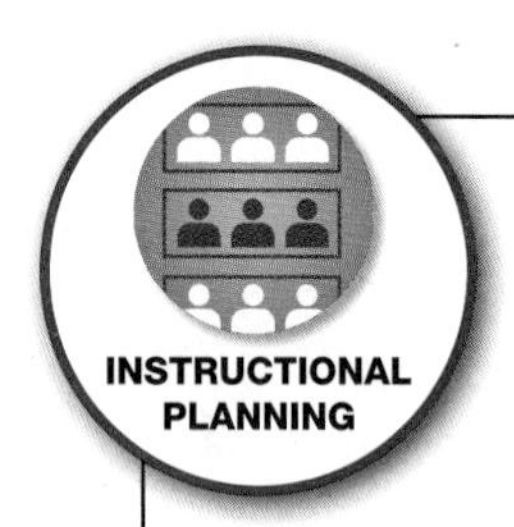

Intervention Grouping Report

CLASS: SCHIRMER 3

School: Lincoln Middle School
Teacher: Margaret Schirmer
Grade: 7

Time Period: 08/24/11 – 02/02/12 ❶

❷ PERFORMANCE STANDARD	STUDENT	GRADE	❸ LEXILE®	❹ DATE	❺ NORMATIVE DATA: PERCENTILE RANK	❻ NCE	❼ STANINE
Advanced	Krynski, Theo	7	1120	01/25/12	78	66	7
Proficient	Collins, Chris	7	868	01/26/12	36	42	4
Basic	Chu, Amy	7	834	01/26/12	32	40	4
Basic	Kramer, Liz	7	809	01/26/12	28	38	4
Basic	Sanchez, Rachel	7	792	01/25/12	26	36	4
Basic	Cooper, Tiffany	7	781	01/25/12	25	36	4
Basic	Ramirez, Gabriella	7	743	01/28/12	21	33	3
Basic	Rupp, Jeremy	7	727	01/27/12	19	32	3
Basic	Imran, Khaleel	7	719	01/25/12	19	32	3
Basic	Evans, Jamal	7	719	01/25/12	19	32	3
Basic	Bracco, Christine	7	709	01/27/12	17	30	3
Basic	Garcia, Matt	7	550	09/01/11	6	17	2
Below Basic	Palermo, Justin	7	438	01/25/12	1	1	1
Below Basic	Fernandez, Luis	7	242	01/25/12	1	1	1
Below Basic	Felix, Tonya	7	BR (10)	01/25/12	1	1	1

Using This Report

Purpose: This report groups students under the four SRI performance standards. The report is used to target for additional support students whose performance is Below Basic or Basic.

Follow-Up: Use the information on the report to set goals for students. Plan appropriate instructional support and intervention for students who are reading below grade level. Encourage students to read independently at their reading level.

How It Helps

I can use this report to create initial groups based on reading performance.

Understand the Data

1 Time Period
Run for This School Year to review current reading performance results. Customize time periods to review results from previous SRI tests.

2 Performance Standard
Student's reading level based on the four SRI performance standards: Advanced, Proficient, Basic, and Below Basic. Performance standard Lexile ranges vary by grade level.

3 Lexile
Students' Lexile score from the most recent SRI test within selected time period.

4 Date
Date of most recent completed SRI test within selected time period.

5 Percentile Rank
Percentage of students from a national sample who received lower scores than this student on a scale of 1 to 99. For example, a student who scores at the 65th percentile performed as well or better than 65 percent of the norm group.

6 NCE (Normal Curve Equivalent)
A comparison of student's rate of progress to the norm, based on a national sample. Students making exactly one year of progress earn a score of 0. Students progressing faster than the norm receive a score from 1 to 99, depending on the rate of increase.

7 Stanine
A standardized score that indicates a student's relative standing in a norm group. Stanines 1, 2, and 3 are below average; stanines 4, 5, and 6 are average; and stanines 7, 8, and 9 are above average.

Use the Data

Who: Teachers (Teacher, Class, or Group report)

When: After each SRI administration

How: You can use the information from this report in the following ways:

Establish Groups

- Consider SRI scores when forming groups for Small-Group Instruction. Use the Groupinator to adjust groups.

Differentiate Instruction

- Students in lower performance standards may benefit from additional scaffolding. Students in higher performance standards may benefit from more independent practice.

Review Related Reports

- SRI Targeted Reading Report (p. 120)
- SRI Student Action Report (p. 126)
- SRI Student Progress Report (p. 128)

Data in Action

Conference With Students Discuss information from this report during individual conferences. Help students set goals for their reading growth. Encourage students to read independently at their reading level.

Analyze the Results | Intervention Grouping Report

Offer appropriate Small-Group support based on current reading performance. If you are using *System 44* in a *READ 180* classroom, form *rBook* groups based on SRI results.

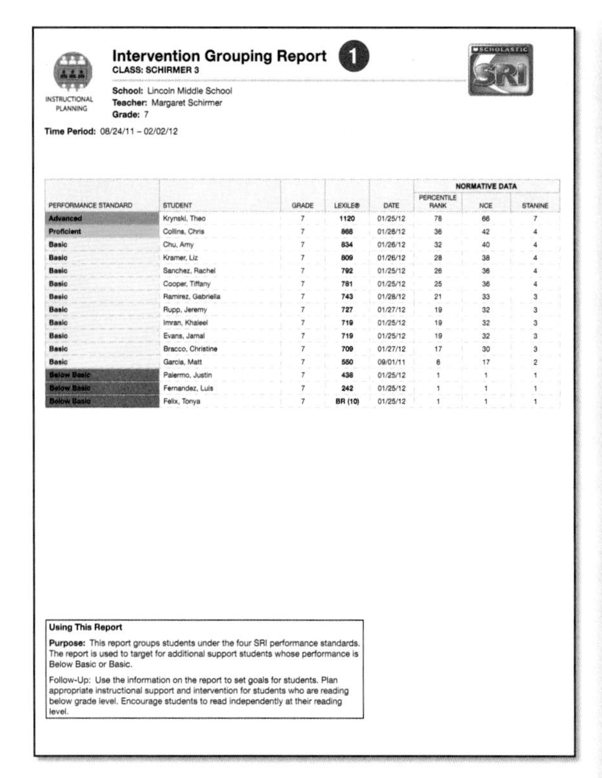

Intervention Grouping Report ❶
CLASS: SCHIRMER 3

INSTRUCTIONAL PLANNING

School: Lincoln Middle School
Teacher: Margaret Schirmer
Grade: 7

Time Period: 08/24/11 – 02/02/12

PERFORMANCE STANDARD	STUDENT	GRADE	LEXILE®	DATE	NORMATIVE DATA: PERCENTILE RANK	NORMATIVE DATA: NCE	NORMATIVE DATA: STANINE
Advanced	Krynski, Theo	7	1120	01/25/12	78	66	7
Proficient	Collins, Chris	7	868	01/26/12	36	42	4
Basic	Chu, Amy	7	834	01/26/12	32	40	4
Basic	Kramer, Liz	7	809	01/26/12	28	38	4
Basic	Sanchez, Rachel	7	792	01/25/12	26	36	4
Basic	Cooper, Tiffany	7	781	01/25/12	25	36	4
Basic	Ramirez, Gabriella	7	743	01/28/12	21	33	3
Basic	Rupp, Jeremy	7	727	01/27/12	19	32	3
Basic	Imran, Khaleel	7	719	01/25/12	19	32	3
Basic	Evans, Jamal	7	719	01/25/12	19	32	3
Basic	Bracco, Christine	7	709	01/27/12	17	30	3
Basic	Garcia, Matt	7	550	09/01/11	6	17	2
Below Basic	Palermo, Justin	7	438	01/25/12	1	1	1
Below Basic	Fernandez, Luis	7	242	01/25/12	1	1	1
Below Basic	Felix, Tonya	7	BR (10)	01/25/12	1	1	1

Using This Report

Purpose: This report groups students under the four SRI performance standards. The report is used to target for additional support students whose performance is Below Basic or Basic.

Follow-Up: Use the information on the report to set goals for students. Plan appropriate instructional support and intervention for students who are reading below grade level. Encourage students to read independently at their reading level.

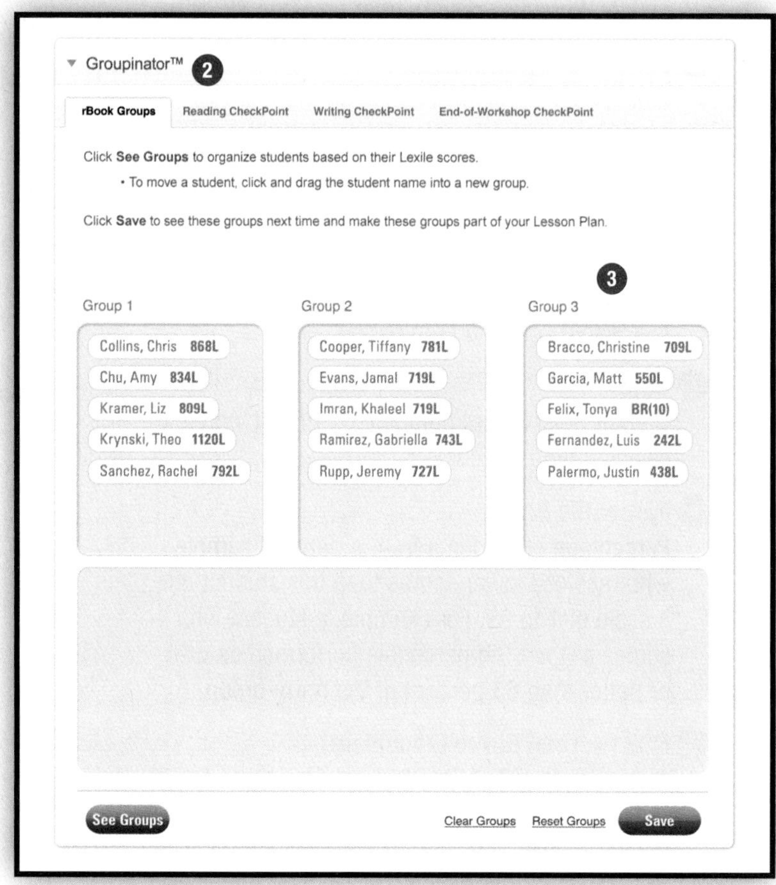

Groupinator: ***rBook*** **Groups**

Data Point	Data Analysis	NEXT STEPS
❶ In *READ 180* classrooms, results from the SRI Intervention Grouping Report are used to form groups for daily *rBook* instruction.	Data from this report is pulled to the Groupinator on the Teacher Dashboard for *rBook* Groups.	Access the Groupinator on the Class Page of the Teacher Dashboard to review *rBook* groups.
❷ The Groupinator uses the data from the SRI Intervention Grouping Report to create groups.	No matter how many performance standards exist in one class, the Groupinator will create three equal groups based on reading level.	Use the SRI Intervention Grouping Report and classroom performance results to make any necessary grouping adjustments.
❸ *rBook* grouping recommendations on the Groupinator can be refreshed after each SRI testing window is closed.	As the year progresses, students' reading levels will change. Regroup students when new data indicates changes in student ability levels.	Click **See Groups** in the Groupinator to review *rBook* grouping recommendations based on current SRI performance.

Review Additional Data

Use Groupinator recommendations to determine appropriate differentiated instructional support during Small-Group Instruction.

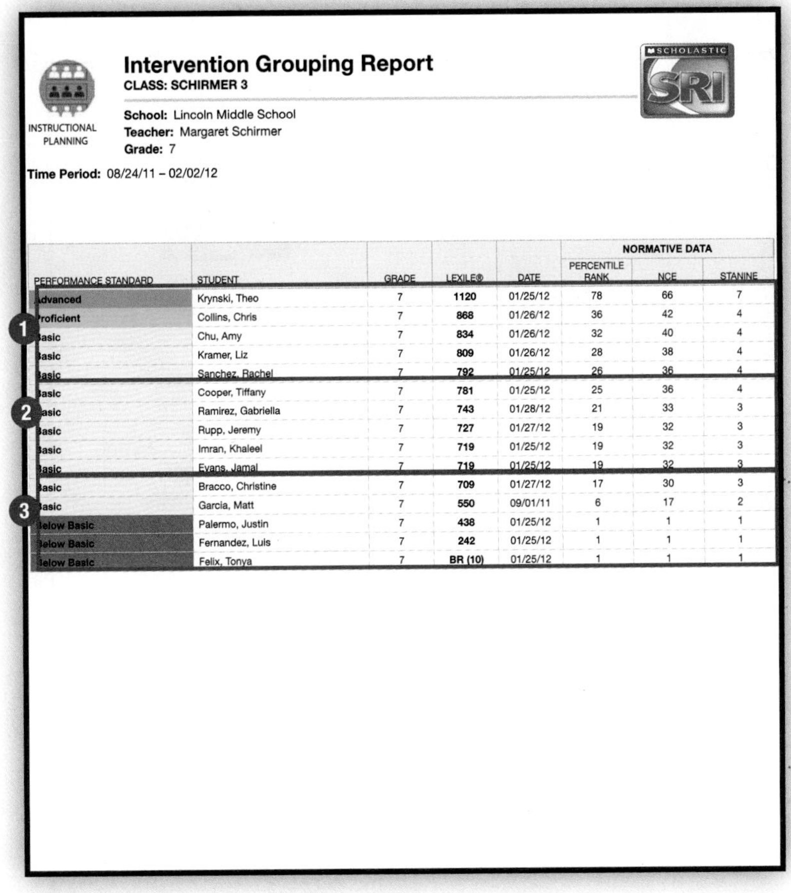

INSTRUCTIONAL PLANNING

Intervention Grouping Report
CLASS: SCHIRMER 3

School: Lincoln Middle School
Teacher: Margaret Schirmer
Grade: 7

Time Period: 08/24/11 – 02/02/12

PERFORMANCE STANDARD	STUDENT	GRADE	LEXILE®	DATE	NORMATIVE DATA: PERCENTILE RANK	NORMATIVE DATA: NCE	NORMATIVE DATA: STANINE
Advanced	Krynski, Theo	7	**1120**	01/25/12	78	66	7
Proficient	Collins, Chris	7	**868**	01/26/12	36	42	4
Basic	Chu, Amy	7	**834**	01/26/12	32	40	4
Basic	Kramer, Liz	7	**809**	01/26/12	28	38	4
Basic	Sanchez, Rachel	7	**792**	01/25/12	26	36	4
Basic	Cooper, Tiffany	7	**781**	01/25/12	25	36	4
Basic	Ramirez, Gabriella	7	**743**	01/28/12	21	33	3
Basic	Rupp, Jeremy	7	**727**	01/27/12	19	32	3
Basic	Imran, Khaleel	7	**719**	01/25/12	19	32	3
Basic	Evans, Jamal	7	**719**	01/25/12	19	32	3
Basic	Bracco, Christine	7	**709**	01/27/12	17	30	3
Basic	Garcia, Matt	7	**550**	09/01/11	6	17	2
Below Basic	Palermo, Justin	7	**438**	01/25/12	1	1	1
Below Basic	Fernandez, Luis	7	**242**	01/25/12	1	1	1
Below Basic	Felix, Tonya	7	**BR (10)**	01/25/12	1	1	1

Enlargement: Intervention Grouping Report

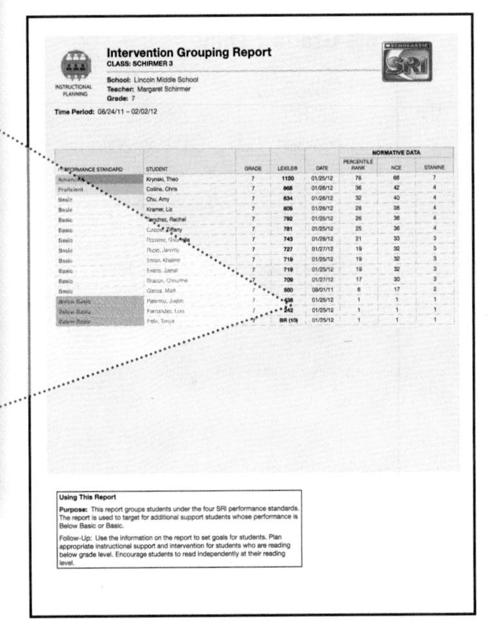

Using This Report

Purpose: This report groups students under the four SRI performance standards. The report is used to target for additional support students whose performance is Below Basic or Basic.

Follow-Up: Use the information on the report to set goals for students. Plan appropriate instructional support and intervention for students who are reading below grade level. Encourage students to read independently at their reading level.

Data Point	Data Analysis	NEXT STEPS
❶ Group 1 includes five students who are reading at three different performance levels—Advanced, Proficient, and Basic.	Amy, Liz, and Rachel are reading at the Basic range. Consider their current classroom performance when finalizing groups.	Assign *rBook* Small-Group Stretch activities to groups with students whose reading levels are nearing grade-level proficiency.
❷ Group 2 includes five students who are all reading at the Basic range.	There are students reading at the Basic range in all groups. If regrouping is necessary, focus on students at this range.	Teach the *rBook* Small-Group lesson as designed to groups with students whose reading levels are mainly in the Basic range.
❸ Group 3 includes five students who are reading at two different performance levels—Basic and Below Basic.	Although Matt is reading at a Basic range, his Lexile indicates that he should stay grouped with students who need additional support.	Assign *rBook* Small-Group Boost activities to groups with students whose reading levels are mainly below the Basic range.

Proficiency Report

Purpose

This report shows SRI proficiency and compares current results to those of other students in the same grade.

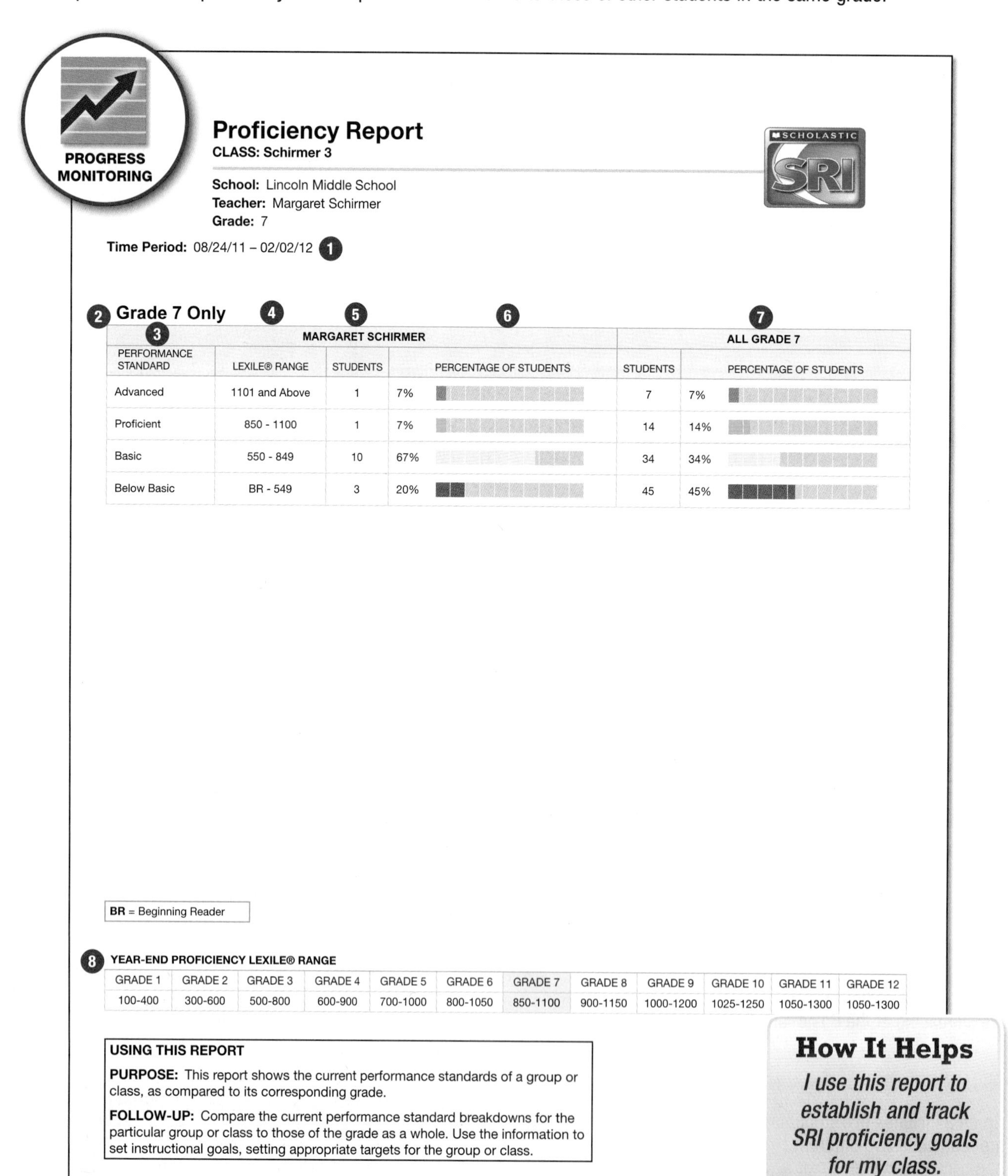

PROGRESS MONITORING

Proficiency Report
CLASS: Schirmer 3

School: Lincoln Middle School
Teacher: Margaret Schirmer
Grade: 7

Time Period: 08/24/11 – 02/02/12 (1)

(2) **Grade 7 Only**

PERFORMANCE STANDARD (3)	MARGARET SCHIRMER: LEXILE® RANGE (4)	STUDENTS (5)	PERCENTAGE OF STUDENTS (6)	ALL GRADE 7 (7): STUDENTS	PERCENTAGE OF STUDENTS
Advanced	1101 and Above	1	7%	7	7%
Proficient	850 - 1100	1	7%	14	14%
Basic	550 - 849	10	67%	34	34%
Below Basic	BR - 549	3	20%	45	45%

BR = Beginning Reader

(8) **YEAR-END PROFICIENCY LEXILE® RANGE**

GRADE 1	GRADE 2	GRADE 3	GRADE 4	GRADE 5	GRADE 6	GRADE 7	GRADE 8	GRADE 9	GRADE 10	GRADE 11	GRADE 12
100-400	300-600	500-800	600-900	700-1000	800-1050	850-1100	900-1150	1000-1200	1025-1250	1050-1300	1050-1300

USING THIS REPORT

PURPOSE: This report shows the current performance standards of a group or class, as compared to its corresponding grade.

FOLLOW-UP: Compare the current performance standard breakdowns for the particular group or class to those of the grade as a whole. Use the information to set instructional goals, setting appropriate targets for the group or class.

How It Helps

I use this report to establish and track SRI proficiency goals for my class.

Understand the Data

1 Time Period
Default time period setting of This School Year displays results from the most recent SRI administration. Customize time period settings to review results from previous tests.

2 Grade
Results displayed by grade level. Classes with students in multiple grade levels will display results in separate charts for each grade level.

3 Performance Standard
Students grouped into four performance standards based on SRI test results and grade level: Advanced, Proficient, Basic, and Below Basic.

4 Lexile Range
Lexile range for students in each performance standard. Lexile ranges for each performance standard vary by grade level.

5 Students
Total number of students meeting each performance standard, based on most recent SRI results within selected time period.

6 Percentage of Students
Percentage of students meeting each performance standard, based on most recent SRI results within selected time period.

7 All Grade
Total students and percentage of students in each performance standard for each grade level. Students included took at least one SRI test. Results include all students in the grade level on the selected SAM server.

8 Year-End Proficiency Lexile Range
Expected year-end Lexile ranges for reading proficiency in each grade. Shaded area represents year-end proficiency range for grade levels from the selected group or class.

Use the Data

Who: Teachers (Teacher, Class, or Group report)

When: After each SRI administration

How: Apply the information in this report in the following ways:

Establish and Track SRI Goals

- Consider scores in context by comparing your group or class SRI results to overall grade level results.
- Establish SRI growth goals based on performance standards and grade levels.
- Track SRI results. Save a copy of this report after each SRI administration and compare your results from one administration to the next.

Share Results

- Share results with administrators. Print this report to update your school administrators on your students' reading progress.
- Celebrate SRI growth with students. Recognize students who have made strong SRI gains, especially students who have moved to a higher performance standard.

Review Related Reports

- SRI Intervention Grouping Report (p. 114)
- SRI Targeted Reading Report (p. 120)
- SRI Student Action Report (p. 126)

Data in Action

Tracking Growth The total number of students in Basic and Below Basic should decrease throughout the year as students move to higher SRI Performance Standards.

Targeted Reading Report

Purpose

This report establishes reading ranges for text difficulty based on the student's Lexile measure.

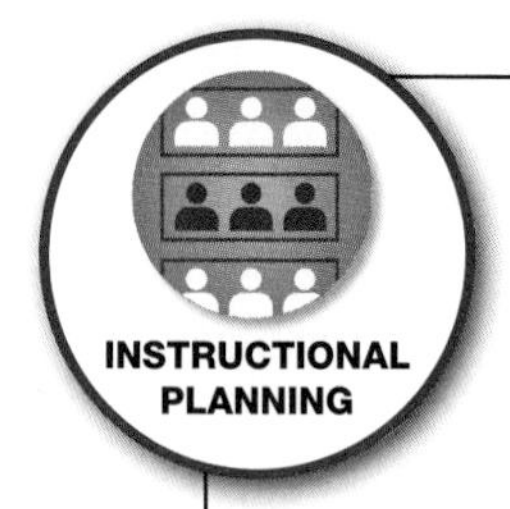

Targeted Reading Report

CLASS: Schirmer 3

School: Lincoln Middle School
Teacher: Margaret Schirmer
Grade: 7

Time Period: 08/24/11 – 02/02/12 ❶

STUDENT	GRADE	❷ LEXILE®	❸ TEST DATE	❹ TEXT DIFFICULTY		
				❺ EASY	❻ ON LEVEL	CHALLENGING ❼
Bracco, Christine	7	**709**	01/27/12	459-609	**609-759**	759-959
Chu, Amy	7	**834**	01/26/12	584-734	**734-884**	884-1084
Collins, Chris	7	**868**	01/26/12	618-768	**768-918**	918-1118
Cooper, Tiffany	7	**781**	01/25/12	531-681	**681-831**	831-1031
Evans, Jamal	7	**719**	01/25/12	469-619	**619-769**	769-969
Felix, Tonya	7	**BR (10)**	01/25/12	N/A	**BR**	BR-260
Fernandez, Luis	7	**242**	01/25/12	BR-142	**142-292**	292-492
Garcia, Matt	7	**550**	01/27/12	300-450	**450-600**	600-800
Imran, Khaleel	7	**719**	01/25/12	469-619	**619-769**	769-969
Kramer, Liz	7	**809**	01/26/12	559-709	**709-859**	859-1059
Krynski, Theo	7	**1120**	09/01/11	870-1020	**1020-1170**	1170-1370
Palermo, Justin	7	**438**	01/27/12	188-338	**338-488**	488-688
Ramirez, Gabriella	7	**743**	01/28/12	493-643	**643-793**	793-993
Rupp, Jeremy	7	**727**	01/27/12	477-627	**627-777**	777-977
Sanchez, Rachel	7	**792**	01/25/12	542-692	**692-842**	842-1042

BR = Beginning Reader

USING THIS REPORT

PURPOSE: This report establishes Lexile reading ranges for text difficulty – easy, average, and challenging – for each student based on the student's Lexile measure.

FOLLOW-UP: Use the reading ranges to assign appropriately leveled text for different instructional purposes and to help students choose books at a comfortable level for independent reading.

How It Helps

I use this report to guide book selection in Modeled and Independent Reading.

Understand the Data

❶ **Time Period**
Default time period setting of This School Year displays results from most recent SRI administration. Customize time period settings to review results from previous tests.

❷ **Lexile**
Each student's current SRI score, measured in Lexile. BR indicates a Beginning Reader, a student with a Lexile below 100.

❸ **Test Date**
Date most recent SRI test was completed within the selected time period.

❹ **Text Difficulty**
Lexile ranges for text, based on the student's current Lexile score.

❺ **Easy**
100L to 250L below the student's current Lexile score.

❻ **On Level**
100L below to 50L above the student's current Lexile score.

❼ **Challenging**
50L to 250L above the student's current Lexile score.

Use the Data

Who: Teachers (Teacher, Class, or Group report)

When: After each SRI administration

How: Apply the information in this report in the following ways:

Guide Independent Reading Choices

- Encourage reluctant readers to select *Easy* books for independent reading to boost confidence.
- Guide students to frequently select *On-Level* books, which are within their fluent and independent range.
- Suggest *Challenging* books when students are highly motivated or have background knowledge about the topic.

Review Related Reports

- SRI Intervention Grouping Report (p. 114)
- SRI Recommended Reading Report (p. 124)
- SRI Student Action Report (p. 126)

Data in Action

Accelerating Reading Growth Review this report after each SRI test. As students' SRI scores increase, ensure that they are accessing more challenging texts during Modeled and Independent Reading and that they are being offered appropriate challenges during Small-Group Instruction.

Incomplete Test Alert

Purpose

This report lists students who did not complete or save the SRI test on their most recent attempt. It includes the date the test was attempted and the student's current grade level.

Incomplete Test Alert

TEACHER: Margaret Schirmer

School: Lincoln Middle School
Grade: 7
Class: Schirmer 3

Time Period: 08/24/11 – 02/02/12

STUDENT	GRADE	ATTEMPTED TEST DATE
Rupp, Jeremy	7	11/09/11

Using This Report

Purpose: This report shows students who did not complete the SRI test on their latest test. It includes the student's grade and the date of the incomplete test.

Follow-Up: Plan each student's next SRI administration, and investigate why each student did not complete the test.

How It Helps

I review this report frequently during SRI testing windows to ensure that all students complete an SRI test. I follow up with students on this report to ensure they are not having trouble with the test.

Student Roster

Purpose

This report lists students assigned to a selected group, class, or teacher. It includes each student's grade, ID, username, and password.

Student Roster

CLASS: SCHIRMER 3

School: Lincoln Middle School
Teacher: Margaret Schirmer
Grade: 7

Time Period: 08/24/11 – 02/02/12

STUDENT	GRADE	STUDENT ID	USERNAME	PASSWORD
Bracco, Christine	7	7299209	cbracco	pas5word
Chu, Amy	7	10135416	achu	pas5word
Collins, Chris	7	7805559	ccollins	pas5word
Cooper, Tiffany	7	7897663	tcooper	pas5word
Evans, Jamal	7	7813157	jevans	pas5word
Felix, Tonya	7	780555	tfelix	pas5word
Fernandez, Luis	7	7513484	lfernandez	pas5word
Garcia, Matt	7	10405447	mgarcia	pas5word
Imran, Khaleel	7	7793169	kimran	pas5word
Kramer, Liz	7	8084279	lkramer	pas5word
Krynksi, Theo	7	7162902	tkrynski	pas5word
Palermo, Justin	7	7471048	jpalermo	pas5word
Ramirez, Gabriella	7	7467053	gramirez	pas5word
Rupp, Jeremy	7	7793706	jrupp	pas5word
Sanchez, Rachel	7	10575041	rsanchez	pas5word
TOTAL STUDENTS = 15				

Using This Report

Purpose: The Student Roster lists the students assigned to a selected group, class, or teacher. It includes each student's grade, ID, username, and password.

Follow-Up: Review the roster to track which students are enrolled in SRI.

How It Helps

I keep a copy of this report on hand in case students forget their passwords. It also helps me ensure that everyone in my System 44 *class is enrolled in SRI.*

Recommended Reading Report

Purpose

This report provides an individualized list of books for each student, based on interests and SRI results.

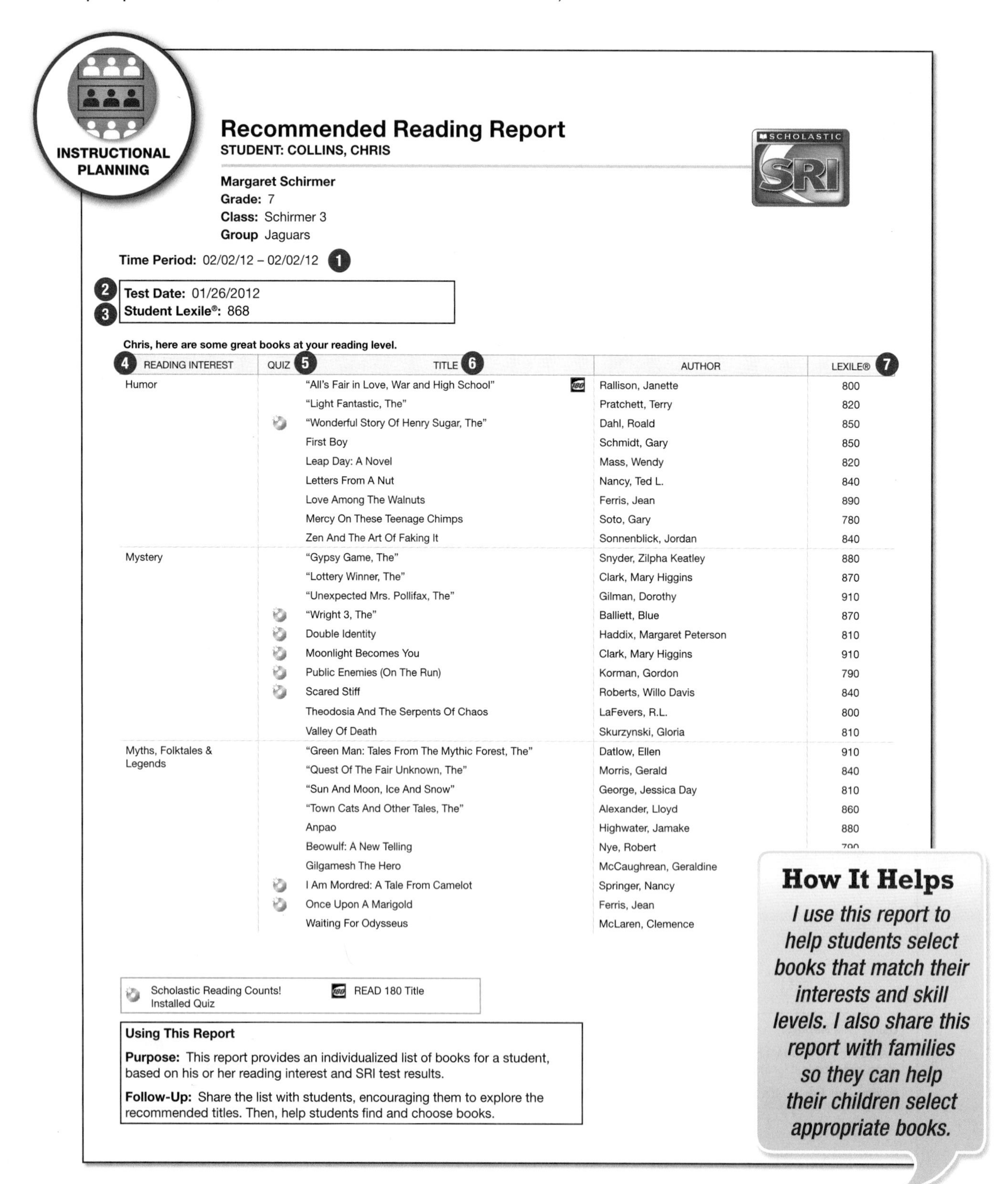

INSTRUCTIONAL PLANNING

Recommended Reading Report

STUDENT: COLLINS, CHRIS

SCHOLASTIC SRI

Margaret Schirmer
Grade: 7
Class: Schirmer 3
Group Jaguars

Time Period: 02/02/12 – 02/02/12 ❶

❷ **Test Date:** 01/26/2012
❸ **Student Lexile®:** 868

Chris, here are some great books at your reading level.

❹ READING INTEREST	QUIZ ❺	TITLE ❻	AUTHOR	LEXILE® ❼
Humor		"All's Fair in Love, War and High School" (READ 180 Title)	Rallison, Janette	800
		"Light Fantastic, The"	Pratchett, Terry	820
	●	"Wonderful Story Of Henry Sugar, The"	Dahl, Roald	850
		First Boy	Schmidt, Gary	850
		Leap Day: A Novel	Mass, Wendy	820
		Letters From A Nut	Nancy, Ted L.	840
		Love Among The Walnuts	Ferris, Jean	890
		Mercy On These Teenage Chimps	Soto, Gary	780
		Zen And The Art Of Faking It	Sonnenblick, Jordan	840
Mystery		"Gypsy Game, The"	Snyder, Zilpha Keatley	880
		"Lottery Winner, The"	Clark, Mary Higgins	870
		"Unexpected Mrs. Pollifax, The"	Gilman, Dorothy	910
	●	"Wright 3, The"	Balliett, Blue	870
	●	Double Identity	Haddix, Margaret Peterson	810
	●	Moonlight Becomes You	Clark, Mary Higgins	910
	●	Public Enemies (On The Run)	Korman, Gordon	790
	●	Scared Stiff	Roberts, Willo Davis	840
		Theodosia And The Serpents Of Chaos	LaFevers, R.L.	800
		Valley Of Death	Skurzynski, Gloria	810
Myths, Folktales & Legends		"Green Man: Tales From The Mythic Forest, The"	Datlow, Ellen	910
		"Quest Of The Fair Unknown, The"	Morris, Gerald	840
		"Sun And Moon, Ice And Snow"	George, Jessica Day	810
		"Town Cats And Other Tales, The"	Alexander, Lloyd	860
		Anpao	Highwater, Jamake	880
		Beowulf: A New Telling	Nye, Robert	[illegible]
		Gilgamesh The Hero	McCaughrean, Geraldine	
	●	I Am Mordred: A Tale From Camelot	Springer, Nancy	
	●	Once Upon A Marigold	Ferris, Jean	
		Waiting For Odysseus	McLaren, Clemence	

● Scholastic Reading Counts! Installed Quiz — READ 180 Title

Using This Report

Purpose: This report provides an individualized list of books for a student, based on his or her reading interest and SRI test results.

Follow-Up: Share the list with students, encouraging them to explore the recommended titles. Then, help students find and choose books.

How It Helps

I use this report to help students select books that match their interests and skill levels. I also share this report with families so they can help their children select appropriate books.

Understand the Data

❶ **Time Period**
Time period setting is This School Year, which displays results from most recent SRI test.

❷ **Test Date**
The student's most recent SRI test date.

❸ **Student Lexile**
The student's current SRI test score.

❹ **Reading Interest**
Topics of interest the student selected at the beginning of the SRI test. Students can select up to three topics of interest.

❺ **Quiz**
Icon next to a book title indicates that *Scholastic Reading Counts!* quiz for that book has been installed and is available.

❻ **Title**
Books related to the student's interests at the appropriate reading level.

❼ **Lexile**
Lexile measure for each book.

Use the Data

Who: Teachers, Students, Parents (Student report)

When: After each SRI administration

How: You can apply the information in this report in the following ways:

Guide Independent Reading

- Print this report after each SRI test administration and use it to help students select books for independent reading.
- Use the SAM Book Expert to gather more information about the books listed in this report. See Using Book Expert on page 51 for more information.

Share Results

- Share this report with school media specialists so they can help students select appropriate books and stock books based on student reading interest and level.
- Send this report home with students along with the SRI Parent Report or with report cards to provide families guidance in helping their children select books.

Review Related Reports

- SRI Student Action Report (p. 126)
- SRI College and Career Readiness Report (p. 132)
- SRI Parent Report (p. 135)

Data in Action

Selecting Book Topics At the beginning of an SRI test, students choose book topics that interest them. Encourage students to select topics carefully so that their Recommended Reading Report reflects books that will truly interest them.

Student Action Report

Purpose

This report tracks a student's SRI history, provides reading ranges, and offers teaching recommendations.

Student Action Report

STUDENT: COLLINS, CHRIS

Teacher: Margaret Schirmer
Grade: 7
Class: Schirmer 3

Time Period: 08/24/11 – 02/02/12 ❶

Chris's SRI Test History

Chris's Lexile(R) measure corresponds to the information indicated in the chart below:

TEST DATE	❷ LEXILE®	❸ PERFORMANCE STANDARD	TEST TYPE	NORMATIVE DATA ❹ PERCENTILE RANK	NCE ❺	❻ STANINE
09/04/11	784	Basic	SRI Computer Test	25	36	4
11/03/11	854	Proficient	SRI Computer Test	35	42	4
01/26/12	868	Proficient	SRI Computer Test	36	42	4

❼ Targeted Reading Placement Chart

For a student with a Lexile(R) measure of **709**, use the Lexile(R) ranges indicated below to help guide book selection, according to your instructional purposes.

LEXILE® RANGE	INDEPENDENT READING	INSTRUCTIONAL READING
918-1118	The text is difficult for Chris.	Chris can build reading skill with direct instructional support.
768-918	Chris can read the text with a high level of engagement and with appropriate levels of challenge.	Chris has sufficient control over vocabulary and syntax to work on applying reading skills.
618-768	Chris can read these texts fluently but with little challenge.	Chris is unchallenged by vocabulary and syntax. This level can be used when teaching new or challenging content.

❽ Recommendations for Chris

To help Chris grow as a reader, encourage Chris to:

- Read books within the target Lexile range (50 Lexiles above and 100 below Lexile measure).
- Use various word attack strategies (context clues, word families, reference materials) to determine the meaning of unknown words.
- Use reading strategies such as drawing conclusions, making and confirming predictions, and making inferences.
- Compare and contrast topics and themes presented across genres.
- Build vocabulary by reading and discussing at least 25 books per year (approximately 750,000 words).

Using This Report

Purpose: This report shows an individual student's SRI test history, a reading placement chart targeting appropriate Lexile ranges for different reading purposes, and teaching recommendations to help the student meet grade-level expectations.

Follow-Up: Review the student's performance and use the placement chart and recommendations for classroom or home assignments.

How It Helps

I use this report to help students select appropriate reading materials and help me determine what support to provide during Whole- and Small-Group Instruction.

Understand the Data

1 Time Period
Default time period setting of This School Year displays results from all SRI tests administered during the school year. Customize date ranges to track progress on selected tests within a school year or review progress over multiple years.

2 Lexile
Includes Lexile scores for all SRI tests taken within the selected time period.

3 Performance Standard
Student's reading level, based on the four SRI performance standards: Below Basic, Basic, Proficient, and Advanced. Lexile ranges for each performance standard vary by grade level.

4 Percentile Rank
Percentage of students from a national sample who received lower scores than this student. Percentiles range from 1 to 99.

5 Normal Curve Equivalent (NCE)
A comparison of the student's rate of progress to the norm, based on a national sample. Students who make exactly one year of growth are keeping pace with the norm and receive an NCE score of zero. Students progressing faster than the norm receive a score from 1–99, depending on the rate of increase.

6 Stanine
A standardized score ranging from 1 to 9. Stanines 1, 2, and 3 are below average; stanines 4, 5, and 6 are average; and stanines 7, 8, and 9 are above average.

7 Targeted Reading Placement Chart
Lexile ranges for independent and instructional reading based on the student's current Lexile.

8 Recommendations
Suggested teaching strategies customized to the student's grade, Lexile score, and SRI performance standard.

Use the Data

Who: Teachers, Students (Student report)

When: After each SRI administration

How: You can use the information in this report in the following ways:

Review Test Results

- Establish SRI growth goals, then conference with students to explain results and track progress toward goals.
- Share results with support specialists at IEP meetings.

Provide Reading Support

- Filter results in the SAM Book Expert according to the Lexile ranges from this report to help students select independent reading materials at appropriate reading levels.

Review Related Reports

- SRI Targeted Reading Report (p. 120)
- SRI Recommended Reading Report (p. 124)
- SRI Student Progress Report (p. 128)

norms

Data in Action

Differentiate Instruction When *44Book* readings are more than 50 Lexile points above the student's current reading level, provide additional support. When *44Book* readings fall 100 Lexile points or more below student's current reading level, reduce scaffolding.

SRI Reports

Student Progress Report | Best Practice Report

Purpose

This report traces historical student progress on SRI tests in relation to year-end proficiency.

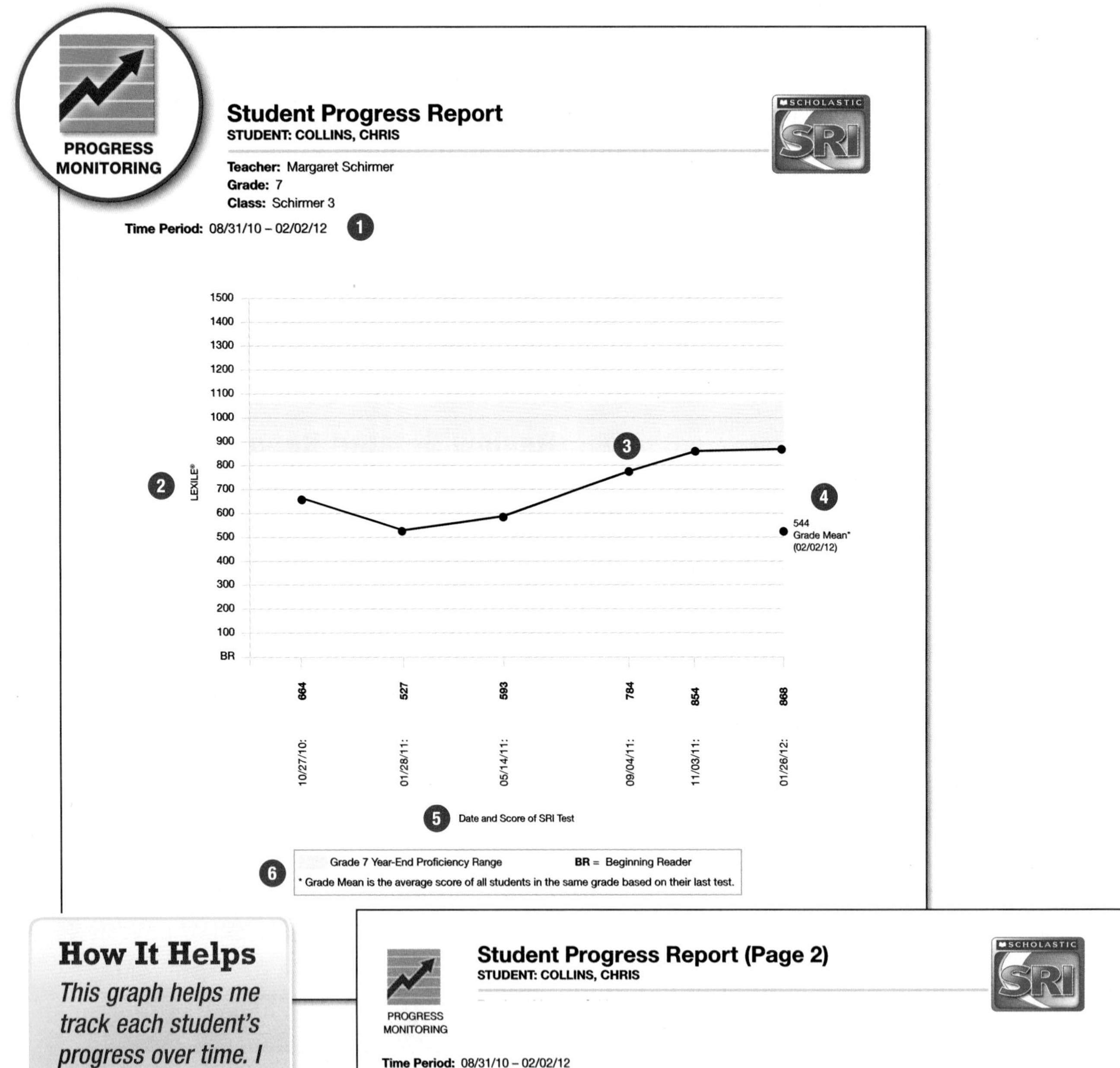

How It Helps

This graph helps me track each student's progress over time. I can share this report with the student, send it home to parents, or use it to point out particular successes to my principal.

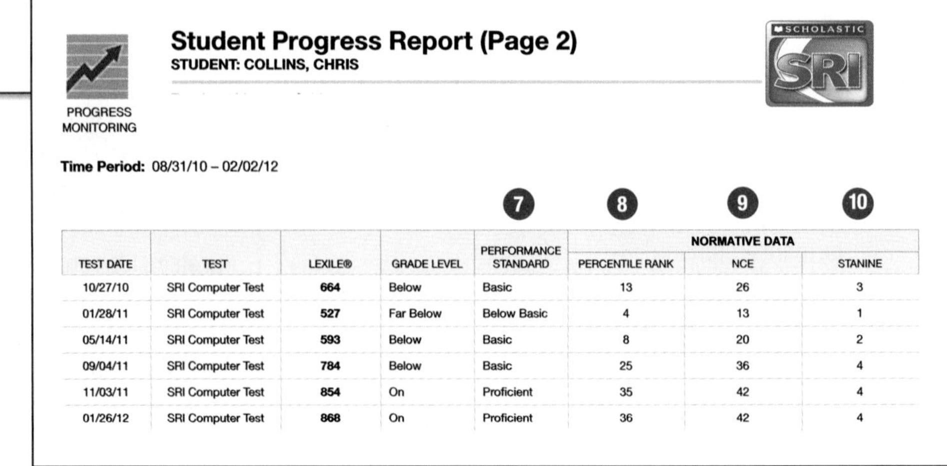

PROGRESS MONITORING

Student Progress Report (Page 2)
STUDENT: COLLINS, CHRIS

SCHOLASTIC SRI

Time Period: 08/31/10 – 02/02/12

TEST DATE	TEST	LEXILE®	GRADE LEVEL	PERFORMANCE STANDARD (7)	NORMATIVE DATA: PERCENTILE RANK (8)	NCE (9)	STANINE (10)
10/27/10	SRI Computer Test	**664**	Below	Basic	13	26	3
01/28/11	SRI Computer Test	**527**	Far Below	Below Basic	4	13	1
05/14/11	SRI Computer Test	**593**	Below	Basic	8	20	2
09/04/11	SRI Computer Test	**784**	Below	Basic	25	36	4
11/03/11	SRI Computer Test	**854**	On	Proficient	35	42	4
01/26/12	SRI Computer Test	**868**	On	Proficient	36	42	4

Understand the Data

1 Time Period
Default time period setting of This School Year displays comprehensive SRI results. Customize time period settings to target recent scores or review results for multiple years.

2 Lexile
Vertical axis shows Lexile in increments of 100.

3 Graph Entries
Each dot represents a student's SRI test result on a particular date.

4 Grade Mean
Dot indicates the average score for all students in that particular grade, based on the latest SRI test results.

5 Date and Score of SRI Test
Horizontal axis displays date and score of all SRI tests completed within the selected time period.

6 Year-End Proficiency Range
Shaded area represents the year-end Lexile proficiency range for the student's current grade level.

7 Performance Standard
Student's reading level based on the four SRI performance standards. Performance standard Lexile ranges vary by grade level.

8 Percentile Rank
Percentage of students from a national sample who received lower scores than this student. For example, a student who scores at the 65th percentile performed as well as or better than 65 percent of the norm group.

9 Normal Curve Equivalent (NCE)
A comparison of student's rate of progress to the norm, based on a national sample. Students progressing faster than the norm would receive a score from 1 to 99, depending on the increase.

10 Stanine
A standardized score that indicates student's relative standing in a norm group. Stanines 1–3 are below average; stanines 4–6 are average; and stanines 7–9 are above average.

Use the Data

Who: Teachers, Students, Families (Student report)

When: After each SRI administration

How: Apply the information in this report in the following ways:

Prepare for Upcoming Test

- Tell students that the SRI measures their reading level so that you can match them with books that they can read and enjoy.
- Prepare students for the SRI test by discussing previous test results. Remind them to use the Skip button if they are given a question they cannot answer. They can skip up to three questions.
- Explain to students that subsequent tests begin at their current Lexile level, so initial questions may seem more challenging.
- Help students set SRI growth goals and understand the year-end Lexile proficiency range.

Review Test Results

- Use customizable certificates available in the SAM Roster to recognize growth.
- Conference with students whose scores dropped and plan appropriate intervention.
- Share results at family-teacher conferences, highlighting reading achievement.

Review Related Reports

- SRI Recommended Reading Report (p. 124)
- SRI Student Action Report (p. 126)
- SRI College and Career Readiness Report (

Data in Action

Test-Taking Strategies Remind students that the SRI will save their place so they can exit the test if they begin to feel tired. They can resume the test the next day.

Analyze the Results | Student Progress Report

DATA STORY

Student: Chris Collins
Current Lexile: 868
Current Grade: 7

Recognize students like Chris who have made large gains in reading comprehension.

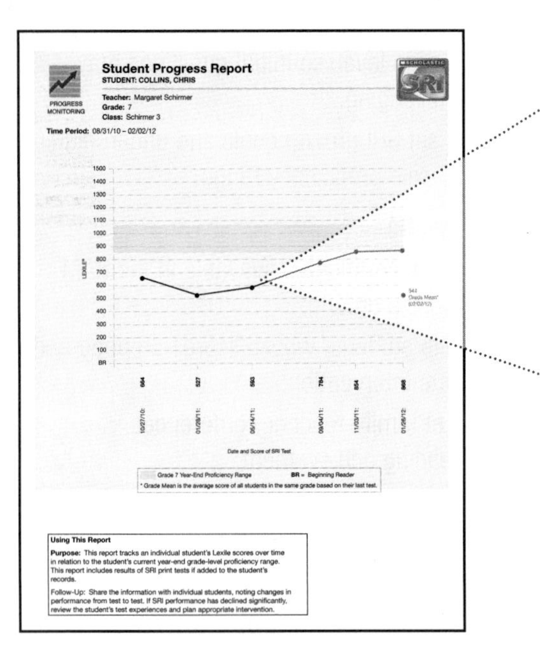

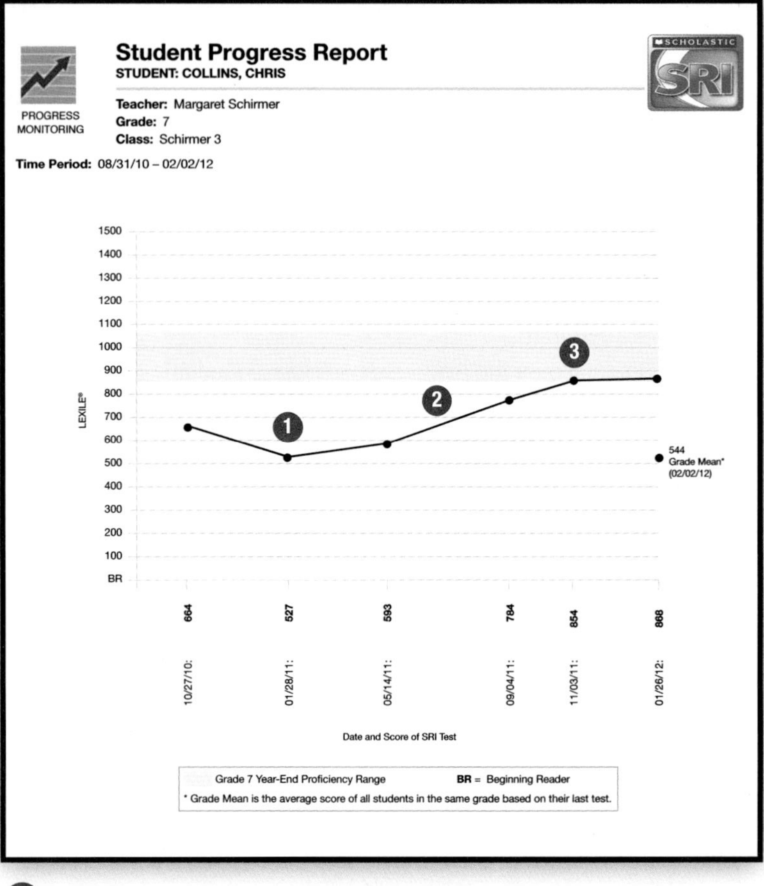

Enlargement: Student Progress Report

Data Point	Data Analysis	NEXT STEPS
1 Chris's data showed a slight decline from the first test to the second test.	Chris was not prepared for the challenging questions of the second test.	Remind students that their second SRI will seem harder because it starts at their current Lexile.
2 Chris's overall SRI growth pattern is positive, with steady increases at each SRI administration.	Chris made over two years' growth during his first year. He is on track for similar results this year.	Use this report to help students set and track SRI growth goals.
3 Chris's SRI graph has reached the blue 7th grade proficiency band.	Since Chris's Lexile score is higher and he is nearing proficiency, he may be ready to exit reading intervention.	Speak with school administration to discuss exit criteria for students who have reached grade-level proficiency.

Student Progress Report
STUDENT: CHU, AMY

PROGRESS MONITORING

SCHOLASTIC SRI

Teacher: Margaret Schirmer
Grade: 7
Class: Schirmer 3

Time Period: 08/06/10 – 02/02/12

LEXILE®: 1700, 1600, 1500, 1400, 1300, 1200, 1100, 1000, 900, 800, 700, 600, 500, 400, 300, 200, 100, BR

539 Grade Mean* (06/02/10)

Test Date	Score
09/04/10:	257
10/30/10:	BR (0)
01/28/11:	746
05/11/11:	698
09/01/11:	443
11/03/11:	837
01/26/12:	834

TEST DATE AND SCORE

Grade 7 Year-End Proficiency Range — **BR** = Beginning Reader

* Grade Mean is the average score of all students in the same grade based on their last test.

Enlargement: Student Progress Report

DATA STORY

Student: Amy Chu
Current Lexile: 834
Current Grade: 7

Identify students like Amy whose results show decline and offer appropriate support.

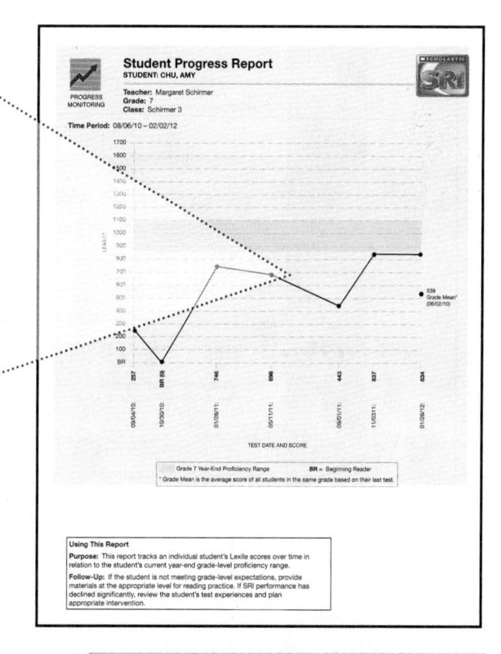

Student Progress Report
STUDENT: CHU, AMY

PROGRESS MONITORING

Teacher: Margaret Schirmer
Grade: 7
Class: Schirmer 3

Time Period: 08/06/10 – 02/02/12

TEST DATE AND SCORE

Grade 7 Year-End Proficiency Range — BR = Beginning Reader

* Grade Mean is the average score of all students in the same grade based on their last test.

Using This Report

Purpose: This report tracks an individual student's Lexile scores over time in relation to the student's current year-end grade-level proficiency range.

Follow-Up: If the student is not meeting grade-level expectations, provide materials at the appropriate level for reading practice. If SRI performance has declined significantly, review the student's test experiences and plan appropriate intervention.

Data Point	Data Analysis	NEXT STEPS
1 Amy had a large drop in score on her second SRI test.	Amy's Estimated Reading Level was not set for her first test, causing a problem with her first SRI test results.	Target *System 44* students for the first SRI test, setting their Estimated Reading Level to Below Grade Level or Far Below Grade Level.
2 Amy had another large drop in score in August of her second year.	Amy did not do much reading over the summer and also may be nervous about the new school year.	Tell students that they can wait a day or two to take the SRI test if they are feeling nervous or having a bad day.
3 Amy's results flatline in January.	Amy has reached grade-level proficiency. Once students have reached proficiency, overall gains may not be as large.	Discuss exit criteria and determine how best to support students once they have exited *System 44*.

College and Career Readiness Report

Purpose

This report tracks student SRI results in relation to narrative, functional, and informational texts.

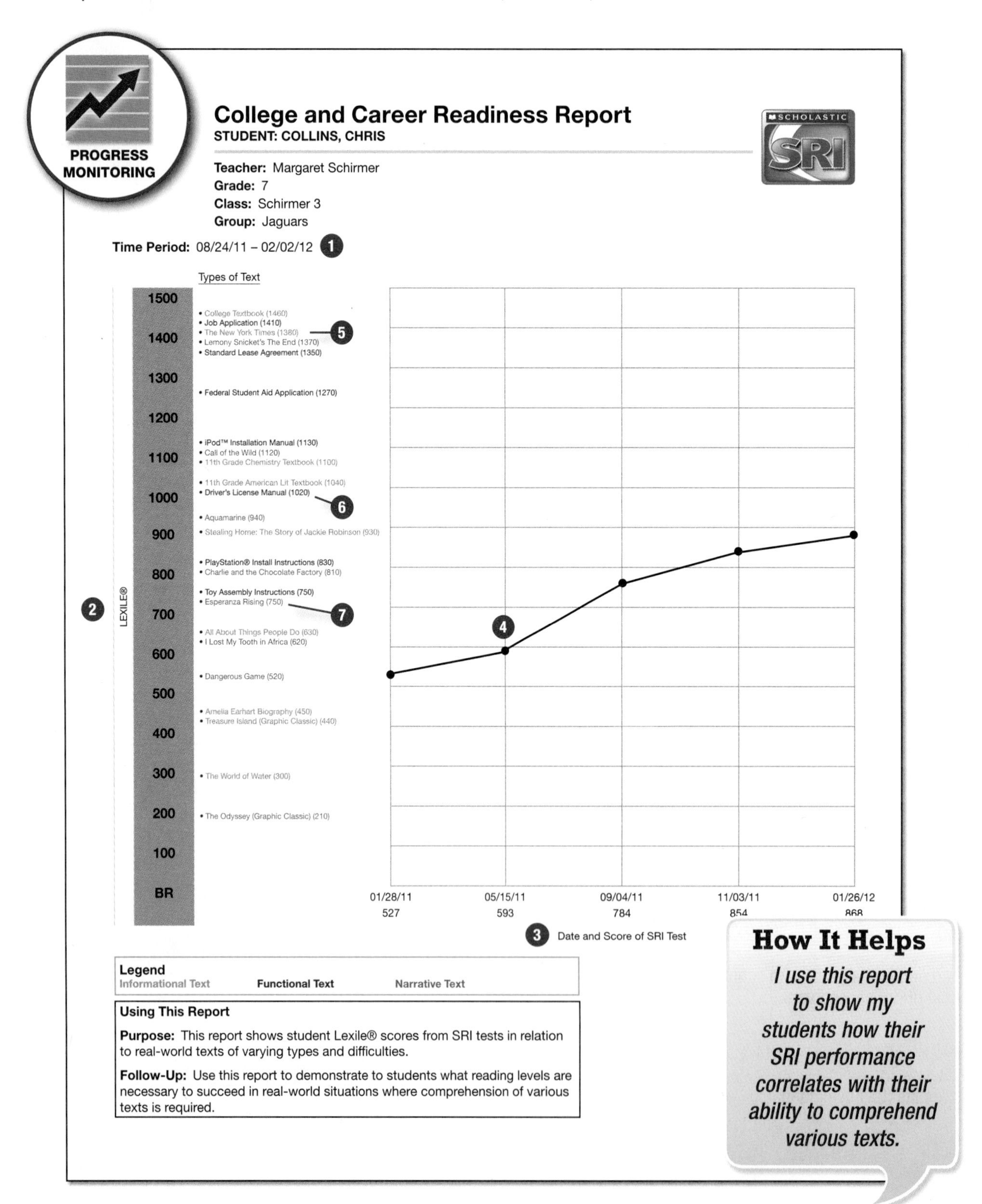

How It Helps

I use this report to show my students how their SRI performance correlates with their ability to comprehend various texts.

Understand the Data

1 Time Period
Default time period setting is This School Year. Customize date ranges to track progress on selected tests within a school year or to review progress over multiple years.

2 Lexile
Vertical axis shows Lexile in increments of 100.

3 Date and Score of SRI Test
Horizontal axis shows dates and scores for all SRI tests within selected time periods.

4 Graph Entries
Data points represent a student's SRI Lexile score on a particular date. Print tests with scores entered in SAM Roster also appear on this report.

5 Informational Text
Green indicates a text that conveys or explains different types of information, such as reference materials and personal narratives.

6 Functional Text
Blue indicates a text that has practical application in everyday life, such as signs, directions, letters, and manuals.

7 Narrative Text
Red indicates a text that aims to entertain, to tell a story, or to provide a literary experience.

Use the Data

Who: Teachers, Students (Student report)

When: After each SRI administration

How: You can apply the information in this report in the following ways:

Prepare for Upcoming Test

- Discuss previous SRI test results with students during one-on-one conferences.
- Help students establish and track SRI growth goals. On average, one year's SRI growth is between 50 and 100 Lexile points, depending on a student's grade level and initial Lexile level.

Review Test Results

- Suggest texts that students can access to challenge comprehension and build fluency.
- Recognize achievement of students who made SRI gains.
- Use the SRI Student Test Printout to examine specific test results with students.
- Conference with families to help them understand the types of materials their children can read at home.

Review Related Reports

- SRI Recommended Reading Report (p. 124)
- SRI Student Test Printout (p. 134)
- SRI Parent Report (p. 135)

Data in Action

Appropriate Growth Expectations Total SRI growth for the year depends on the student's grade level and initial Lexile. Review the SRI Growth Goals Report to help students set individual growth goals.

Student Test Printout

Purpose

This report displays results of the student's SRI test, including passages, answers, and student responses.

Student Test Printout

STUDENT: CHU, AMY

Teacher: Margaret Schirmer
Grade: 7
Class: Schirmer 3

Time Period: 08/24/11 – 02/02/12

Test Date: 01/26/2012
Test Time: 20 Minutes
Student Lexile®: 834

Q: We ran, and rested, and ran again. Rather than endure the extra effort of scaling the far side, we followed the valley to the west. In the darkness we stumbled and fell over the uneven ground, bruising ourselves. Behind us the light followed, relentlessly weaving to and fro. During one pause we saw that the Tripods had split up, one going up the other side of the valley and another marching to the east. But the third was coming our way and gaining on us.

The Tripods were ______ us.

- ✓chasing
- carrying
- calling
- cheating

Christopher, John. THE WHITE MOUNTAINS. 1967. Reprint, New York: Simon & Schuster Children's Publishing Division, 1988.

Q: Chavez kept trying to persuade the other workers to join together and demand a pay raise. But people were still too afraid of losing their jobs. Then he began teaching Mexican migrant workers how to speak English. If they knew English, they could take the steps to become American citizens.

Chavez wanted to ______ them.

- please
- ✓help
- tease
- remove

Cedeno, Maria E. CESAR CHAVEZ: LABOR LEADER. Brookfield, CT: The Millbrook Press, 1993.

Using This Report

Purpose: This report provides a printout of the last SRI test the student has completed. It includes each passage and all four answer choices, with the student's answer choice and the correct answer choice both indicated. Each passage source is also listed.

Follow-Up: Review the printout of the test with the student, pointing out items the student answered incorrectly. Work through those items with students to help them understand why they came up with incorrect answers.

How It Helps

I use this report to review the test with students, discussing items answered incorrectly. We work together to understand why particular questions were missed.

Parent Report

Purpose

This report introduces SRI to parents or caregivers, provides their child's SRI test results, and offers suggestions for how parents can help their child build fundamental reading skills at home.

STUDENT: BRACCO, CHRISTINE

Teacher: Margaret Schirmer
Grade: 7
Class: Schirmer 3
Group: Group A

January 17, 2013

Dear Parent or Caregiver,

This year, I will use the *Scholastic Reading Inventory* (SRI), a classroom-based test that will help us keep track of Christine's reading progress.

Your student completes a short, computerized test in about 20 minutes and receives results in a reading measurement called a Lexile measure (L).

Here is Christine's result:

Test Date	*SRI Test Results*
January 16, 2013	650L

Grade 7 End-of-Year Proficiency Target Range: 850L–1100L

Here are some things that you can do at home to support Christine's reading progress:

- Set a goal for Christine to read at least 20 minutes a day.
- Look for fiction and nonfiction books that are near your student's Lexile level. You can access a free book matching site at Book Expert Online (www.scholastic.com/bookexpert) or access the free resources at Find-A-Book (www.lexile.com/fab). This website lets you know if your book selection is available at your local public library.
- Encourage Christine's interests! If your student has deep knowledge on a certain topic, then he/she should be able to read books and articles on this topic at a higher reading level actively and with greater confidence. Your student's reading ability can be "stretched" with more complex texts on familiar topics.
- Familiarize Christine with informational texts. With your supervision, your student should look at the newspaper, informational websites, product manuals, assembly directions, how-to guides, and other materials that may contain technical words and formats.

Thank you for taking the time to help build Christine's reading skills. Please feel free to contact me if you have any questions, comments, or concerns.

Sincerely,

____

How It Helps

I send the Parent Report home after the first test to introduce families to SRI. I send it home after each subsequent test to update families on their child's reading progress.

Award Report

Purpose

This report lists students who have passed the number of quizzes required to earn an award.

Award Report
CLASS: SCHIRMER 3

SCHOLASTIC READING COUNTS!

School: Lincoln Middle School
Teacher: Margaret Schirmer
Grade: 7

Time Period: 08/24/11 – 02/02/12 

Gold Award (25 Books)

STUDENT	BOOKS READ
NO DATA TO REPORT	

Silver Award (15 Books) 

STUDENT	BOOKS READ
Evans, Jamal	15

Bronze Award (10 Books)

STUDENT	BOOKS READ
Cooper, Tiffany	10

Red Award (5 Books)

STUDENT	BOOKS READ
Bracco, Christine	7
Chu, Amy	6
Felix, Tonya	6
Imran, Khaleel	9
Palermo, Justin	7
Sanchez, Rachel	9

USING THIS REPORT

PURPOSE: This report shows students who have earned the points required to qualify for an award. Use the report to monitor students' progress toward meeting their independent reading goals.

FOLLOW-UP: Plan incentives and provide additional student motivation by displaying the report in the classroom.

How It Helps

I set up my award values at the beginning of the year and use this report to acknowledge students who have achieved awards at monthly reading celebrations.

Understand the Data

1 Time Period
Default time period of This School Year displays results for all quizzes passed during the school year. Customize time period settings to review results for specific periods of time.

2 Award Status
Lists students who have passed enough quizzes to earn Gold, Silver, Bronze, Red, and Blue awards. Award values can be managed in the SAM Roster.

3 Books or Points
Lists awards based on whether student goal is set as books read or points earned. Only *Scholastic Reading Counts!* quizzes with passing scores count toward award status.

Use the Data

Who: Teachers (Teacher, Class, or Group report)

When: Once or twice a month

How: Apply the information in the following ways:

Celebrate Reading Achievement

- Monitor student progress toward goals by printing this report and sharing results with the class once or twice a month. Create a chart or bulletin board to post award status and updates.
- Recognize reading achievement by customizing and printing S*cholastic Reading Counts!* certificates in the SAM Roster.

Share Results

- Print this report to update your school administration on your students' reading progress. Invite administrators to your classroom to congratulate students who have met or exceeded their goals.
- Encourage students to use the My Reads section of the Student Dashboard to track their own status. Celebrate students who are on track to meet or exceed their goals. Offer support to students who are struggling to meet their goals.

Review Related Reports

- *SRC!* Books Read Report (p. 138)
- *SRC!* Points Report (p. 144)
- *SRC!* Student Reading Report (p. 156)

Data in Action

Quiz Award Values The Awards Settings in the *Scholastic Reading Counts!* Settings section of the SAM Roster tab allows you to establish values for each award.

Books Read Report | Best Practice Report

Purpose

This report includes a table and bar graph to track total *Scholastic Reading Counts!* quizzes passed.

Books Read Report

CLASS: Schirmer 3

School: Lincoln Middle School
Teacher: Margaret Schirmer
Grade: 7

Time Period: 08/24/11 – 02/02/12 ❶

STUDENT	❷ LEXILE®	❸ AVG. BOOK LEXILE®	❹ NUMBER OF QUIZZES PASSED	❺ GOAL	❻ TOTAL WORDS READ
Bracco, Christine	709	753	7	20	135,889
Chu, Amy	834	678	6	15	65,964
Collins, Chris	868	820	6	15	10,276
Cooper, Tiffany	781	735	10	17	83,026
Evans, Jamal	719	755	15	18	66,750
Felix, Tonya	BR (10)	375	6	30	17,093
Fernandez, Luis	242	690	2	30	9,664
Garcia, Matt	550	485	2	22	5,078
Imran, Khaleel	719	626	9	20	276,999
Kramer, Liz	809	750	2	18	10,888
Krynski, Theo	1120	730	4	13	8,550
Palermo, Justin	438	381	7	23	16,833
Ramirez, Gabriella	743	720	1	18	5,360
Rupp, Jeremy	727	N/A	0	18	0
Sanchez, Rachel	792	773	9	17	156,931
❼ **TOTALS**	**700 (AVG)**	**638 (AVG)**	**86**	**294**	**869,301**

Using This Report

Purpose: This report consists of a table and bar graph that show the number of books read and related book information by teacher, grade, class, or group.

Follow-Up: Use the table and bar graph to share information with parents and to supplement student portfolios.

How It Helps

I use this report to track how many quizzes my students have passed and recognize their reading achievements.

Understand the Data

1 Time Period
Run for This School Year to review *Scholastic Reading Counts!* participation for the full year. Customize time period settings to analyze quarterly or monthly results.

2 Lexile
Student's SRI score from most recent test, regardless of time period settings.

3 Average Book Lexile
Average Lexile measure for all books with quizzes taken, including multiple quiz attempts and quizzes not passed.

4 Number of Quizzes Passed
Total *Scholastic Reading Counts!* quizzes passed within selected time period.

5 Goal
Goal for total book quizzes passed for the year, if books are established as the goal in SAM Roster.

6 Total Words Read
Total words read for each *Scholastic Reading Counts!* quiz passed.

7 Totals
Totals for the group or class, including quizzes passed, total books set as goal if established in SAM, total words read, as well as average book Lexile and average student Lexile.

Use the Data

Who: Teachers (Teacher, Class, or Group report)

When: Monthly or quarterly

How: Apply the information from this report in the following ways:

Establish and Track Goals

- Set class goals for books read and/or words read for each grading period. Post class goals and progress toward goal. Consider having groups or classes compete for the most words or books read.
- Set individual student goals for books read or quizzes passed each grading period. Help students track individual progress in their *44Book* My Achievements section or on a conferencing log.

Share Results

- Run this report once a month and update students and classes on overall performance.
- Share this report with school administration to demonstrate progress and participation in the independent reading rotation.

Review Related Reports

- *SRC!* Reading Progress Report (p. 148)
- *SRC!* Student Quiz Success Report (p. 154)
- *SRC!* Student Reading Report (p. 156)

Data in Action

Independent Reading Assessment Regular assessment of independent reading fosters on-task behavior. In addition to using *SRC!* quizzes, incorporate daily reading logs and other measures of written accountability, such as QuickWrites and Graphic Organizers.

Analyze Results | Books Read Report

Students who select books at appropriate interest and level should experience quiz success.

Student: Matt Garcia
Quizzes Passed: 2
Quizzes Taken: 13

Matt has not passed many quizzes. Identify the areas of challenge and offer support.

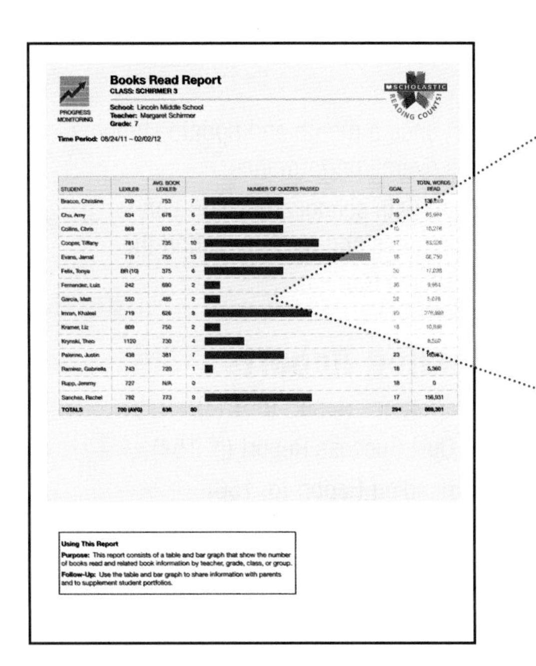

Books Read Report
CLASS: SCHIRMER 3
PROGRESS MONITORING
School: Lincoln Middle School
Teacher: Margaret Schirmer
Grade: 7
Time Period: 08/24/11 – 02/02/12

Using This Report
Purpose: This report consists of a table and bar graph that show the number of books read and related book information by teacher, grade, class, or group.
Follow-Up: Use the table and bar graph to share information with parents and to supplement student portfolios.

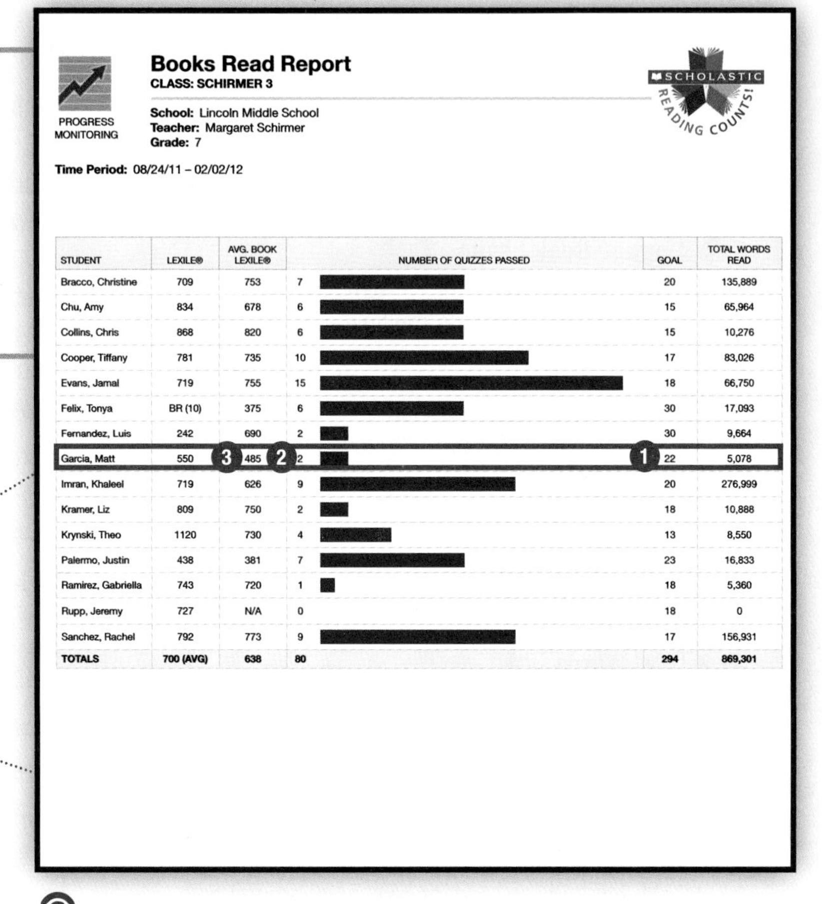

Books Read Report
CLASS: SCHIRMER 3

PROGRESS MONITORING

School: Lincoln Middle School
Teacher: Margaret Schirmer
Grade: 7

SCHOLASTIC READING COUNTS!

Time Period: 08/24/11 – 02/02/12

STUDENT	LEXILE®	AVG. BOOK LEXILE®	NUMBER OF QUIZZES PASSED	GOAL	TOTAL WORDS READ
Bracco, Christine	709	753	7	20	135,889
Chu, Amy	834	678	6	15	65,964
Collins, Chris	868	820	6	15	10,276
Cooper, Tiffany	781	735	10	17	83,026
Evans, Jamal	719	755	15	18	66,750
Felix, Tonya	BR (10)	375	6	30	17,093
Fernandez, Luis	242	690	2	30	9,664
Garcia, Matt	550	485	2	22	5,078
Imran, Khaleel	719	626	9	20	276,999
Kramer, Liz	809	750	2	18	10,888
Krynski, Theo	1120	730	4	13	8,550
Palermo, Justin	438	381	7	23	16,833
Ramirez, Gabriella	743	720	1	18	5,360
Rupp, Jeremy	727	N/A	0	18	0
Sanchez, Rachel	792	773	9	17	156,931
TOTALS	**700 (AVG)**	**638**	**80**	**294**	**869,301**

Enlargement: Books Read Report

Data Point	Data Analysis	NEXT STEPS
1 Matt's goal for the year is 22 books.	Since it is nearly halfway through the year, Matt should be nearly halfway to his goal.	Set individual student quiz goals based on ability and reading level. Help students regularly monitor their quiz progress.
2 Matt has passed two quizzes so far.	Matt is struggling with *Scholastic Reading Counts!* quizzes. He is not passing quizzes.	Review the *SRC!* Student Reading Report to investigate specific quiz results.
3 The average Lexile for Matt's books is within 100 Lexile points of his current Lexile.	The quizzes Matt has passed are in his independent reading range. When reading books at appropriate levels, Matt can pass the accompanying quiz.	Ensure that students are reading books within their independent reading range. Review the SRI Targeted Reading Report for ranges.

Review Additional Data

Use the *SRC!* Student Reading Report to review specific quiz results for students who struggle.

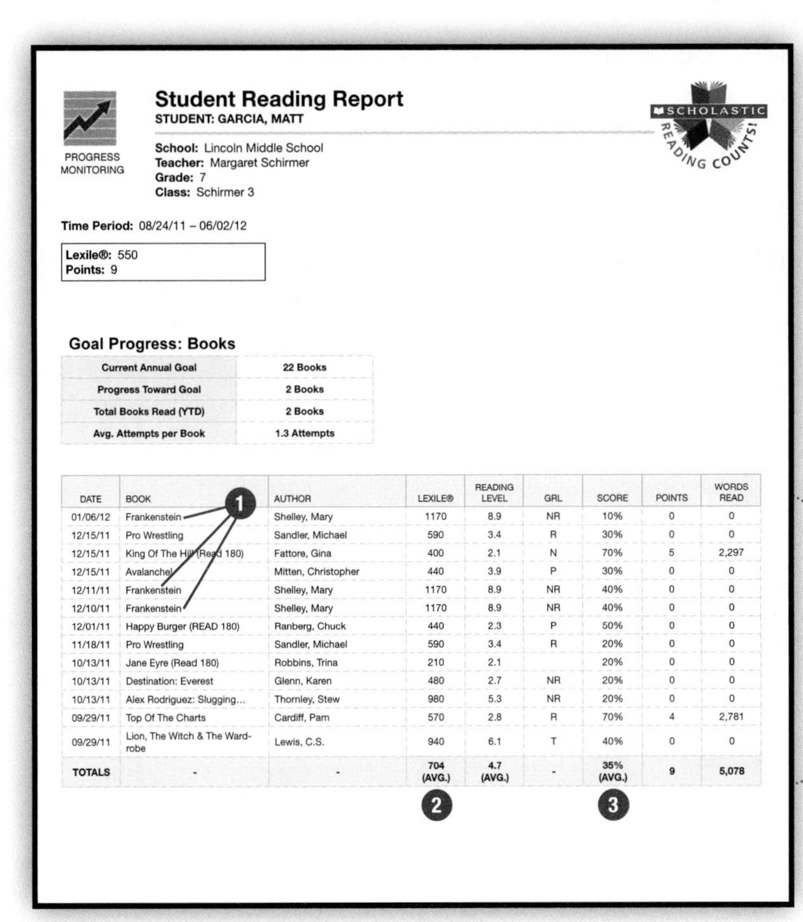

Student Reading Report
STUDENT: GARCIA, MATT

PROGRESS MONITORING

School: Lincoln Middle School
Teacher: Margaret Schirmer
Grade: 7
Class: Schirmer 3

Time Period: 08/24/11 – 06/02/12

Lexile®: 550
Points: 9

Goal Progress: Books

Current Annual Goal	22 Books
Progress Toward Goal	2 Books
Total Books Read (YTD)	2 Books
Avg. Attempts per Book	1.3 Attempts

DATE	BOOK	AUTHOR	LEXILE®	READING LEVEL	GRL	SCORE	POINTS	WORDS READ
01/06/12	Frankenstein	Shelley, Mary	1170	8.9	NR	10%	0	0
12/15/11	Pro Wrestling	Sandler, Michael	590	3.4	R	30%	0	0
12/15/11	King Of The Hill (Read 180)	Fattore, Gina	400	2.1	N	70%	5	2,297
12/15/11	Avalanche!	Mitten, Christopher	440	3.9	P	30%	0	0
12/11/11	Frankenstein	Shelley, Mary	1170	8.9	NR	40%	0	0
12/10/11	Frankenstein	Shelley, Mary	1170	8.9	NR	40%	0	0
12/01/11	Happy Burger (READ 180)	Ranberg, Chuck	440	2.3	P	50%	0	0
11/18/11	Pro Wrestling	Sandler, Michael	590	3.4	R	20%	0	0
10/13/11	Jane Eyre (Read 180)	Robbins, Trina	210	2.1		20%	0	0
10/13/11	Destination: Everest	Glenn, Karen	480	2.7	NR	20%	0	0
10/13/11	Alex Rodriguez: Slugging...	Thornley, Stew	980	5.3	NR	20%	0	0
09/29/11	Top Of The Charts	Cardiff, Pam	570	2.8	R	70%	4	2,781
09/29/11	Lion, The Witch & The Ward-robe	Lewis, C.S.	940	6.1	T	40%	0	0
TOTALS	-	-	704 (AVG.)	4.7 (AVG.)	-	35% (AVG.)	9	5,078

Enlargement: Student Reading Report

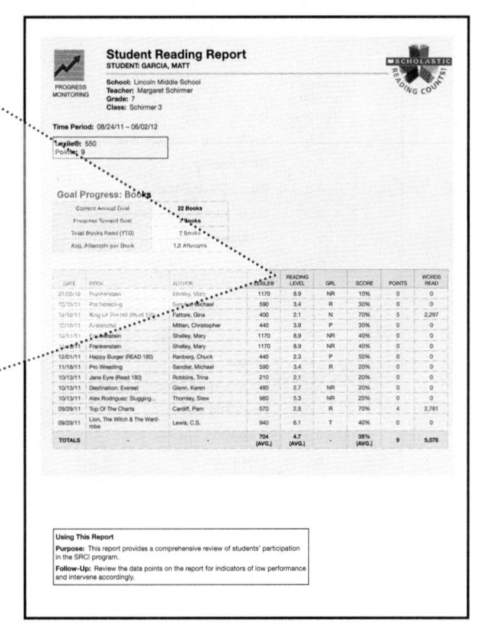

Using This Report

Purpose: This report provides a comprehensive review of students' participation in the SRC! program.

Follow-Up: Review the data points on the report for indicators of low performance and intervene accordingly.

Data Point	Data Analysis	NEXT STEPS
❶ Matt has attempted a quiz on the same book three times.	His second attempt at a quiz was only one day after his first attempt.	If a student has an unsuccessful quiz attempt, provide additional support prior to allowing the student to take a quiz again.
❷ Matt's average book Lexile is 704 and his current Lexile is 550.	Matt has been attempting to read books far above his current independent reading level.	Review student reading logs to ensure appropriate book selection. Use the *SRC!* Recommended Reading Report to help students select books.
❸ Matt's average quiz score is 35%.	Matt has attempted 13 quizzes but has only passed two.	Use *Teaching Resources for Modeled and Independent Reading* to hold book conferences before the student attempts the quiz.

Book Frequency and Rating Report

Purpose

This report ranks books according to how students rated them during a selected time period. It includes the book Lexile, the point value for each book, and a summary of how many *Scholastic Reading Counts!* quizzes have been taken and passed.

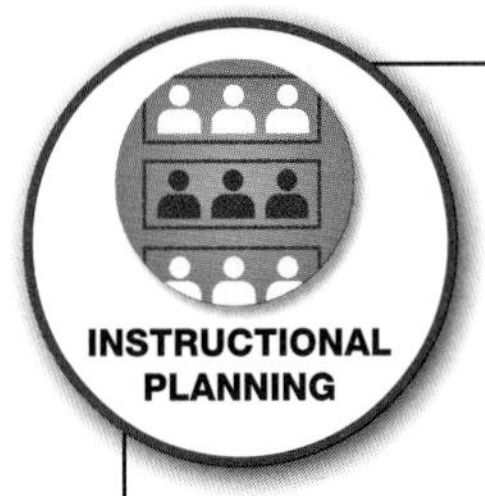

Book Frequency and Rating Report
SCHOOL: LINCOLN MIDDLE SCHOOL

Time Period: 08/24/11 – 02/02/12

AVG. STUDENT RATING	BOOK	AUTHOR	LEXILE®	POINTS	QUIZZES PASSED/ TAKEN
5.0	Behind The Bedroom Wall	Williams, Laura E.	660	6	1/3
5.0	BMX Racing	Gutman, Bill	770	3	1/1
5.0	Bone: Ghost Circles	Smith, Jeff	N/A	6	1/1
5.0	Bone: Out From Boneville	Smith, Jeff	360	4	1/1
5.0	Breaking Dawn	Meyer, Stephanie	690	40	2/2
5.0	Captain Underpants/Invasion Of	Pilkey, Dav	730	3	2/2
5.0	Captain Underpants/Perilous	Pilkey, Dav	640	3	1/1
5.0	Cat In the Hat, The	Seuss, Dr.	260	2	1/1
5.0	Charlie & The Chocolate ...	Dahl, Roald	810	8	1/1
5.0	Eclipse	Meyer, Stephanie	670	33	2/2
5.0	Finding The Titanic (Read 180)	Ballard, Robert D.	540	3	1/3
5.0	Freak The Mighty	Philbrick, Rodman	1000	10	1/1
5.0	Friendship, The	Talyor, Mildred D.	750	3	1/1
5.0	New Moon	Meyer, Stephanie	690	29	4/4
5.0	Old Yeller	Gipson, Fred	910	8	1/2
5.0	Old Yeller (Anthology)	Gipson, Fred	880	2	1/1
5.0	Runaway Train	Campbell, Julia	420	3	1/1
5.0	Stealing Home: The Story Of...	Denenberg, Barry	930	6	3/3
5.0	Summer On Wheels	Soto, Gary	750	9	1/1
5.0	There's A Girl In-Hammerlock	Spinelli, Jerry	520	10	1/3
5.0	Twilight	Meyer, Stephanie	720	25	4/6
5.0	Watsons Go To Birmingham-1963	Curtis, Christopher Paul	1000	12	1/1
5.0	Winning Season: Emergency Quar	Wallace, Rich	720	6	1/1
5.0	Winning Season: The Roar Of...	Wallace, Rich	680	6	1/1
4.8	Money Hungry	Flake, Sharon G.	650	9	4/5
4.8	Quinceanera Means Sweet 15	Chambers, Veronica	630	12	4/4
4.7	Donner Party (Read 180)	Olson, Todd	330	5	2/3
4.5	Bone: Rock Jaw	Smith, Jeff	N/A		

Using This Report

Purpose: This report ranks books according to how students rated them during a selected time period. It includes the Lexile level and point value for each book.

Follow-Up: Use the report to guide students' independent reading selections. Encourage students to choose other books on related themes or by the same authors as the most popular books.

How It Helps

I use this report to spark conversations between students about the books they have enjoyed. I also share this report with my media specialist so that these books are available in the library.

Most Frequent Quizzes Report

Purpose

This report provides information on how frequently specific *Scholastic Reading Counts!* quizzes have been taken. It includes the book or article title, Lexile, quiz success rate, and quiz results for individual students.

Most Frequent Quizzes Report

CLASS: Schirmer 3

School: Lincoln Middle School
Teacher: Margaret Schirmer
Grade: 7

Time Period: 08/24/11 – 02/02/12

Adventures of Capt. Underpants

Lexile®	720
Points	3
Times Taken	6
Times Passed	6

STUDENT NAME	STUDENT LEXILE	DATE TAKEN	SCORE (%)
Cooper, Tiffany	781	10/08/11	90
Evans, Jamal	719	01/08/12	90
Imran, Khaleel	719	12/15/11	100
Kramer, Liz	809	12/01/12	100
Palermo, Justin	438	11/12/11	90
Ramirez, Gabriella	743	10/23/11	90
TOTALS	**754 (AVG.)**		**93% (AVG.)**

Oh Yuck! (READ 180)

Lexile®	990
Points	3
Times Taken	5
Times Passed	4

STUDENT NAME	STUDENT LEXILE	DATE TAKEN	SCORE (%)
Collins, Chris	868	10/29/11	50
Collins, Chris	868	11/02/11	90
Garcia, Matt	485	01/21/12	70
Imran, Khaleel	719	10/23/11	80
Krynski, Theo	1120	12/03/11	80
TOTALS	**894 (AVG.)**		**74% (AVG.)**

Using This Report

Purpose: This report provides information on quizzes student have taken most often. It includes the Lexile measure and point value for each book, overall quiz success rate, and quiz scores for individual students.

Follow-Up: Suggest related titles to students. Monitor student quiz scores and offer additional support to students who are having difficulty with the quizzes.

How It Helps

I use this report to track book popularity and suggest related book titles. I can also monitor student quiz results so that I can offer additional support as needed.

Points Report

Purpose

This report tracks points students have earned for passing *Scholastic Reading Counts!* quizzes.

Points Report

CLASS: SCHIRMER 3

School: Lincoln Middle School
Teacher: Margaret Schirmer
Grade: 7

Time Period: 08/24/11 – 02/02/12 ❶

STUDENT	❷ LEXILE®	❸ AVG. BOOK LEXILE®	❹ POINTS EARNED	❺ POINTS AVAILABLE	❻ GOAL	❼ TOTAL WORDS READ
Bracco, Christine	709	753	41	41	N/A	135,889
Chu, Amy	834	678	32	32	N/A	65,964
Collins, Chris	868	820	32	9	N/A	10,276
Cooper, Tiffany	781	735	26	26	N/A	83,026
Evans, Jamal	719	755	23	23	N/A	66,750
Felix, Tonya	BR (10)	375	24	24	N/A	17,093
Fernandez, Luis	242	690	7	7	N/A	9,664
Garcia, Matt	550	485	9	9	N/A	5,078
Imran, Khaleel	719	626	85	85	N/A	276,999
Kramer, Liz	809	750	6	6	N/A	10,888
Krynski, Theo	1120	730	15	15	N/A	8,550
Palermo, Justin	438	381	32	32	N/A	16,833
Ramirez, Gabriella	743	720	3	3	N/A	5,360
Rupp, Jeremy	727	N/A	0	0	N/A	0
Sanchez, Rachel	792	773	55	55	N/A	156,931
❽ **TOTALS**	**700 (AVG)**	**638 (AVG)**	**352**	**329**	**0**	**869,301**

Using This Report

Purpose: This report tracks the number of points students have earned during a selected time period. It includes student Lexile scores, point goals, total number of words read, and average Lexile measure of books read.

Follow-Up: Congratulate students who have met or are nearing their goals. Provide support to students who are experiencing difficulty meeting their goals.

How It Helps

I use this report to motivate my students. By establishing annual point goals and tracking their progress, I can celebrate reading success with students.

Understand the Data

❶ **Time Period**
Default time period of This School Year displays results for all quizzes passed during the school year. Customize time period settings to review results within shorter time frames.

❷ **Lexile**
Student's most recent SRI score within the selected time period.

❸ **Average Book Lexile**
Average Lexile for all books with quizzes passed.

❹ **Points Earned**
Total number of points earned for *Scholastic Reading Counts!* quizzes passed.

❺ **Points Available**
Total number of points that have not been redeemed, if tracked in SAM Roster.

❻ **Goal**
Reading goal for the year for each student, if points is selected as goal in SAM Roster.

❼ **Total Words Read**
Words read for books when each *Scholastic Reading Counts!* quiz is passed.

❽ **Totals**
Class or group totals for points established for points earned, points available, goal, and words read. Also includes class or group average student Lexile and average book Lexile for quizzes passed.

Use the Data

Who: Teachers (Teacher, Class, or Group report)

When: Once or twice a month

How: Apply the information in the following ways:

Monitor Quiz Progress

- Establish annual points goals for students in the *Scholastic Reading Counts!* Settings in the SAM Roster.
- Determine whether to establish the same goal for the entire class or assign individual goals based on student reading levels.
- Encourage students to track their own points status. Celebrate students who are on track to meet or exceed their goals. Offer support to students who are having trouble meeting their goals.

Share Results

- Print this report to update your school administration on your students' reading progress. Invite administrators to your classroom to congratulate students who have met their goals.
- Institute reading contests between groups, classes, or even with another *System 44* classroom. Track total points read by the group or class throughout the year.

Review Related Reports

- *SRC!* Books Read Report (p. 138)
- *SRC!* Quiz Alert (p. 146)
- *SRC!* Student Reading Report (p. 156)

Data in Action

Redeeming Quiz Points The Points Recording Tool in the *Scholastic Reading Counts!* Grading section of the SAM Roster allows you to track when students have redeemed their points for class incentives.

Quiz Alert

Purpose

This report highlights a variety of challenges individual students may be experiencing with *Scholastic Reading Counts!* quizzes. A summary is provided in the top chart with details about each student's specific quiz challenge included in the charts below.

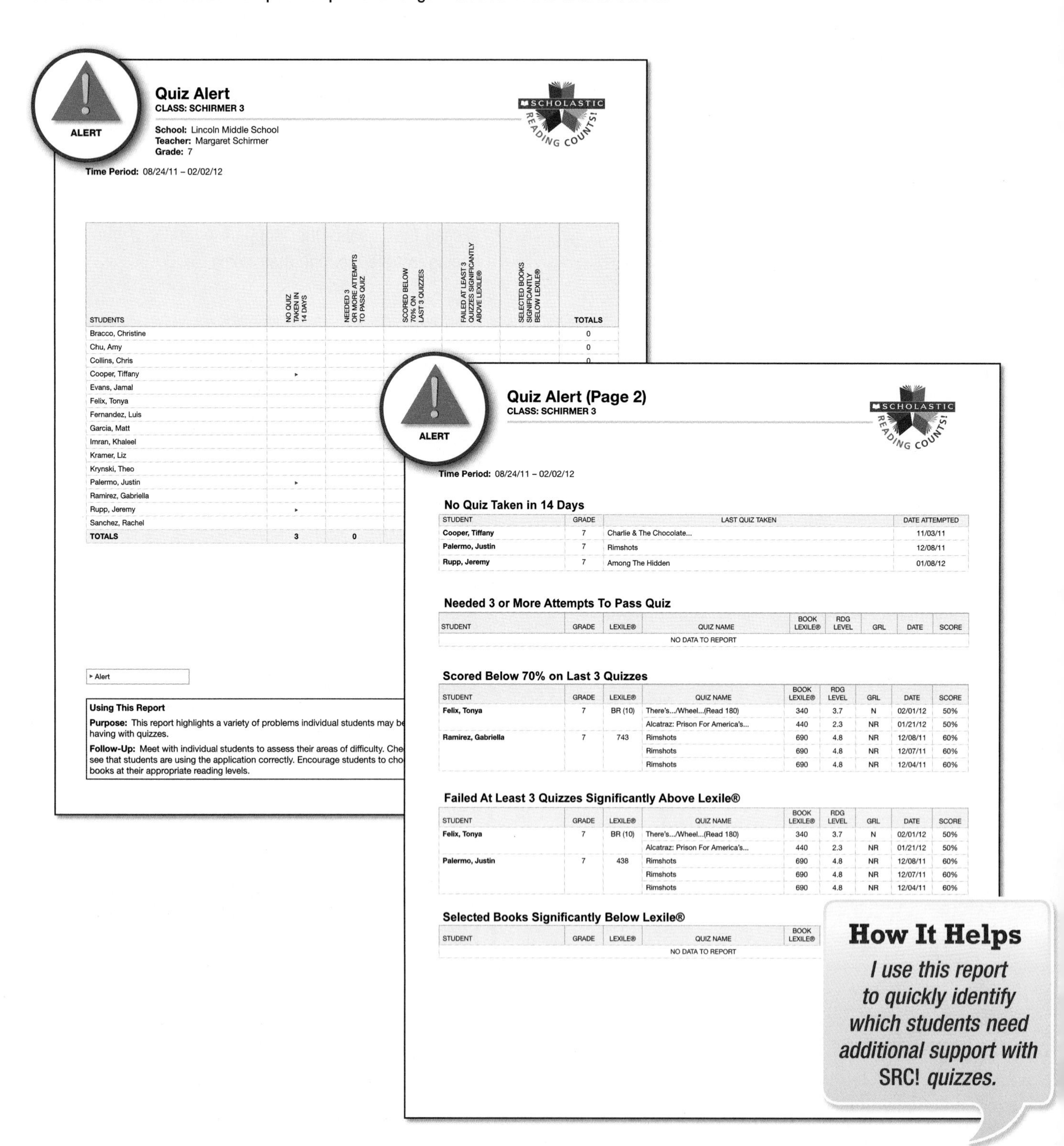

ALERT

Quiz Alert
CLASS: SCHIRMER 3

School: Lincoln Middle School
Teacher: Margaret Schirmer
Grade: 7

Time Period: 08/24/11 – 02/02/12

STUDENTS	NO QUIZ TAKEN IN 14 DAYS	NEEDED 3 OR MORE ATTEMPTS TO PASS QUIZ	SCORED BELOW 70% ON LAST 3 QUIZZES	FAILED AT LEAST 3 QUIZZES SIGNIFICANTLY ABOVE LEXILE®	SELECTED BOOKS SIGNIFICANTLY BELOW LEXILE®	TOTALS
Bracco, Christine						0
Chu, Amy						0
Collins, Chris						0
Cooper, Tiffany	▸					
Evans, Jamal						
Felix, Tonya						
Fernandez, Luis						
Garcia, Matt						
Imran, Khaleel						
Kramer, Liz						
Krynski, Theo						
Palermo, Justin	▸					
Ramirez, Gabriella						
Rupp, Jeremy	▸					
Sanchez, Rachel						
TOTALS	3	0				

▸ Alert

Using This Report
Purpose: This report highlights a variety of problems individual students may b[e] having with quizzes.
Follow-Up: Meet with individual students to assess their areas of difficulty. Che[ck to] see that students are using the application correctly. Encourage students to cho[ose] books at their appropriate reading levels.

ALERT

Quiz Alert (Page 2)
CLASS: SCHIRMER 3

Time Period: 08/24/11 – 02/02/12

No Quiz Taken in 14 Days

STUDENT	GRADE	LAST QUIZ TAKEN	DATE ATTEMPTED
Cooper, Tiffany	7	Charlie & The Chocolate...	11/03/11
Palermo, Justin	7	Rimshots	12/08/11
Rupp, Jeremy	7	Among The Hidden	01/08/12

Needed 3 or More Attempts To Pass Quiz

STUDENT	GRADE	LEXILE®	QUIZ NAME	BOOK LEXILE®	RDG LEVEL	GRL	DATE	SCORE
			NO DATA TO REPORT					

Scored Below 70% on Last 3 Quizzes

STUDENT	GRADE	LEXILE®	QUIZ NAME	BOOK LEXILE®	RDG LEVEL	GRL	DATE	SCORE
Felix, Tonya	7	BR (10)	There's.../Wheel...(Read 180)	340	3.7	N	02/01/12	50%
			Alcatraz: Prison For America's...	440	2.3	NR	01/21/12	50%
Ramirez, Gabriella	7	743	Rimshots	690	4.8	NR	12/08/11	60%
			Rimshots	690	4.8	NR	12/07/11	60%
			Rimshots	690	4.8	NR	12/04/11	60%

Failed At Least 3 Quizzes Significantly Above Lexile®

STUDENT	GRADE	LEXILE®	QUIZ NAME	BOOK LEXILE®	RDG LEVEL	GRL	DATE	SCORE
Felix, Tonya	7	BR (10)	There's.../Wheel...(Read 180)	340	3.7	N	02/01/12	50%
			Alcatraz: Prison For America's...	440	2.3	NR	01/21/12	50%
Palermo, Justin	7	438	Rimshots	690	4.8	NR	12/08/11	60%
			Rimshots	690	4.8	NR	12/07/11	60%
			Rimshots	690	4.8	NR	12/04/11	60%

Selected Books Significantly Below Lexile®

STUDENT	GRADE	LEXILE®	QUIZ NAME	BOOK LEXILE®
			NO DATA TO REPORT	

Reading Growth Acknowledgment

Purpose

This report acknowledges students who have passed quizzes on books that have Lexile measures above the students' current Lexile scores. It lists the quiz passed, the score received, and the Lexile of the book.

Reading Growth Acknowledgment

CLASS: SCHIRMER 3

School: Lincoln Middle School
Teacher: Margaret Schirmer
Grade: 7

Time Period: 08/24/11 – 02/02/12

Reading Level Growth Acknowledgment

Student is able to pass quizzes at levels significantly above his or her Lexile® level.

STUDENT	GRADE	LEXILE®	QUIZ NAME	BOOK LEXILE®	RDG LEVEL	GRL	DATE	SCORE
Felix, Tonya	7	BR (10)	Alcatraz: Prison For America's	440	2.3	NR	02/05/12	90%
			UFOs: Fact Or Fiction?	440	2.8	O	12/03/11	80%
			King Of The Hill (Read 180)	400	2.1	N	11/17/11	90%
			Band, The	220	2.1	M	11/10/11	100%
			Frankenstein (Read 180)	300	2.1	NR	11/05/11	70%
			Still The Greatest/Rigoberta...	450	2.5	O	10/21/11	70%
Garcia, Matt	7	485	Captain Underpants/Attack Of	780	4.2	P	02/01/12	90%
			Hiroshima (Read 180)	660	4.3	S	01/21/12	80%
			Oh Yuck! (Read 180)	990	6.8	X	11/12/11	70%

Using This Report

Purpose: This report acknowledges students who have passed quizzes on books that have Lexile® measures above the student's current Lexile® score.

Follow-Up: Congratulate the student and offer encouragement for further success.

How It Helps

I use this report to acknowledge students who are challenging themselves and excelling in the SRC! *program.*

Reading Progress Report | Best Practice Report

Purpose

This report provides an overview of students' *Scholastic Reading Counts!* quiz participation and progress.

Reading Progress Report
CLASS: SCHIRMER 3

School: Lincoln Middle School
Teacher: Margaret Schirmer
Grade: 7

Time Period: 08/24/11 – 02/02/12 (1)

(2) Year to Date Totals

Quizzes Taken	128
Quizzes Passed	86
Quiz Success Rate	64.3%
Points Earned	655
Words Read	869,301

STUDENT	GRADE	(3) LEXILE®	(4) QUIZZES PASSED/ TAKEN	(5) QUIZ SUCCESS RATE	(6) AVG. QUIZ SCORE	(7) BOOKS READ	(8) POINTS EARNED	(9) ANNUAL GOAL	(10) % OF GOAL ACHIEVED
Bracco, Christine	7	709	7/8	88%	84%	7	41	20(B)	47%
Chu, Amy	7	834	6/7	86%	86%	6	32	15(B)	40%
Collins, Chris	7	868	6/8	75%	▸ 62%	6	32	15(B)	40%
Cooper, Tiffany	7	781	10/12	83%	▸ 65%	10	26	17(B)	58%
Evans, Jamal	7	719	15/17	88%	▸ 49%	15	23	18(B)	83%
Felix, Tonya	7	BR (10)	6/13	46%	83%	6	24	30(B)	20%
Fernandez, Luis	7	242	2/3	67%	▸ 67%	2	7	30(B)	7%
Garcia, Matt	7	550	2/13	15%	▸ 35%	2	9	22(B)	9%
Imran, Khaleel	7	719	9/10	90%	89%	9	85	20(B)	45%
Kramer, Liz	7	809	2/5	40%	▸ 54%	2	6	18(B)	11%
Krynski, Theo	7	1120	4/4	100%	83%	4	15	13(B)	31%
Palermo, Justin	7	438	7/8	88%	76%	7	32	23(B)	30%
Ramirez, Gabriella	7	743	1/5	20%	▸ 62%	1	3	18(B)	6%
Rupp, Jeremy	7	727	0/0	N/A	N/A	0	0	18(B)	0%
Sanchez, Rachel	7	792	9/15	60%	73%	9	55	17(B)	53%
(11) **TOTALS**	-	**700 (AVG.)**	**86/128**	**64% (AVG.)**	▸ **64% (AVG.)**	**86**	**352**	-	**31% (AVG.)**

(B)=Books ▸ Indicates Score Below 70%

Using This Report

Purpose: This report provides an overview of students' progress in the program. In addition to tracking group quiz success rates, the report shows individual quiz performance and achievement.

Follow-Up: Use the information in the report to plan incentives and to help students monitor their progress. You may also use the report to guide instruction and create reading groups.

How It Helps

I use this report to monitor my students' independent reading progress and plan any necessary interventions.

Understand the Data

1. **Time Period**
Run for This School Year to review annual progress. Customize time period settings to review quarterly or monthly results.

2. **Year to Date Totals**
Cumulative quiz results for selected time period.

3. **Lexile**
Student's SRI score from the most recent test, regardless of time period settings.

4. **Quizzes Passed/Taken**
Ratio of total quizzes passed and total quiz attempts for each student.

5. **Quiz Success Rate**
Percentage of quizzes passed of all quizzes attempted during selected time period.

6. **Average Quiz Score**
Average score on all quizzes taken. Red arrows indicate quiz averages below 70%.

7. **Books Read**
Total *SRC!* quizzes passed for each student within selected time period.

8. **Points Earned**
Total points earned for each student within selected time period. Student must pass a quiz to earn points.

9. **Annual Goal**
Reading goal for the year, measured in books (B) or points (P), if established in SAM Roster.

10. **Percent of Goal Achieved**
Percentage of goal student has achieved within selected time period.

11. **Totals**
Class or group total books read, quizzes taken, and points earned for passed quizzes within selected time period. Also includes class or group averages of student Lexile, quiz success rate, quiz score, and percent of goal achieved.

Use the Data

Who: Teachers (Teacher, Class, or Group report)

When: Once or twice a month

How: Apply the information from this report in the following ways:

Establish and Track Goals

- Use the SAM Roster to enter book goals or points earned for each student.
- Discuss individual student goals for books read or points earned each grading period during conferences. Help students track individual progress in their *44Book* My Achievements section or on a conferencing log.

Share Results

- Run this report once a month and update students on overall performance.
- Share this report with school administrators to demonstrate progress and participation in Modeled and Independent Reading.

Review Related Reports

- *SRC!* Books Read Report (p. 138)
- *SRC!* Points Report (p. 144)
- *SRC!* Student Reading Report (p. 156)

Data in Action

Scheduling *SRC!* Quizzes To ensure regular use of *Scholastic Reading Counts!* quizzes, establish expectations for total pages read per day or quizzes passed per quarter. Help students determine when a book should be complete and write projected completion dates on a calendar.

Analyze Results | Reading Progress Report

With appropriate preparation and support, students should maintain strong quiz success rates and scores.

DATA STORY

Student: Rachel Sanchez
Quizzes Passed: 9
Quizzes Taken: 15

Rachel struggles to pass quizzes. Identify causes and ways to provide additional support.

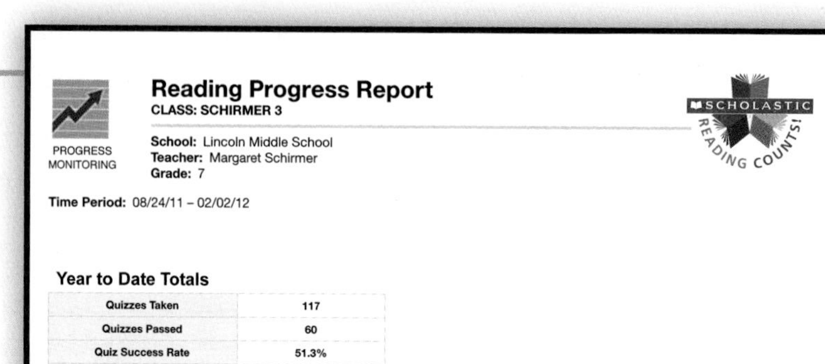

Reading Progress Report
CLASS: SCHIRMER 3

PROGRESS MONITORING

School: Lincoln Middle School
Teacher: Margaret Schirmer
Grade: 7

Time Period: 08/24/11 – 02/02/12

Year to Date Totals

Quizzes Taken	117
Quizzes Passed	60
Quiz Success Rate	51.3%
Points Earned	329
Words Read	743,252

STUDENT	GRADE	LEXILE®	QUIZZES PASSED/ TAKEN	QUIZ SUCCESS RATE	AVG. QUIZ SCORE	BOOKS READ	POINTS EARNED	ANNUAL GOAL	% OF GOAL ACHIEVED
Bracco, Christine	7	709	7/8	88%	84%	7	43	20(B)	35%
Chu, Amy	7	834	6/7	86%	86%	6	32	15(B)	40%
Collins, Chris	7	868	6/8	75%	▸ 62%	6	32	15(B)	40%
Cooper, Tiffany	7	781	10/12	83%	▸ 65%	10	118	17(B)	58%
Evans, Jamal	7	719	15/17	88%	▸ 49%	15	200	18(B)	83%
Felix, Tonya	7	BR (10)	6/13	46%	83%	6	24	30(B)	20%
Fernandez, Luis	7	242	2/3	67%	▸ 67%	2	7	30(B)	7%
Garcia, Matt	7	550	2/13	15%	▸ 35%	2	9	22(B)	9%
Imran, Khaleel	7	719	9/10	90%	89%	9	78	20(B)	45%
Kramer, Liz	7	809	2/5	40%	▸ 54%	2	6	18(B)	11%
Krynski, Theo	7	1120	4/4	100%	83%	4	15	13(B)	31%
Palermo, Justin	7	438	7/8	88%	76%	7	32	23(B)	30%
Ramirez, Gabriella	7	743	1/5	20%	▸ 62%	1	3	18(B)	6%
Rupp, Jeremy	7	727	0/0	N/A	N/A	0	0	18(B)	0%
Sanchez, Rachel	7	792	9/15	60%	73%	9	55	17(B)	53%
TOTALS	-	**700 (AVG.)**	**86/128**	**54% (AVG.)**	▸ **64% (AVG.)**	**86**	**655**	-	**31% (AVG.)**

(B)=Books ▸ Indicates Score Below 70%

Enlargement: Reading Progress Report

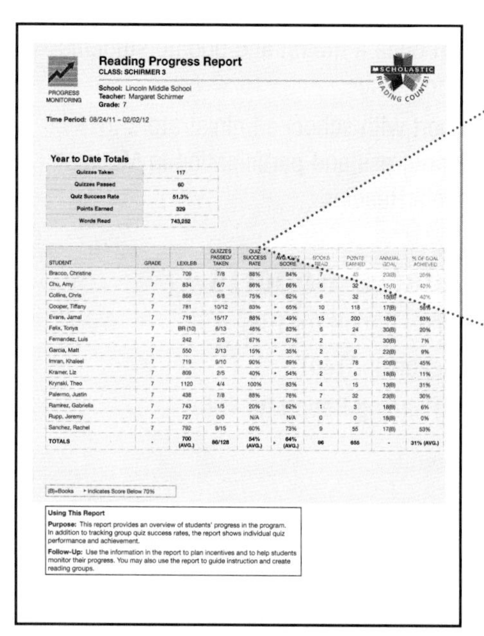

Using This Report

Purpose: This report provides an overview of students' progress in the program. In addition to tracking group quiz success rates, the report shows individual quiz performance and achievement.

Follow-Up: Use the information in the report to plan incentives and to help students monitor their progress. You may also use the report to guide instruction and create reading groups.

Data Point	Data Analysis	NEXT STEPS
❶ Rachel has taken 15 quizzes but only passed nine.	Rachel is attempting quizzes but is not experiencing quiz success.	When students struggle to pass multiple quizzes, run and analyze the *SRC!* Student Reading Report to identify the cause.
❷ Rachel's quiz success rate is 60% while her average quiz score is 73%.	Rachel has passed 60% of the quizzes she attempted. Her average score on the quizzes she has taken is 73%.	Review student reading logs, Graphic Organizers, and QuickWrites before allowing students to take a quiz.
❸ Rachel is 53% of the way to achieving her book goal.	It is halfway through the year, and Rachel is halfway to her goal.	Set individual goals based on student's initial Lexile.

Review Additional Data

Cross-reference the *Scholastic Reading Counts!* Student Reading Report to analyze specific performance results.

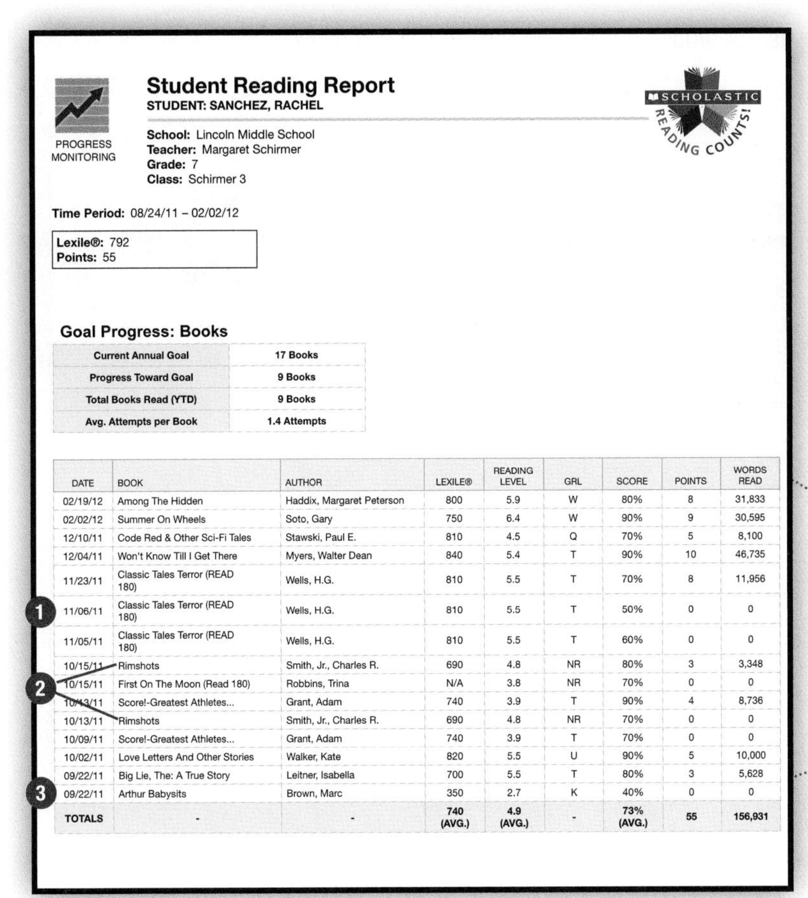

Student Reading Report
STUDENT: SANCHEZ, RACHEL

PROGRESS MONITORING

SCHOLASTIC READING COUNTS!

School: Lincoln Middle School
Teacher: Margaret Schirmer
Grade: 7
Class: Schirmer 3

Time Period: 08/24/11 – 02/02/12

Lexile®: 792
Points: 55

Goal Progress: Books

Current Annual Goal	17 Books
Progress Toward Goal	9 Books
Total Books Read (YTD)	9 Books
Avg. Attempts per Book	1.4 Attempts

DATE	BOOK	AUTHOR	LEXILE®	READING LEVEL	GRL	SCORE	POINTS	WORDS READ
02/19/12	Among The Hidden	Haddix, Margaret Peterson	800	5.9	W	80%	8	31,833
02/02/12	Summer On Wheels	Soto, Gary	750	6.4	W	90%	9	30,595
12/10/11	Code Red & Other Sci-Fi Tales	Stawski, Paul E.	810	4.5	Q	70%	5	8,100
12/04/11	Won't Know Till I Get There	Myers, Walter Dean	840	5.4	T	90%	10	46,735
11/23/11	Classic Tales Terror (READ 180)	Wells, H.G.	810	5.5	T	70%	8	11,956
11/06/11	Classic Tales Terror (READ 180)	Wells, H.G.	810	5.5	T	50%	0	0
11/05/11	Classic Tales Terror (READ 180)	Wells, H.G.	810	5.5	T	60%	0	0
10/15/11	Rimshots	Smith, Jr., Charles R.	690	4.8	NR	80%	3	3,348
10/15/11	First On The Moon (Read 180)	Robbins, Trina	N/A	3.8	NR	70%	0	0
10/13/11	Score!-Greatest Athletes...	Grant, Adam	740	3.9	T	90%	4	8,736
10/13/11	Rimshots	Smith, Jr., Charles R.	690	4.8	NR	70%	0	0
10/09/11	Score!-Greatest Athletes...	Grant, Adam	740	3.9	T	70%	0	0
10/02/11	Love Letters And Other Stories	Walker, Kate	820	5.5	U	90%	5	10,000
09/22/11	Big Lie, The: A True Story	Leitner, Isabella	700	5.5	T	80%	3	5,628
09/22/11	Arthur Babysits	Brown, Marc	350	2.7	K	40%	0	0
TOTALS	-	-	740 (AVG.)	4.9 (AVG.)	-	73% (AVG.)	55	156,931

Enlargement: Student Reading Report

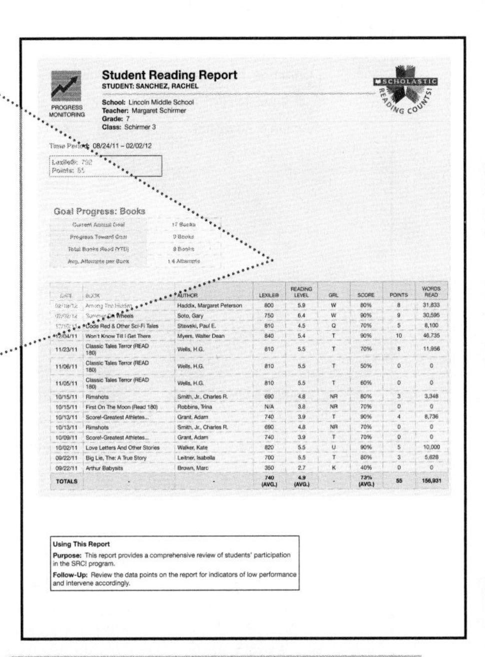

Using This Report

Purpose: This report provides a comprehensive review of students' participation in the SRC! program.

Follow-Up: Review the data points on the report for indicators of low performance and intervene accordingly.

Data Point	Data Analysis	NEXT STEPS
1 Rachel took a quiz on the same book three times.	Rachel made a second attempt at the same quiz only one day after her first attempt.	Students must wait at least 24 hours before retaking a quiz. Have students use this time to review their book and accompanying work.
2 In another case, Rachel also took a quiz on the same book twice.	Rachel took a few days to review her book, then passed the quiz on her second attempt.	Before allowing a student to retake a quiz, review the book and previous quiz results with the student to provide additional support.
3 Rachel did not pass a quiz on a book that was well within her independent reading range.	Rachel took two quizzes on different books on the same day.	Promote quiz success by ensuring that students have read each book and completed all accompanying activities prior to taking a quiz.

Recommended Reading Report

Purpose

This report provides an individualized reading list for students based on their interest choices.

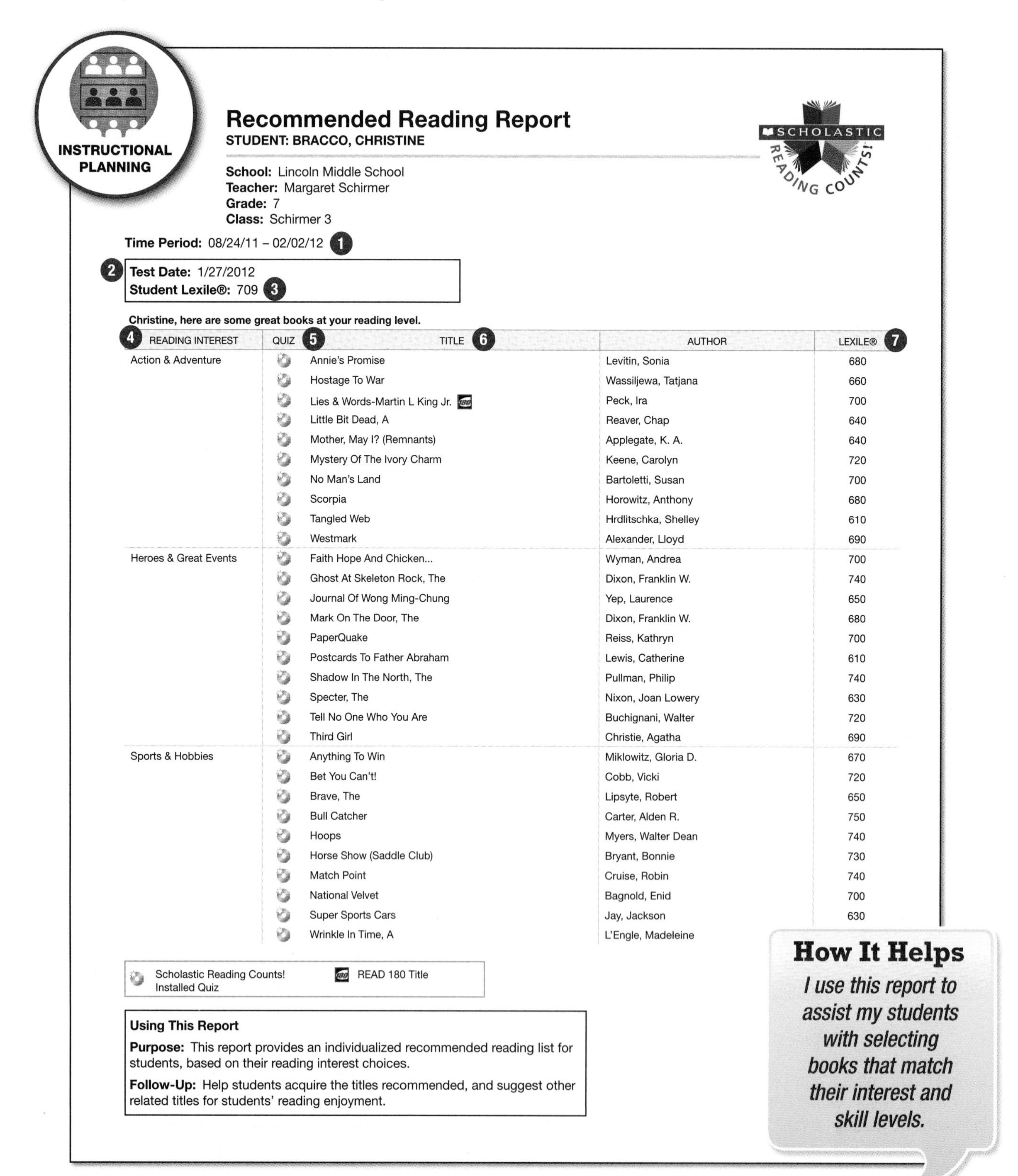

INSTRUCTIONAL PLANNING

Recommended Reading Report
STUDENT: BRACCO, CHRISTINE

School: Lincoln Middle School
Teacher: Margaret Schirmer
Grade: 7
Class: Schirmer 3

Time Period: 08/24/11 – 02/02/12 ❶

❷ **Test Date:** 1/27/2012
Student Lexile®: 709 ❸

Christine, here are some great books at your reading level.

❹ READING INTEREST	QUIZ ❺	TITLE ❻	AUTHOR	LEXILE® ❼
Action & Adventure	●	Annie's Promise	Levitin, Sonia	680
	●	Hostage To War	Wassiljewa, Tatjana	660
	●	Lies & Words-Martin L King Jr. (READ 180)	Peck, Ira	700
	●	Little Bit Dead, A	Reaver, Chap	640
	●	Mother, May I? (Remnants)	Applegate, K. A.	640
	●	Mystery Of The Ivory Charm	Keene, Carolyn	720
	●	No Man's Land	Bartoletti, Susan	700
	●	Scorpia	Horowitz, Anthony	680
	●	Tangled Web	Hrdlitschka, Shelley	610
	●	Westmark	Alexander, Lloyd	690
Heroes & Great Events	●	Faith Hope And Chicken...	Wyman, Andrea	700
	●	Ghost At Skeleton Rock, The	Dixon, Franklin W.	740
	●	Journal Of Wong Ming-Chung	Yep, Laurence	650
	●	Mark On The Door, The	Dixon, Franklin W.	680
	●	PaperQuake	Reiss, Kathryn	700
	●	Postcards To Father Abraham	Lewis, Catherine	610
	●	Shadow In The North, The	Pullman, Philip	740
	●	Specter, The	Nixon, Joan Lowery	630
	●	Tell No One Who You Are	Buchignani, Walter	720
	●	Third Girl	Christie, Agatha	690
Sports & Hobbies	●	Anything To Win	Miklowitz, Gloria D.	670
	●	Bet You Can't!	Cobb, Vicki	720
	●	Brave, The	Lipsyte, Robert	650
	●	Bull Catcher	Carter, Alden R.	750
	●	Hoops	Myers, Walter Dean	740
	●	Horse Show (Saddle Club)	Bryant, Bonnie	730
	●	Match Point	Cruise, Robin	740
	●	National Velvet	Bagnold, Enid	700
	●	Super Sports Cars	Jay, Jackson	630
	●	Wrinkle In Time, A	L'Engle, Madeleine	

● Scholastic Reading Counts! Installed Quiz — READ 180 Title

Using This Report

Purpose: This report provides an individualized recommended reading list for students, based on their reading interest choices.

Follow-Up: Help students acquire the titles recommended, and suggest other related titles for students' reading enjoyment.

How It Helps

I use this report to assist my students with selecting books that match their interest and skill levels.

Understand the Data

1 Time Period
Time period setting of This School Year displays results based on student's current Lexile score.

2 Test Date
Student's most recent SRI test date.

3 Student Lexile
Student's most recent SRI score. Book choices are filtered based on this score.

4 Reading Interest
Topics, or genres, the student selected at the beginning of the SRI test.

5 Quiz
Icon next to a book title indicates that a *Scholastic Reading Counts!* quiz has been installed and is available for the book.

6 Title
Books at appropriate reading levels and correlated to student interest.

7 Lexile
Lexile measure for each book.

Use the Data

Who: Teachers, Students, Families (Student report)

When: After each SRI administration

How: Apply information from this report in the following ways:

Guide Independent Reading

- Print this report after each SRI test and use it to help students select books for Modeled and Independent Reading.
- Use the SAM Book Expert to share more information about books listed in this report with students.

Share Results

- Share this report with media specialists so that they can help students select appropriate books and can stock book titles based on student interest and reading level.
- Send this report home with students along with the *Scholastic Reading Counts!* parent letters or with report cards to provide caregivers with guidance in helping their children select appropriate books.

Review Related Reports

- *SRC!* Student Reading Report (p. 156)
- *SRC!* Parent Report I (p. 158)
- *SRC!* Parent Report II (p. 159)

Data in Action

Adjusting Report Settings The SRI Settings in the SAM Roster tab allows you to limit the books that appear on this report to display only book titles with installed *Scholastic Reading Counts!* quizzes.

Student Quiz Success Report

Purpose

This report provides data for each student on *Scholastic Reading Counts!* quizzes passed.

Student Quiz Success Report
STUDENT: BRACCO, CHRISTINE

School: Lincoln Middle School
Teacher: Margaret Schirmer
Grade: 7
Class: Schirmer 3

Time Period: 08/24/11 – 02/02/12 ❶

Lexile®: 709 ❷
Total Points: 41
Quizzes Passed: 7

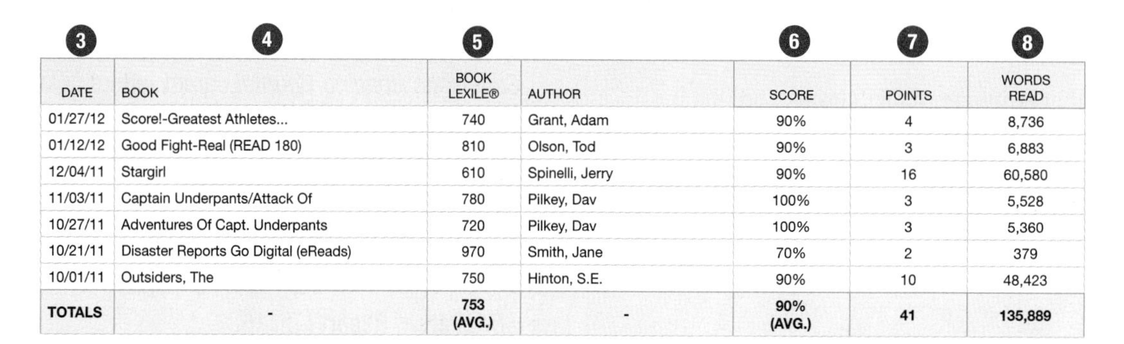

❸ DATE	❹ BOOK	❺ BOOK LEXILE®	AUTHOR	❻ SCORE	❼ POINTS	❽ WORDS READ
01/27/12	Score!-Greatest Athletes...	740	Grant, Adam	90%	4	8,736
01/12/12	Good Fight-Real (READ 180)	810	Olson, Tod	90%	3	6,883
12/04/11	Stargirl	610	Spinelli, Jerry	90%	16	60,580
11/03/11	Captain Underpants/Attack Of	780	Pilkey, Dav	100%	3	5,528
10/27/11	Adventures Of Capt. Underpants	720	Pilkey, Dav	100%	3	5,360
10/21/11	Disaster Reports Go Digital (eReads)	970	Smith, Jane	70%	2	379
10/01/11	Outsiders, The	750	Hinton, S.E.	90%	10	48,423
TOTALS	-	**753 (AVG.)**	-	**90% (AVG.)**	**41**	**135,889**

How It Helps

I share data from this report with my students so that they can celebrate their successes. I track words read for all of my students on our bulletin board.

Understand the Data

❶ **Time Period**
Default time period setting of This School Year displays all quizzes passed during the year. Customize time period settings to review results for more targeted periods of time.

❷ **Lexile**
Student's most recent SRI score within the selected time period.

❸ **Date**
Date each *Scholastic Reading Counts!* quiz was passed for all books.

❹ **Book**
Book title for each quiz passed. Quizzes that were attempted but not passed are not included on this report.

❺ **Book Lexile**
Lexile measure of each book.

❻ **Score**
Percentage of questions answered correctly.

❼ **Points**
Each book is assigned a set point value. Students earn points for each *Scholastic Reading Counts!* quiz passed.

❽ **Words Read**
Total words read for all books when each *Scholastic Reading Counts!* quiz is passed.

Use the Data

Who: Teachers, Students, Families (Student report)

When: Once or twice a month

How: Apply the information in the following ways:

Conference With Students

- Print this report each month and conference with students regarding their progress. Celebrate success and encourage continued reading growth.
- Establish goals for words read, pages read, or books read for each student. Have students use this report to track progress toward goals.

Share Results

- Add this report to student portfolios as a record of independent reading achievement.
- Print this report to share at conferences with families to provide more detail on students' reading progress.

Review Related Reports

- *SRC!* Reading Progress Report (p. 148)
- *SRC!* Student Reading Report (p. 156)
- *SRC!* Parent Report II (p. 159)

Data in Action

Reading Achievement Many students enrolled in *System 44* have experienced failure in reading in the past. Use this report to help students overcome feelings of reading frustration. Build confidence and self-esteem by regularly celebrating quiz successes.

Student Reading Report

Purpose

This report summarizes each student's *Scholastic Reading Counts!* quiz participation.

Student Reading Report

STUDENT: BRACCO, CHRISTINE

School: Lincoln Middle School
Teacher: Margaret Schirmer
Grade: 7
Class: Schirmer 3

Time Period: 08/24/11 – 02/02/12 ❶

Lexile®: 709
Points: 41

❷ **Goal Progress: Books**

Current Annual Goal	20 Books
Progress Toward Goal	7 Books
Total Books Read (YTD)	7 Books
Avg. Attempts per Book	1.0 Attempt

❸ DATE	❹ BOOK	AUTHOR	❺ BOOK LEXILE®	❻ READING LEVEL	❼ GRL	❽ SCORE	❾ POINTS	❿ WORDS READ
01/27/12	Score!-Greatest Athletes...	Grant, Adam	740	3.9	T	90%	4	8,736
01/21/12	Tornadoes (Natural Disaters)	Thompson, Luke	980	6.8	U	40%	0	0
01/12/12	Good Fight-Real (READ 180)	Olson, Tod	810	5.5	NR	90%	3	6,883
12/04/11	Stargirl	Spinelli, Jerry	590	6.1	V	90%	16	60,580
11/03/11	Captain Underpants/Attack Of	Pilkey, Dav	780	4.2	P	100%	3	5,528
10/27/11	Adventures Of Capt. Under-pants	Pilkey, Dav	720	3.5	P	100%	3	5,360
10/21/11	Disaster Reports Go Digital (eReads)	Smith, Jane	970	6.8	NR	70%	2	379
10/01/11	Outsiders, The	Hinton, S.E.	750	5.1	Z	90%	10	48,423
TOTALS	-	-	**793 (AVG.)**	**5.2 (AVG.)**	-	**84% (AVG.)**	**41**	**135,889**

Using This Report

Purpose: This report provides a comprehensive review of students' participation in the SRC! program.

Follow-Up: Review the data points on the report for indicators of low performance and intervene accordingly.

How It Helps

I share this report with my students so that they can monitor their progress. We discuss any challenges they are experiencing, and then they track their progress in their 44Books.

Understand the Data

1 Time Period
Default time period setting of This School Year displays all quizzes passed during the year. Customize time period settings to review results for more targeted periods of time.

2 Goal Progress
Student's annual goal, if established in SAM. Also includes progress toward goal, listed as points or books, depending on SAM settings.

3 Date
Date of each *Scholastic Reading Counts!* quiz attempt. Each book quiz can be attempted up to three times.

4 Book
Book title for each quiz attempt. Books with multiple quiz attempts will appear multiple times.

5 Book Lexile
Lexile measure of each book.

6 Reading Level
Grade- and month-based reading level of the book (e.g., 4.2 indicates the second month of fourth grade).

7 Guided Reading Level (GRL)
Complexity of the book, based on length, plot, vocabulary, and other features. There are 18 levels for Grades K–4, ranging from A through R.

8 Score
Percentage of questions answered correctly.

9 Points
Each book is assigned a set point value. Students earn points for each *Scholastic Reading Counts!* quiz passed. A score of 0 indicates a quiz attempted but not passed.

10 Words Read
Total words read for all books when each *Scholastic Reading Counts!* quiz is passed.

Use the Data

Who: Teachers, Students, Families (Student report)

When: Once or twice a month

How: You can use the information in this report in the following ways:

Conference With Students

- Print this report each month to conference with students about their progress. Discuss and address challenges a student might be having with comprehension or taking quizzes.
- Establish goals for words read, books read, or quizzes passed for each student. Help students track progress toward goals with this report.

Share Results

- Add this report to student portfolios as a record of independent reading achievement.
- Print this report to share at conferences with families to provide more detail on students' reading progress.

Review Related Reports

- *SRC!* Reading Progress Report (p. 148)
- *SRC!* Student Quiz Success Report (p. 154)

Data in Action

Regular Reading Accountability Students benefit from consistent monitoring of work completed in Modeled and Independent Reading. Implement daily goals for pages read or quarterly goals for books read or quizzes passed. Help students track progress on daily reading logs.

Parent Report I

Purpose

This report introduces parents or caregivers to *SRC!* and includes their child's independent reading goal, if established in SAM. It also includes recommendations for supporting reading at home.

STUDENT: IMRAN, KHALEEL

School: Lincoln Middle School
Teacher: Margaret Schirmer
Grade: 7
Class: Schirmer 3

September 4, 2011

Dear Parent or Caregiver,

Khaleel will be participating in *Scholastic Reading Counts!*, an independent reading program with a library of thousands of best-loved titles. Through *Scholastic Reading Counts!* we will be able to track what Khaleel is reading independently. Khaleel will also be encouraged and rewarded for reading more and achieving more!

Participating in *Scholastic Reading Counts!* includes:

- Choosing books to read.
- Taking quizzes on the computer to check comprehension.
- Receiving instant feedback, including reward points and congratulations screens for passing quizzes successfully.

Personal Goal (# of books or points/year)

Name	*Grade*	*Lexile®*	*Personal Goal*
Imran, Khaleel	7	710	20 Books / Year

Supporting reading at home will help Khaleel become a lifelong reader. Here are some useful tips:

- If Khaleel has an interest in a specific sport or hobby, encourage him/her to read about it.
- Talk about what your child is reading. Ask questions about the plot or about fun facts if it's nonfiction.
- Try to find a variety of reading materials for your child to experience: fiction, nonfiction, magazines, newspapers, humorous books, recipes, maps, etc.

Thank you for making Reading Count! for Khaleel this school year and always.

Sincerely,

How It Helps

I send Parent Report I home at the beginning of the year to introduce families to the program and suggest ways they can help with reading at home.

Parent Reports II and III

Purpose

Parent Report II updates parents or caregivers on their child's progress in *SRC!* Parent Report III provides a final summary of a student's performance. Both reports include tips to encourage reading at home.

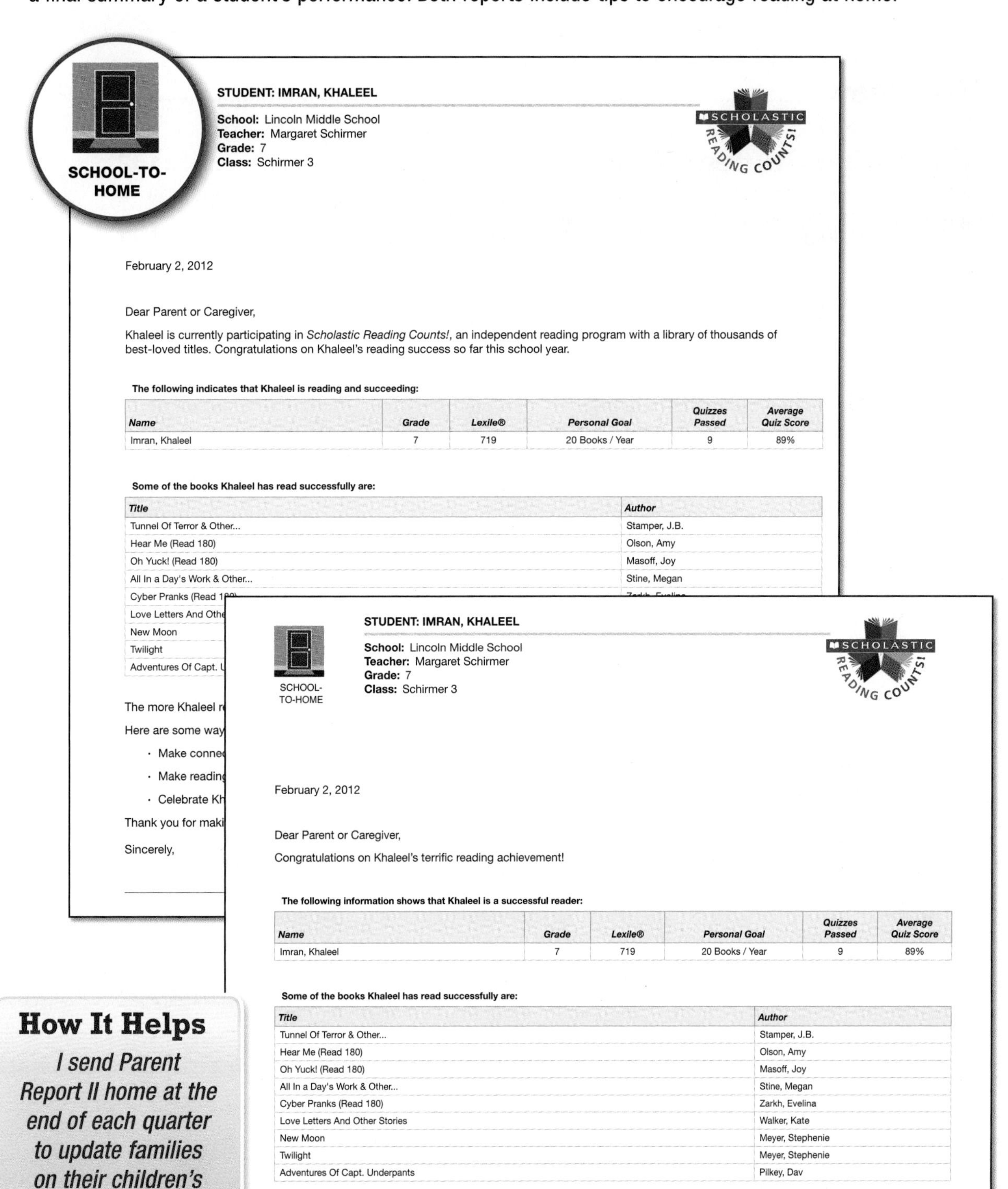

SCHOOL-TO-HOME

STUDENT: IMRAN, KHALEEL

School: Lincoln Middle School
Teacher: Margaret Schirmer
Grade: 7
Class: Schirmer 3

February 2, 2012

Dear Parent or Caregiver,

Khaleel is currently participating in *Scholastic Reading Counts!*, an independent reading program with a library of thousands of best-loved titles. Congratulations on Khaleel's reading success so far this school year.

The following indicates that Khaleel is reading and succeeding:

Name	Grade	Lexile®	Personal Goal	Quizzes Passed	Average Quiz Score
Imran, Khaleel	7	719	20 Books / Year	9	89%

Some of the books Khaleel has read successfully are:

Title	Author
Tunnel Of Terror & Other...	Stamper, J.B.
Hear Me (Read 180)	Olson, Amy
Oh Yuck! (Read 180)	Masoff, Joy
All In a Day's Work & Other...	Stine, Megan
Cyber Pranks (Read 1	
Love Letters And Oth	
New Moon	
Twilight	
Adventures Of Capt. U	

The more Khaleel r

Here are some way

- Make conne
- Make readin
- Celebrate Kh

Thank you for maki

Sincerely,

SCHOOL-TO-HOME

STUDENT: IMRAN, KHALEEL

School: Lincoln Middle School
Teacher: Margaret Schirmer
Grade: 7
Class: Schirmer 3

February 2, 2012

Dear Parent or Caregiver,

Congratulations on Khaleel's terrific reading achievement!

The following information shows that Khaleel is a successful reader:

Name	Grade	Lexile®	Personal Goal	Quizzes Passed	Average Quiz Score
Imran, Khaleel	7	719	20 Books / Year	9	89%

Some of the books Khaleel has read successfully are:

Title	Author
Tunnel Of Terror & Other...	Stamper, J.B.
Hear Me (Read 180)	Olson, Amy
Oh Yuck! (Read 180)	Masoff, Joy
All In a Day's Work & Other...	Stine, Megan
Cyber Pranks (Read 180)	Zarkh, Evelina
Love Letters And Other Stories	Walker, Kate
New Moon	Meyer, Stephenie
Twilight	Meyer, Stephenie
Adventures Of Capt. Underpants	Pilkey, Dav

Here are some tips to use at home to keep Khaleel reading and succeeding:

- Encourage Khaleel to write letters, postcards, or emails.

How It Helps

I send Parent Report II home at the end of each quarter to update families on their children's reading progress.

Data-Driven Decision Making

Overview

You can use the data collected by *System 44* to make instructional decisions for each student in the program.

While program reports are your main resource for data-driven decision making, *System 44* provides several additional resources that help you leverage data into actionable decisions. These resources will help you:

- Determine periodic grades.
- Monitor oral reading fluency growth.
- Evaluate exit readiness.

These resources are accessible on the Scholastic Achievement Manager (SAM) and provide efficient ways for you to make student data truly useful. Use this section to learn how these progress-monitoring resources support ongoing data-driven decision making in the classroom.

Assigning Student Grades

When grading, consider the complete picture of a student's progress and performance in *System 44.* Evaluate students according to usage and mastery of the program and transfer of new skills, as well as participation and effort.

The chart below shows where to find relevant data to include in grading estimations. All *System 44* reports can be accessed using the Scholastic Achievement Manager (SAM). Percentages are automatically generated by the software. See the previous section of this book, Reporting in *System 44* (p. 68), for detailed information about each report.

System 44 Software

Performance Indicator	Where to Look	Program Expectations
Decoding Accuracy Score	Reading Progress Report	70% or higher
Decoding Fluency Score	Reading Progress Report	70% or higher
Spelling Score	Reading Progress Report	70% or higher
Comprehension Score	Reading Progress Report	70% or higher
Fluency Recording Score	Reading Progress Report	Score = 3 (out of 6) or higher

The chart below includes questions to consider when evaluating students' direct instruction performance.

System 44 Direct Instruction

Performance Indicator	Questions to Consider
Participation	• Is the student paying attention? • Is the student responding thoughtfully to questions? • Is the student collaborating with peers?
Metacognitive Skills	• Is the student applying S.M.A.R.T. concepts to learning? • Is the student maintaining new skills?
Effort and Motivation	• Is the student trying his/her best? • Is the student engaged and focused? • Is the student responding to corrective feedback? • Is the student demonstrating success with classroom expectations? (See Behavioral Goals Rubrics in the *44Book.*)
Homework	• Is the student completing homework as assigned? • Is the student completing homework accurately?

System 44 Grading Form

Access the *System 44* Grading Form on SAM (**Keyword:** **44 Grading**). Complete one for each student when determining periodic grades. Refer to the example below showing how one teacher grades performance criteria.

Name ____________________ Date ____________

SYSTEM 44

System 44 Grading Form

▶ Follow these steps when grading *System 44* students.

1. **Estimate** a student's performance on each criterion as a percentage. Record the percentages in the Grade column. Example: 90%.
2. **Prioritize** by assigning each criterion a weight. Ask,"Which of these criteria do I consider the most important?" For accurate class assessment, apply the same weight to each criterion for every student. Record this percentage in the Weight column.
3. **Multiply** each grade by the weight of importance. Convert percentages to decimals when multiplying, e.g., 95% = .95. Record this number in the Subtotal column. Then add subtotals together and multiply by 100. Record the Final Grade. Convert to letter grades if required.

Criterion	Grade	Weight	Subtotal
Software Performance			
Decoding Accuracy Score			
Decoding Fluency Score			
Spelling Score			
Comprehension Score			
Fluency Recording Score			
Direct Instruction Performance			
Participation			
Metacognitive Skills			
Effort and Motivation			
Homework			
Total			__(100)=__

FINAL GRADE: ________%
FINAL LETTER GRADE: ________

Resource Links
SAM Keyword: 44 Grading

Use with **Assessment and Reporting Guide,** *pages 102–103.*

System 44 • Grading Worksheet

Calculating Grades

1. **Determine grades** for direct instruction by converting estimations of students' performance in each of the criteria below into a percentage. Record this number under the Grade column for each criteria.
2. **Prioritize performance criteria** by giving each a weight. Ask yourself, "Which of these criteria do I consider the most important?" For an accurate class assessment, be sure to apply the same weight to each criterion for every student. Record this percentage under the Weight column for each criterion. The percentages should add up to 100%.
3. **Calculate Final Grade**. Multiply each grade by the weight of importance. Use decimal points when multiplying (e.g., 95% = .95). Then add those subtotals together and multiply by 100. Record that number under Final Grade and convert to a letter grade if required.

Criterion	Grade	Weight	Subtotal
Software Performance			
Decoding Accuracy Score	95%	15%	.1425
Decoding Fluency Score	90%	15%	.135
Spelling Score	88%	10%	.088
Comprehension Score	90%	10%	.09
Fluency Recording Score	100%	5%	.05
Direct Instruction Performance			
Participation	75%	15%	.1125
Metacognitive Skills	90%	10%	.09
Effort and Motivation	85%	10%	.085
Homework	90%	10%	.09

FINAL GRADE: 88%
FINAL LETTER GRADE: ____

Data-Driven Decision Making

Monitoring Oral Reading Fluency

Oral reading fluency is one of the strongest predictors of reading comprehension. Fluent reading requires rapid recognition of words, decoding accuracy, and oral expressiveness (prosody).

Assessing Oral Reading Fluency

Oral reading fluency is typically measured using grade-level text and reported as number of Words Correct Per Minute (WCPM). There are rigorously developed national norms, so teachers can regularly monitor students' progress and compare WCPM to grade-level benchmarks at Fall, Winter, and Spring.

The Hasbrouck & Tindal (2006) norms for Grades 1–8 with Fall, Winter, and Spring WCPM show percentiles. In addition, the Hasbrouck & Tindal norms include average weekly improvement data. Hasbrouck & Tindal suggest that any student scoring 10 or more words below the 50th percentile using the average score of two unpracticed readings from grade-level materials requires a fluency-building program such as *System 44*.

2006 Hasbrouck & Tindal Oral Reading Fluency Data

Grade	Percentile	Fall WCPM*	Winter WCPM*	Spring WCPM*	Avg. Weekly Improvement**
1	90		81	111	1.9
	75		47	82	2.2
	50		23	53	1.9
	25		12	28	1.0
	10		6	15	0.6
2	90	106	125	142	1.1
	75	79	100	117	1.2
	50	51	72	89	1.2
	25	25	42	61	1.1
	10	11	18	31	0.6
3	90	128	146	162	1.1
	75	99	120	137	1.2
	50	71	92	107	1.1
	25	44	62	78	1.1
	10	21	36	48	0.8
4	90	145	166	180	1.1
	75	119	139	152	1.0
	50	94	112	123	0.9
	25	68	87	98	0.9
	10	45	61	72	0.8
5	90	166	182	194	0.9
	75	139	156	168	0.9
	50	110	127	139	0.9
	25	85	99	109	0.8
	10	61	74	83	0.7
6	90	177	195	204	0.8
	75	153	167	177	0.8
	50	127	140	150	0.7
	25	98	111	122	0.8
	10	68	82	93	0.8
7	90	180	192	202	0.7
	75	156	165	177	0.7
	50	128	136	150	0.7
	25	102	109	123	0.7
	10	79	88	98	0.6
8	90	185	199	199	0.4
	75	161	173	177	0.5
	50	133	146	151	0.6
	25	106	115	124	0.6
	10	77	84	97	0.6

**Average words per week growth
*WCPM = Words Correct Per Minute

Hasbrouck, J. & Tindal, G. A. (2006). Oral reading fluency norms: A valuable assessment tool for reading teachers. *The Reading Teacher, 59(7),* 636-644.

Building Fluency With *System 44*

Most students in *System 44* are not yet prepared to read grade-level text with fluency. Nevertheless, it is important for them to practice the fundamentals of fluency (pacing, phrasing, and prosody) as they develop essential decoding and word recognition skills. Practice and evaluate student fluency using a variety of instructional-level text included in *System 44*:

- *Decodable Digest* passages
- Success Passages
- books from the *System 44* Library

Grade-level Oral Fluency Assessments are also available. They appear in the Stretch Texts & Fluency Practice section of the Upper Elementary and Secondary *44Books*. For teachers who are using *System 44* with *READ 180*, Oral Fluency Assessments appear in *READ 180 Resources for Differentiated Instruction, Book 1.*

Use the OFA Tracking Log in the *44Book* to monitor your students' fluency progress. Refer to the opposite page for an explanation of this resource.

System 44 Oral Fluency Assessment

Conduct Oral Fluency Assessments (OFAs) approximately every six weeks to regularly monitor progress. Use this resource to record and track *System 44* students' growth in oral reading fluency over time.

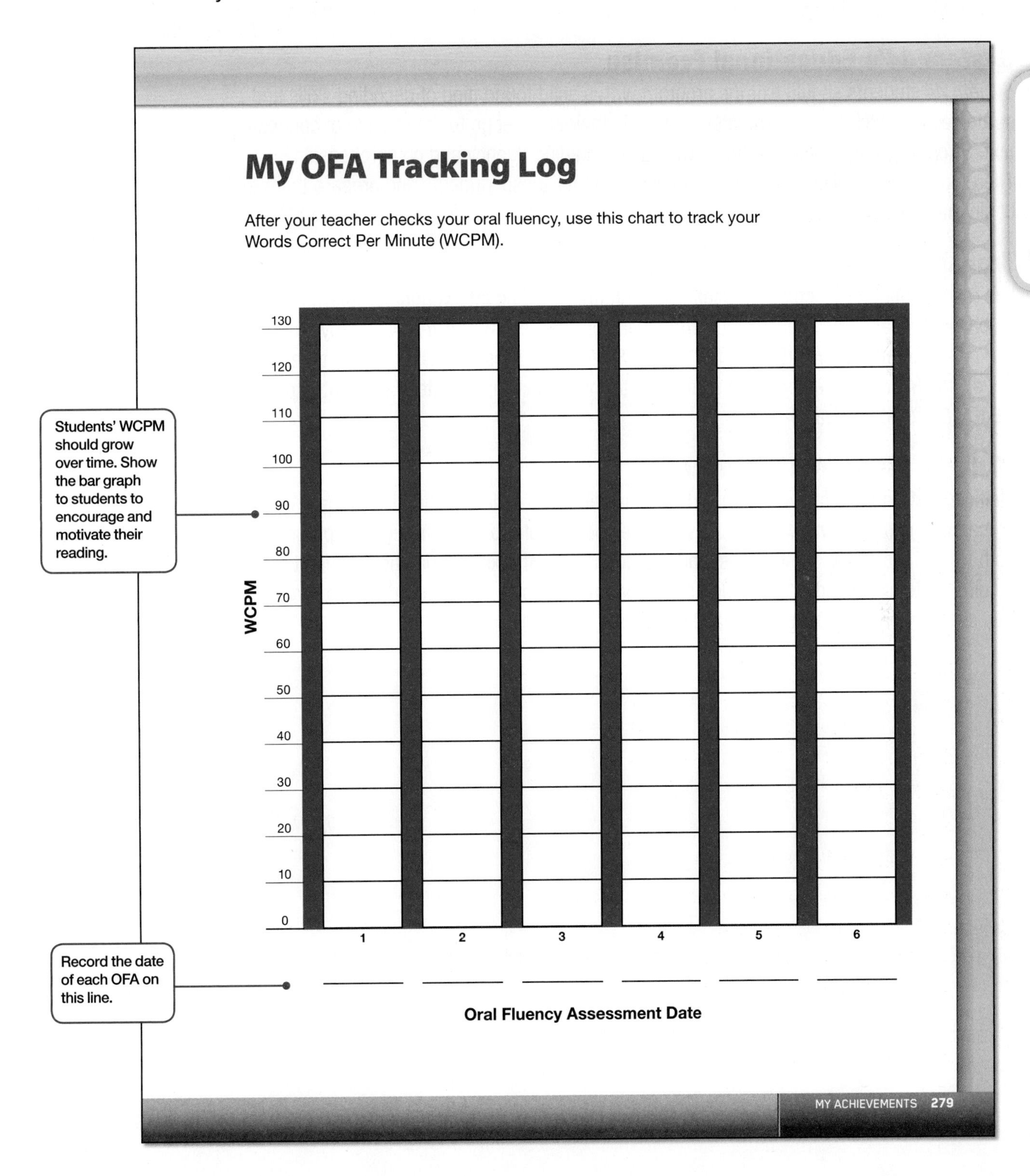

Exiting *System 44*

It is important to evaluate student readiness to exit *System 44*, as well as to develop an ongoing transition and support plan. Due to *System 44*'s differentiated placement and pacing, students will be prepared to exit the program at different times during the school year.

System 44's Educational Promise

System 44 students should exit the program with a solid foundation of decoding skills and strategies on which to build, transfer, and apply their knowledge to the reading of connected text. Strong decoding skills are the bridge to oral reading fluency and comprehension. Therefore, *System 44* will narrow the decoding gap for these students and prepare them to begin making grade-level gains.

Transition Plan

It is recommended that students transition to another reading intervention program that will emphasize vocabulary, fluency, and comprehension after exiting *System 44*. Many students can move directly into *READ 180* after exiting *System 44*. These students should take the *Scholastic Reading Inventory* (SRI) again to determine their appropriate placement into the *READ 180* Topic Software.

Multiple Measures of Success

Multiple performance measures should be considered when determining if a student is prepared to exit *System 44*. These may include successful progress through the program, both formal and informal measures, and teacher judgment. Exit criteria should reflect the requirements and standards of your district and encompass enough information to provide a true sense of each student's skills and readiness.

System 44 Exit Criteria

You may choose to refer to the Exit Criteria rubric below when determining if a student is prepared to exit *System 44*. For each of the criteria listed, select the rating that best reflects current student performance. Base your evaluation on data from *System 44* reports, the SRI, Summative Assessments, and your own observations in the classroom.

Readiness to Exit

A minimum rating of 8 or higher must be achieved to indicate that a student is prepared to exit *System 44* and enter a reading intervention program. If including Oral Reading Fluency and Maintained Learning in your decision, a rating of 14–18 should be achieved. Between 1–4 Bonus Points may be added depending on each student's last recorded SRI Lexile measure.

System 44 Exit Criteria	Scale	Rating
1. Mastery of the Software Scope & Sequence	Refer to the Student Mastery Report **1** = Less than 75% of Total Scope & Sequence Mastered **2** = 75% or more of Total Scope & Sequence Mastered **3** = All Instructional Categories 100% Mastered	
2. Most Recent Decoding Status	Refer to the Student Progress Report **1** = Pre- or Beginning Decoder **2** = Developing Decoder **3** = Advancing Decoder	
3. Fluent Decoding and Word Recognition Skills	Refer to the Reading Progress Report **1** = Avg. Decoding Fluency Score < 70% **2** = Avg. Decoding Fluency Score 70%–85% **3** = Avg. Decoding Fluency Score > 85%	
4. Oral Reading Fluency Improvement	Refer to the Reading Progress Report **1** = Avg. Beginning Fluency **2** = Avg. Emerging Fluency **3** = Avg. Developing Fluency **4** = Avg. Proficient Fluency **5** = Avg. Strong Fluency **6** = Avg. Exemplary Fluency **N/A** = Not applicable to school or student	
5. Maintained Learning	Refer to the Summative Assessment Score Sheets and Answer Keys **1** = *System 44* Midyear Test Score > 75% **2** = *System 44* End-of-Year Test Score > 75% **3** = Both Summative Assessment Scores > 75% **N/A** = Not applicable to school or student	
6. ***BONUS POINTS:*** ***Growth in Reading Comprehension (Lexile Measures)***	**1** = BR–200 Lexile Growth **2** = 210–300 Lexile Growth **3** = 310–400 Lexile Growth **4** = > 400 Lexile Growth **N/A** = Not applicable to school or student	
	Total Rating =	______
	READY TO EXIT *SYSTEM 44*	**YES/NO**

Administrator Reports

Meeting Administrators' Needs

As students participate in *System 44*, the Scholastic Achievement Manager (SAM) gathers data about program usage and performance. This data enables you to monitor the effectiveness of program implementation within your school or district. You can track program usage and reading progress for classes, teachers, grades, schools, or your entire district to ensure that students are getting the maximum benefits from *System 44*.

SAM reports are available for the following components:

- *Scholastic Phonics Inventory* (SPI)
- *System 44* software
- *Scholastic Reading Inventory* (SRI)
- *Scholastic Reading Counts! (SRC!)*

Putting Report Data to Work

SAM reports are designed for flexible use. You can specify a time period for data you wish to view, sort, save, and print. The *System 44* Software Manual contains detailed instructions on how to adjust SAM settings and access SAM resources. You can also review aggregated SAM results in Data Snapshots on the Leadership Dashboard.

Proven Results for Student Groups

System 44 is proven to meet the needs of students across a range of demographic groups whose reading achievement is below the proficient level. The program provides concrete, reliable information that will enable you to track progress for groups of students across a school or district. More specifically, to help meet your state requirements, *System 44* offers:

- A reliable mechanism for monitoring, evaluating, and reporting progress.
- Differentiated instruction to meet student needs.
- Reports that disaggregate student data by demographic group.
- The ability to export data to demonstrate performance across schools and districts.

A compendium of *System 44* research summarizes the results from 20 studies. Several studies in this document illustrate the impact on student achievement when *System 44* is implemented "on model." *Raising Reading Achievement for America's Most Challenged Older Students* can be downloaded at **www.scholastic.com/research**.

Using the Leadership Dashboard

The Leadership Dashboard streamlines the process of progress monitoring and determining where to provide strategic implementation support. Use your Leadership Dashboard to monitor student progress, set up weekly Notifications, and identify factors critical to a successful implementation.

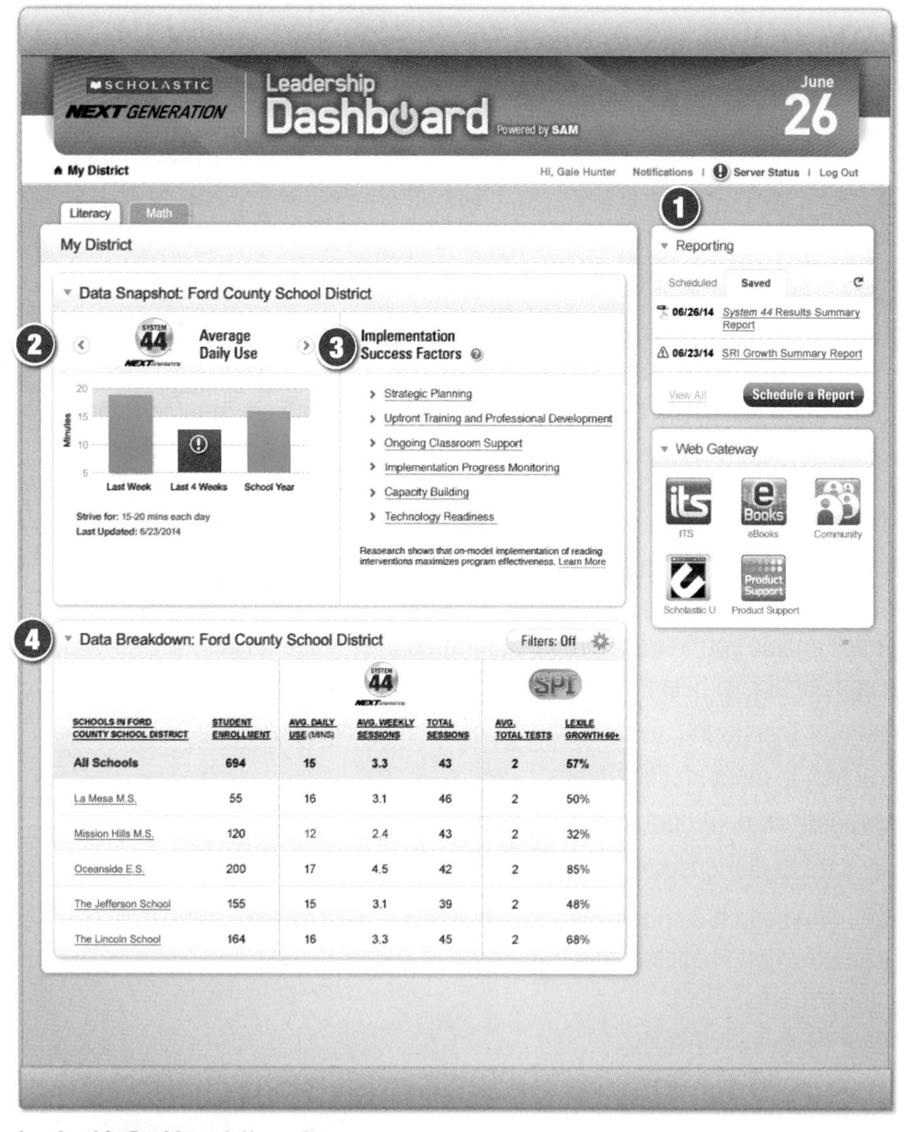

Leadership Dashboard: Home Page

1 Receive Notifications and Schedule Reports

Manage **weekly Notifications** or schedule the Dashboard to run SAM reports.

2 Review Aggregated Results

Review **aggregated student results** by district, school, or class.

3 Support Implementation

Provide **strategic implementation support** by quickly identifying schools or classes that are experiencing challenges.

4 Review Student Results

Review results from each component of *System 44* for all schools or classes.

Leadership Dashboard Notifications

Use the Leadership Dashboard to manage weekly Notification digests. Review the Notifications and use the information to determine which SAM reports to schedule for further analysis.

Launch the Notifications Wizard

Log in to the Leadership Dashboard anytime to set or modify Notifications settings. From the Leadership Dashboard Home Page, click **Notifications**.

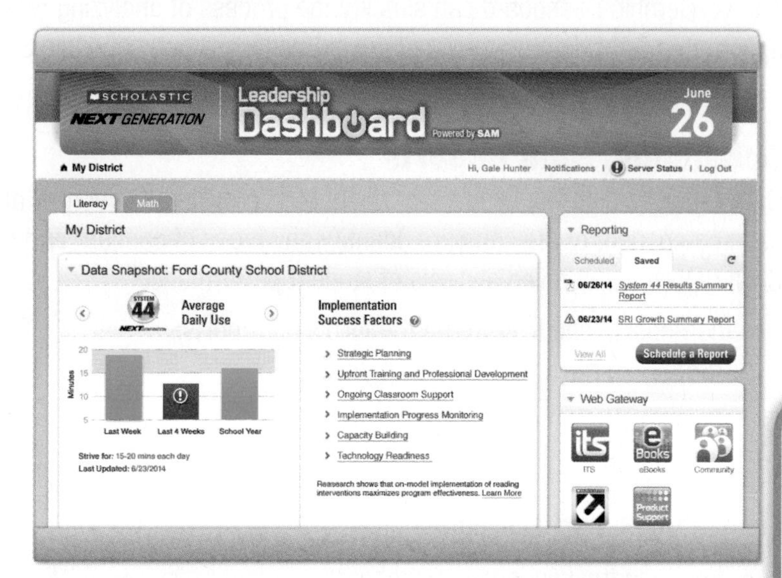

Leadership Dashboard: Home Page

Manage Notifications

1. Click the **Notifications** link on the Home Page of the Leadership Dashboard.
2. Place a check mark next to any Notifications you wish to receive.
3. Click **Save** to schedule the Notifications.
4. A Notification digest will be sent to your inbox once a week and will contain information for the Notifications you selected.
5. Return to this screen to adjust Notifications options at any time.

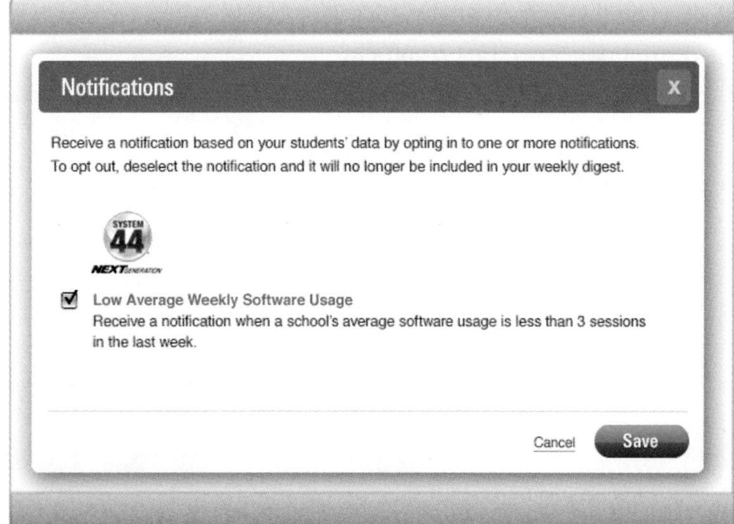

Leadership Dashboard: Notifications Wizard

Using the Leadership Dashboard to Schedule Reports

The Leadership Dashboard can simplify the process of analyzing reports. Review the aggregated SAM data on the Leadership Dashboard and schedule SAM reports to be sent to your email inbox.

Scheduling SAM Reports

Data Snapshots on the Leadership Dashboard provide an overview of student participation in each component of the software. Identify any areas of concern and schedule accompanying SAM reports for detailed analysis of student performance.

Use the Report Scheduler to run the following reports:

- *System 44* Results Summary Report
- SRI Growth Summary Report

Launch the Report Scheduler

1. Log in to the Leadership Dashboard anytime to schedule a SAM report.
2. Review the Data Snapshots for your district or school. Use results to determine which reports to review.
3. From the Leadership Dashboard Home Page, click **Schedule a Report** to launch the Report Scheduler.

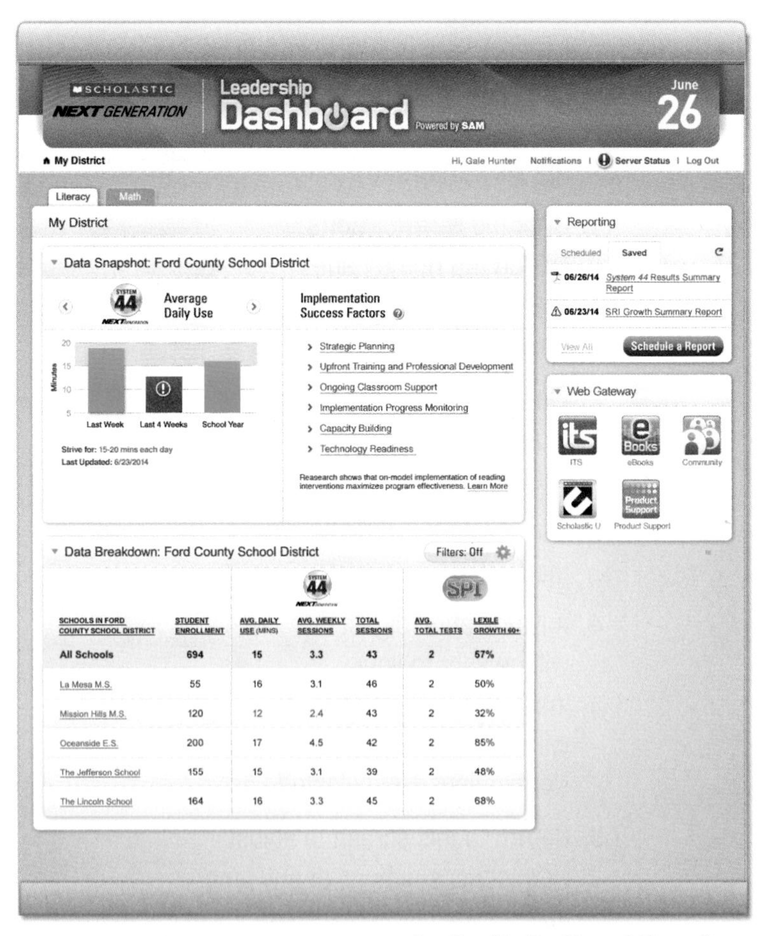

Leadership Dashboard: Home Page

Using the Leadership Dashboard Report Scheduler

The Report Scheduler on the Leadership Dashboard contains many of the same features and functions as reports settings found in SAM. Use these settings to schedule a report.

Schedule a Report

1. **Who:** Select the district or a school.
2. **What:** Select a program and a report.
3. **Time Period:** Select whether to run the report for the last two weeks or the school year. The selected time period is dependent on the date you schedule the report to be run.
4. **When:** Select the date to run the report.
5. **Confirm:** Review your selections. Click **DONE** to schedule the report.

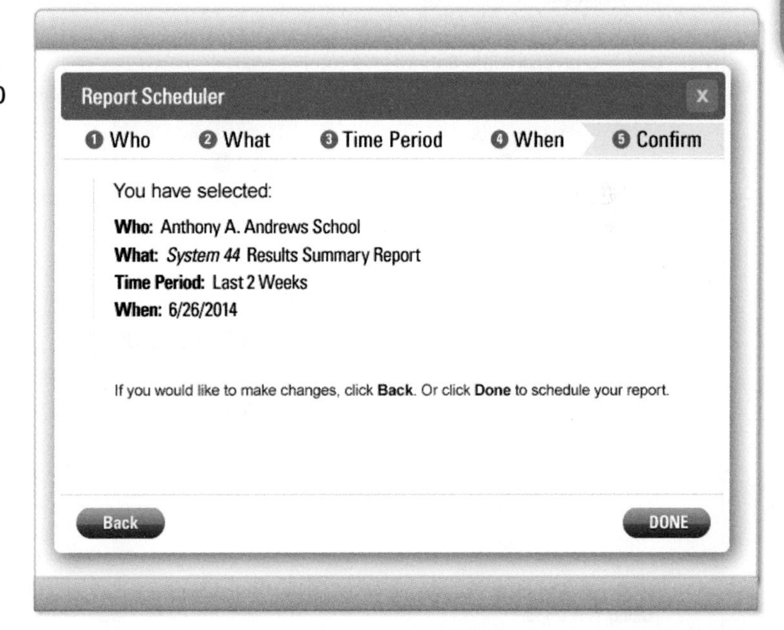

Leadership Dashboard: Report Scheduler

Review a Report

When the report is ready, you will receive an email notification. The report will be available in the Report Scheduler as a PDF. Use this guide to analyze student results. Use that analysis to provide instructional support and implementation feedback. For more information about implementation, review the Implementation Success Factors section of the Leadership Dashboard.

District/School Status Report

Purpose

Use this report to review student SPI performance on a district- or school-wide basis.

District/School Status Report

DISTRICT: LINCOLN UNIFIED SCHOOL DISTRICT

Time Period: 08/24/11 – 09/24/11 ❶

Total Schools: 8
Total Students Tested: 660

Lincoln Unified School District (660 total students)

❷ SPI DECODING STATUS	❸ STUDENTS	❹ PERCENTAGE OF STUDENTS
Advancing Decoder	390	59%
Developing Decoder	145	22%
Pre- or Beginning Decoder	125	19%

Cesar Chavez Middle School (108 total students)

SPI DECODING STATUS	STUDENTS	PERCENTAGE OF STUDENTS
Advancing Decoder	65	60%
Developing Decoder	31	29%
Pre- or Beginning Decoder	12	11%

Mead Elementary School (67 total students)

SPI DECODING STATUS	STUDENTS	PERCENTAGE OF STUDENTS
Advancing Decoder	39	58%
Developing Decoder	12	18%
Pre- or Beginning Decoder	16	24%

Using This Report

Purpose: This report allows administrators to review student performance on SPI on a district- or school-wide basis.

Follow-Up: Evaluate the need for reading intervention and allocate resources accordingly. If you are using Scholastic programs, Pre-, Beginning, and Developing Decoders are candidates for *System 44*; Advancing Decoders are candidates for *READ 180*.

How It Helps

This report helps me evaluate the need for reading intervention so I can allocate resources accordingly.

Understand the Data

1 Time Period
The information in this report is based on the last SPI test taken within the selected time period. To view a particular test administration, adjust the time period accordingly.

2 SPI Decoding Status
Students are placed into one of three groups based on SPI performance: Pre- or Beginning Decoder, Developing Decoder, and Advancing Decoder. For a description of each Decoding Status, see page 33.

3 Students
The number of students in each group.

4 Percentage of Students
The percentage of students in each group.

Use the Data

Who: Administrators

When: At the beginning of the school year, following the initial administration of SPI

How: Apply the information from this report in the following ways:

Allocate Resources

- Identify instructional programs to meet the needs of students in each group.
- Ensure that resources are allocated properly to address students' needs.

Follow Up

- Conference with principals or teachers to discuss ways to meet the needs of their students.

Review Related Reports

- SPI Screening and Placement Report (p. 80)
- SRI District/School Proficiency Report (p. 186)

Data in Action

Advancing Decoders While Advancing Decoders can decode with adequate fluency, they may experience challenges with other aspects of reading, such as comprehension or vocabulary. For more information about these students' reading proficiency, administer the *Scholastic Reading Inventory* (SRI) and run the District/School Proficiency Report.

District/School Growth Report

Purpose

This report shows changes in student performance and progress on SPI over time by district, school, or class.

District/School Growth Report

DISTRICT: LINCOLN UNIFIED SCHOOL DISTRICT

Time Period: 08/24/11 – 02/02/12 

Total Schools: 8
Total Students Tested: 660

Lincoln Unified School District (660 total students)

	FIRST TEST IN TIME PERIOD		LAST TEST IN TIME PERIOD	
SPI DECODING STATUS	STUDENTS	PERCENTAGE OF STUDENTS	STUDENTS	PERCENTAGE OF STUDENTS
Advancing Decoder	390	59%	443	67%
Developing Decoder	145	22%	180	27%
Pre- or Beginning Decoder	125	19%	37	6%

Cesar Chavez Middle School (108 total students)

	FIRST TEST IN TIME PERIOD		LAST TEST IN TIME PERIOD	
SPI DECODING STATUS	STUDENTS	PERCENTAGE OF STUDENTS	STUDENTS	PERCENTAGE OF STUDENTS
Advancing Decoder	65	60%	76	70%
Developing Decoder	31	29%	29	27%
Pre- or Beginning Decoder	12	11%	3	3%

Mead Elementary School (67 total students)

	FIRST TEST IN TIME PERIOD		LAST TEST IN TIME PERIOD	
SPI DECODING STATUS	STUDENTS	PERCENTAGE OF STUDENTS	STUDENTS	PERCENTAGE OF STUDENTS
Advancing Decoder	39	58%	44	66%
Developing Decoder	12	18%	19	28%
Pre- or Beginning Decoder	16	24%	4	6%

Using This Report

Purpose: This report shows changes in student performance and progress on SPI over time by district, school, or class.

Follow-Up: Identify groups that are not showing adequate growth and may require additional support or resources.

How It Helps

I use this report to identify groups that are not showing adequate growth and may require additional support or resources.

Understand the Data

❶ **Time Period**
The information in this report is based on the first and last SPI test taken within the selected time period. Be sure to choose a time period that spans at least two test dates.

❷ **SPI Decoding Status**
Students are placed into one of three groups based on SPI performance: Pre- or Beginning Decoder, Developing Decoder, and Advancing Decoder. For a description of each Decoding Status, see page 33.

❸ **First Test in Time Period**
The number and percentage of students in each group for the first SPI test in the selected time period.

❹ **Last Test in Time Period**
The number and percentage of students in each group for the last SPI test in the selected time period.

Use the Data

Who: Administrators

When: At the middle and end of the school year, after subsequent administrations of SPI

How: Apply the information from this report in the following ways:

Acknowledge Success

- If students in a particular school or class are performing especially well, explore the instructional strategies being used and share them with other teachers.

Follow Up

- Conference with principals or teachers to discuss ways to meet the needs of their students.
- Redistribute resources, if necessary, to address changing student needs.

Review Related Reports

- SPI Summary Progress Report (p. 82)
- SRI Proficiency Growth Report (p. 190)

Data in Action

SPI Testing Windows SPI contains three equivalent test forms and should be administered at the beginning, middle, and end of the school year. Establish SPI testing windows and communicate these to schools and teachers to enable data comparisons within and across schools.

Results Summary Report

Purpose

This report shows *System 44* usage and performance data and results for SPI and SRI.

Results Summary Report

DISTRICT: LINCOLN UNIFIED SCHOOL DISTRICT

Time period: 09/06/11 – 02/02/12 (1)

Total System 44 Next Generation Licenses: 400

Lincoln Unified School District

ENROLLMENT		MEDIAN USAGE PER STUDENT				SOFTWARE COMPLETION			MOST RECENT SPI PERFORMANCE (8)	
SCHOOL	(2) STUDENTS IN SYSTEM 44	(3) SESSION LENGTH (MIN.)	(4) TOTAL SESSIONS	(5) SESSIONS PER WEEK	(6) PERCENT OF TOPICS COMPLETED	STUDENTS WITH 0-49% OF TOPICS COMPLETED	(7) STUDENTS WITH 50-79% OF TOPICS COMPLETED	STUDENTS WITH 80-100% OF TOPICS COMPLETED	Pre-and Beginning Decoders / Developing Decoders / Advancing Decoders (0% 25% 50% 75% 100%)	(9) AVERAGE SRI SCORE (LEXILE®)
Cesar Chavez Middle School	136	16	54	4	40%	91	39	6	38 / 64 / 34	221
Mead Elementary School	102	18	72	5	53%	48	41	13	25 / 54 / 23	274
The Lincoln School	155	17	68	4	51%	87	47	21	28 / 77 / 50	310
TOTAL	**393**	**17**	**64**	**4**	**48%**	**226**	**127**	**40**	**91 / 195 / 107**	**268**

Cesar Chavez Middle School

Teacher	Students	Session Length	Total Sessions	Sessions per Week	Percent Completed	0-49%	50-79%	80-100%	SPI Performance	SRI
Cole, Mercedes	40	16	52	4	38%	26	12	2	16 / 14 / 10	240
Strauss, Dave	30	15	45	4	33%	23	7	0	8 / 18 / 4	201
Wood, John	66	19	60	5	44%	42	20	4	14 / 32 / 20	223
TOTAL	**136**	**16**	**54**	**4**	**40%**	**91**	**39**	**6**	**38 / 64 / 34**	**221**

USING THIS REPORT

Purpose: Use this report to compare System 44 Next Generation usage data and the most recent SPI and SRI results for schools and classes.

Follow-Up: Run this report at the end of each SPI/SRI test window to track progress and usage.

WHAT IS THE MEDIAN?

In statistics, median is separates the higher h from the lower half. Fi list of numbers by arra lowest value to highes the middle one.

How It Helps

This report provides an overview of school and class participation in System 44 *and helps monitor fidelity of implementation.*

Understand the Data

1 Time Period
To view cumulative progress, set the time period to This School Year. Customize date ranges for a more targeted review of usage.

2 Enrollment
Total number of students enrolled in *System 44* who have completed at least one software session.

3 Session Length (Minutes)
Median number of minutes that students spend on the software each session (day). Students should average 15–19 minutes per session.

4 Total Sessions
Median total number of sessions (days) that students logged on to the software.

5 Sessions Per Week
Median number of sessions (days) that students logged on to *System 44* each week. Students should average two to four sessions per week.

6 Percent of Topics Completed
Median percent of Topics completed. *System 44* software includes 160 Topics.

7 Software Completion
Number of students who have completed less than half of the Topics, between 50% and 79% of Topics, and at least 80% of Topics.

8 Most Recent SPI Performance
Number of students with each decoding status on the last test within the selected time period.

9 Average SRI Score (Lexile)
Average student Lexile measures for the last test within the selected time period.

Use the Data

Who: Administrators

When: Monthly or after every SPI test administration

How: Apply the information in this report in the following ways:

Establish Participation Criteria

- If your school or district has implemented *System 44* for a full year, the total sessions benchmark is 96 (3 days per week × 32 weeks). Work with *System 44* coordinators and teachers to set benchmarks for specific time periods.

Follow Up

- If median usage is below 15 minutes per session or 3 sessions per week, check in with schools or individual teachers to explore implementation issues. Ensure that all classrooms have access to fully functioning technology.
- Conference with teachers whose classes are not meeting minimum participation benchmarks. Discuss classroom management techniques to ensure that students log on to the software every day.

Review Related Reports

- *System 44* Reading Progress Report (p. 88)
- SPI District/School Growth Report (p. 176)
- SRI Growth Summary Report (p. 188)

Data in Action

Monitoring Program Completion Students who have completed less than 50% of Topics in the spring may need another year in *System 44*. Prepare to transition students who have completed at least 80% of Topics into *READ 180* or another Tier 2 intervention program.

Response to Intervention Summary Report

Purpose

Use this report to track *System 44* progress and usage. Use the Median RTI as a benchmark for progress and mastery.

Response to Intervention Summary Report

DISTRICT: LINCOLN UNIFIED SCHOOL DISTRICT

Time Period: 09/06/11 – 05/15/12 ❶

Students in SYSTEM 44: 393

Lincoln Unified School District

ENROLLMENT		MEDIAN USAGE PER STUDENT					
SCHOOL	STUDENTS IN SYSTEM 44	TOTAL TIME (MIN.)	❷ NO. OF SESSIONS	❸ MASTERY TO DATE (OUT OF 25 SERIES)	NO. OF TOPICS MASTERED	❹ NO. OF TOPICS FAST TRACKED	❺ MIN./ TOPIC
Cesar Chavez Middle School	136	1,305	135	13	95	15	15
Mead Elementary School	102	1,365	125	14	99	0	20
The Lincoln School	155	945	100	9	63	0	14
❻ **MEDIAN RTI**		**1,179**	**119**	**12**	**84**	**5**	**16**

Cesar Chavez Middle School

ENROLLMENT		MEDIAN USAGE PER STUDENT					
TEACHER	STUDENTS IN SYSTEM 44	TOTAL TIME (MIN.)	NO. OF SESSIONS	MASTERY TO DATE (OUT OF 25 SERIES)	NO. OF TOPICS MASTERED	NO. OF TOPICS FAST TRACKED	MIN./ TOPIC
Cole, Mercedes	40	1,850	150	13	91	20	13
Strauss, Dave	30	1,150	105	14	100	3	20
Wood, John	66	950	102	13	93	10	13
MEDIAN RTI		**1,305**	**135**	13	**94**	**15**	**15**

Using This Report

Purpose: Use this report to track System 44 progress and usage across a district or school. Use the Median RTI as a benchmark for progress and mastery.

Follow-Up: Be aware of any System 44 user group whose students' progress appears to be slow or who does not show consistent program usage. Consider contacting responsible parties to determine if the user group is implementing the program with fidelity or if it needs additional support.

How It Helps

I use this report to identify groups that are showing slow progress or inconsistent program usage.

Understand the Data

1 Time Period
This report is based on students' cumulative usage and mastery to the date it is run.

2 Number of Sessions
Median number of days the students logged on to the software.

3 Mastery to Date
Median number of instructional Series mastered to date (out of 25 Series).

4 Number of Topics Fast-Tracked
Median number of Topics students Fast-Tracked. (Note: When students pass a Fast-Track assessment, they skip the following Topic of instruction.)

5 Minutes/Topic
Median of the average number of minutes it takes students to complete Topics. Does not include Fast-Tracked Topics.

6 Median RTI
Represents the median usage and mastery for the district or school.

Use the Data

Who: Administrators

When: Every six weeks

How: Apply the information from this report in the following ways:

Monitor Progress

- Compare the students for each school or teacher to the Median RTI.
- If students in a particular school or class are performing especially well, explore the instructional strategies being used and share them with other teachers.

Follow Up

- Conference with principals or teachers to discuss ways to meet the needs of their students.

Review Related Reports

- *System 44* Reading Progress Report (p. 90)
- SPI District/School Growth Report (p. 176)

Data in Action

Median RTI Response to Intervention is a teaching framework that recommends regular progress monitoring and a comparison of students to a determined benchmark. Use the Median RTI to compare the students from each school or teacher against their peers for both usage and mastery. If students are below the Median RTI, review their software usage, Rate of Completion (see p. 102), and number of Topics Fast-Tracked.

Demographic Growth Summary Report

Purpose

This report provides a demographic summary of SRI performance over time.

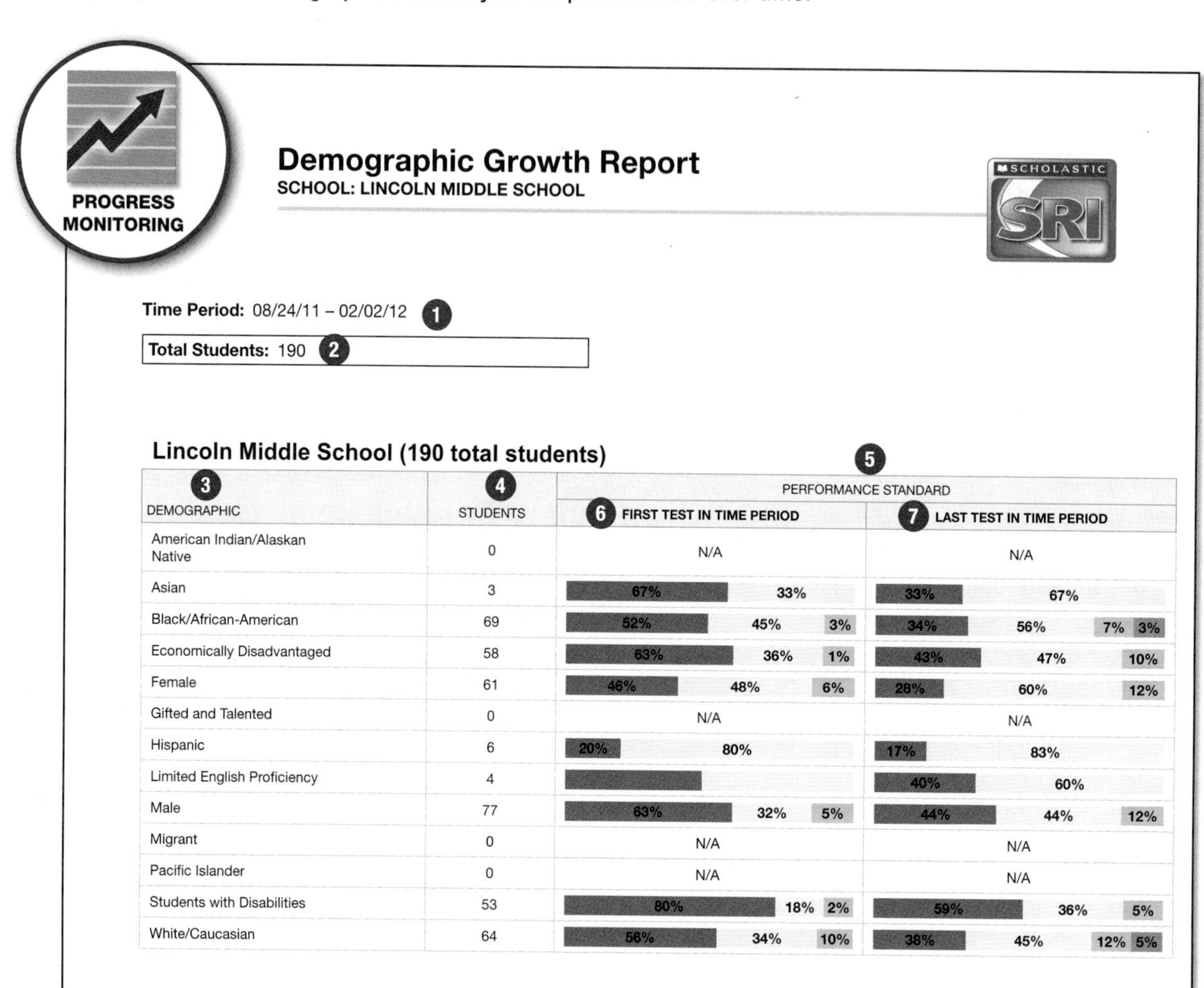

PROGRESS MONITORING

Demographic Growth Report
SCHOOL: LINCOLN MIDDLE SCHOOL

SCHOLASTIC SRI

Time Period: 08/24/11 – 02/02/12 ❶

Total Students: 190 ❷

Lincoln Middle School (190 total students)

❸ DEMOGRAPHIC	❹ STUDENTS	❺ PERFORMANCE STANDARD: ❻ FIRST TEST IN TIME PERIOD	❺ PERFORMANCE STANDARD: ❼ LAST TEST IN TIME PERIOD
American Indian/Alaskan Native	0	N/A	N/A
Asian	3	67% 33%	33% 67%
Black/African-American	69	52% 45% 3%	34% 56% 7% 3%
Economically Disadvantaged	58	63% 36% 1%	43% 47% 10%
Female	61	46% 48% 6%	28% 60% 12%
Gifted and Talented	0	N/A	N/A
Hispanic	6	20% 80%	17% 83%
Limited English Proficiency	4		40% 60%
Male	77	63% 32% 5%	44% 44% 12%
Migrant	0	N/A	N/A
Pacific Islander	0	N/A	N/A
Students with Disabilities	53	80% 18% 2%	59% 36% 5%
White/Caucasian	64	56% 34% 10%	38% 45% 12% 5%

Below Basic | Basic | Proficient | Advanced

Using This Report

Purpose: This report provides a demographic breakdown of SRI performance over time.

Follow-Up: Identify demographic groups that are in need of extra help based on their SRI performance standard percentages.

How It Helps

This report helps me identify demographic groups that are in need of extra help based on their SRI performance standard results.

Understand the Data

1 Time Period
Default time period setting of This School Year displays results from the first and most recent SRI administrations. Customize time period settings to compare results between any two SRI test administrations.

2 Total Students
Total students for each class, grade, or school who have taken at least two SRI tests within the selected time frame.

3 Demographic
Demographic subgroups established during student enrollment in SAM Roster. Students included in this report may appear in more than one subgroup.

4 Students
Total students in each demographic group who have taken at least two SRI tests within selected time periods.

5 Performance Standard
Percentage of students in each SRI performance standard: Advanced, Proficient, Basic, and Below Basic. Performance standards are color-coded according to the key at the bottom of the report.

6 First Test Score in Time Period
Percentage of students who fall within each performance standard on the first test within the selected time period for each demographic group.

7 Last Test Score in Time Period
Percentage of students who fall within each performance standard on the last test within the selected time period for each demographic group.

Use the Data

Who: Administrators

When: After subsequent SRI administrations

How: Apply the information in this report in the following ways:

Monitor Progress

- During the year, track performance standard changes to ensure that students' reading results are improving.

Acknowledge Success

- If students in a particular school or class are doing especially well, explore the instructional strategies being used and share them with other teachers or schools.

Provide Additional Support

- Provide additional implementation training and in-classroom support for classes or schools that continue to fall below expectations.

Review Related Reports

- SRI Demographic Proficiency Report (p. 184)
- SRI Growth Summary Report (p. 188)
- SRI Proficiency Summary Report (p. 192)

Data in Action

Setting Up Demographic Subgroups To review results by demographic group, add demographic information when creating student accounts in the SAM Roster. This can be done during initial student data import or can be completed manually by modifying student profiles.

Demographic Proficiency Report

Purpose

This report provides a demographic breakdown of SRI performance for schools, grades, and classes.

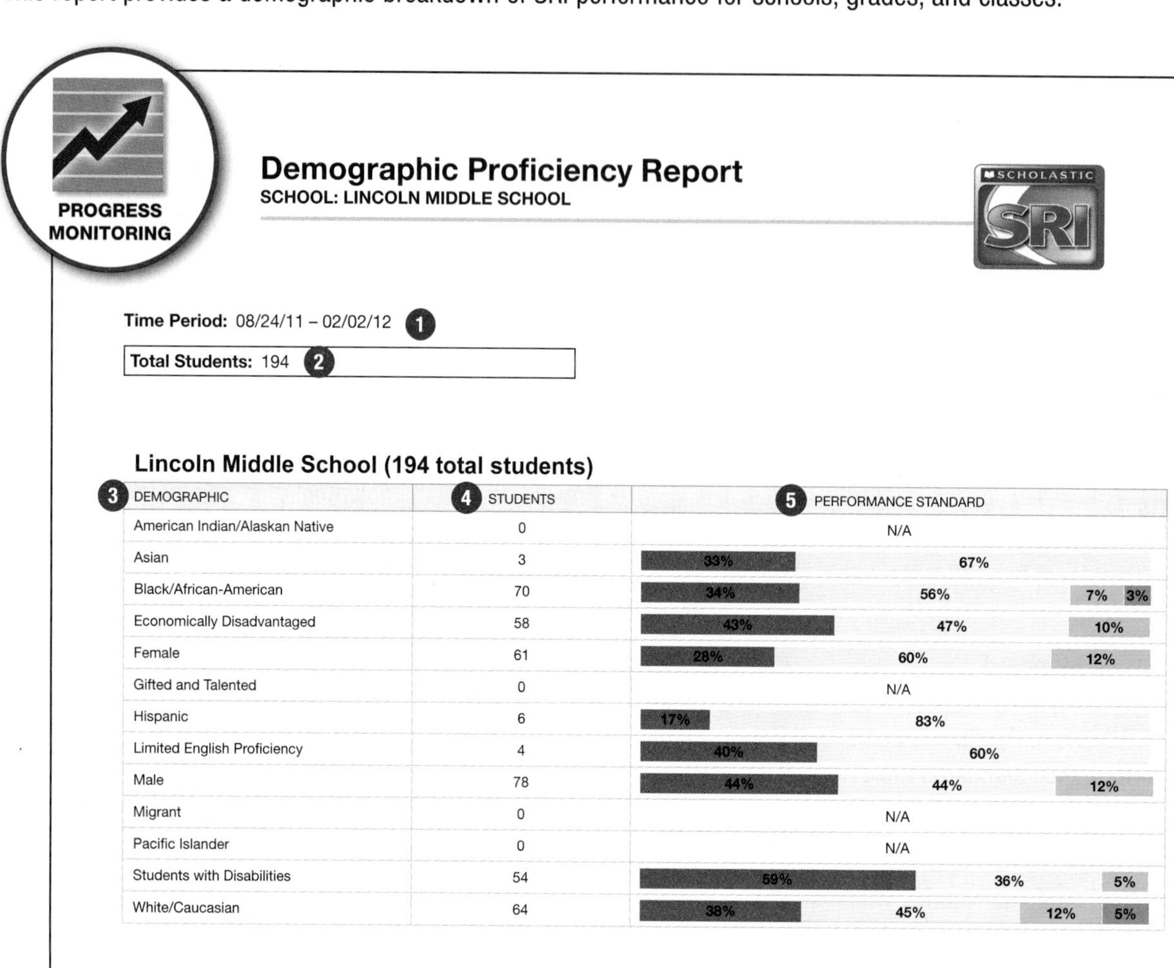

PROGRESS MONITORING

Demographic Proficiency Report
SCHOOL: LINCOLN MIDDLE SCHOOL

SCHOLASTIC SRI

Time Period: 08/24/11 – 02/02/12 ❶

Total Students: 194 ❷

Lincoln Middle School (194 total students)

❸ DEMOGRAPHIC	❹ STUDENTS	❺ PERFORMANCE STANDARD
American Indian/Alaskan Native	0	N/A
Asian	3	33% 67%
Black/African-American	70	34% 56% 7% 3%
Economically Disadvantaged	58	43% 47% 10%
Female	61	28% 60% 12%
Gifted and Talented	0	N/A
Hispanic	6	17% 83%
Limited English Proficiency	4	40% 60%
Male	78	44% 44% 12%
Migrant	0	N/A
Pacific Islander	0	N/A
Students with Disabilities	54	59% 36% 5%
White/Caucasian	64	38% 45% 12% 5%

Below Basic | Basic | Proficient | Advanced

Using This Report

Purpose: This report provides a demographic breakdown of SRI performance.

Follow-Up: Identify demographic groups that are in need of extra help based on their SRI performance standard percentages.

How It Helps

I use this report to identify demographic groups that are in need of extra support based on SRI performance.

Understand the Data

1 Time Period
Default time period setting of This School Year displays results from most recent SRI administration. Customize time period settings to review results from previous tests.

2 Total Students
Total number of students who have taken at least one SRI test within the selected time period.

3 Demographic
Student demographic groups for Adequate Yearly Progress. Note that students may be included in more than one subgroup.

4 Students
Total students within each Demographic Group.

5 Performance Standard
Percentages of students within each of the four performance standards: Advanced, Proficient, Basic, and Below Basic. Performance standard results are color-coded according to the key at the bottom of the report.

Use the Data

Who: Administrators

When: After each SRI administration

How: You can apply the information in this report in the following ways:

Monitor Progress

- Establish expected annual proficiency goals. Communicate expectations for students moving from lower to higher performance standards throughout the year.

Acknowledge Success

- If students in a particular school or class are doing especially well, explore the instructional strategies being used and share them with other teachers or schools.

Provide Additional Support

- Provide additional implementation training and in-classroom support for classes or schools who fall below expectations.

Review Related Reports

- SRI Demographic Growth Summary Report (p. 182)
- SRI Growth Summary Report (p. 188)
- SRI Proficiency Summary Report (p. 192)

Data in Action

Setting Up Demographic Subgroups To review results by demographic group, add demographic information when creating student accounts in the SAM Roster. This can be done during initial student data import or can be completed manually by modifying student profiles.

District/School Proficiency Report

Purpose

This report provides an overview of the performance of students who completed an SRI test.

District/School Proficiency Report

SCHOOL: LINCOLN MIDDLE SCHOOL

Time Period: 08/24/11 – 02/02/12 (1)

(2) **Total Grades:** 3
(3) **Total SRI Students:** 195

Lincoln Middle School (195 total students)

(4) PERFORMANCE STANDARD	(5) STUDENTS	(6) PERCENTAGE OF STUDENTS
Advanced	5	3%
Proficient	24	12%
Basic	94	48%
Below Basic	72	37%

Grade 6 (43 total students)

PERFORMANCE STANDARD	STUDENTS	PERCENTAGE OF STUDENTS
Advanced	0	0%
Proficient	4	8%
Basic	22	51%
Below Basic	17	40%

Grade 7 (78 total students)

PERFORMANCE STANDARD	STUDENTS	PERCENTAGE OF STUDENTS
Advanced	1	1%
Proficient	14	17%
Basic	30	38%
Below Basic	41	53%

(7) **YEAR-END PROFICIENCY LEXILE® RANGE**

GRADE 1	GRADE 2	GRADE 3	GRADE 4	GRADE 5	GRADE 6	GRADE 7	GRADE 8	GRADE 9	GRADE 10	GRADE 11	GRADE 12
100-400	300-600	500-800	600-900	700-1000	800-1050	850-1100	900-1150	1000-1200	1025-1250	1050-1300	1050-1300

Using This Report

Purpose: This report allows administrators or principals to review the performance of students using SRI on a district-wide or school-wide basis.

Follow-Up: Identify schools or classes whose performance on SRI is less than optimal. Review SRI usage with the respective principal or teacher.

How It Helps

This report helps me review SRI performance results.

Understand the Data

1 Time Period
Default time period setting of This School Year displays results from the most recently completed SRI test. Customize time period settings to review results from other SRI tests.

2 Total Schools/Grades
Total number of schools or grade levels with students who have completed at least one SRI test.

3 Total SRI Students
Total number of students who have completed at least one SRI test.

4 Performance Standard
Students are grouped into four performance standards based on their SRI results: Advanced, Proficient, Basic, or Below Basic. Performance standard bands vary based on grade level.

5 Students
Total students within each performance standard based on results from most recent SRI test completed within selected time period.

6 Percentage of Students
Percentage of students within each performance standard based on results from most recent SRI test completed within selected time period.

7 Year-End Proficiency Lexile Range
Expected year-end Lexile range for reading proficiency. Proficiency Lexile ranges vary by grade level. Shaded grade levels indicate the grade levels of students included in the report.

Use the Data

Who: Administrators

When: After each SRI test

How: Apply the information from this report in the following ways:

Monitor Progress

- Establish expected annual proficiency goals. Communicate expectations for students moving from lower to higher performance standards throughout the school year.

Acknowledge Success

- If students in a particular school or class are doing especially well, explore the instructional strategies being used and share them with other teachers or schools.

Provide Additional Support

- Provide additional implementation training and in-classroom support for classes or schools who fall below expectations.

Review Related Reports

- SRI Demographic Proficiency Report (p. 184)
- SRI Proficiency Growth Report (p. 190)
- SRI Proficiency Summary Report (p. 192)

Data in Action

Set Goals Encourage principals and teachers to set goals for students' SRI performance. Monitor progress toward goals and celebrate successes.

Growth Summary Report

Purpose

This report measures Lexile growth between two SRI test dates in a selected time period.

Growth Summary Report

SCHOOL: LINCOLN MIDDLE SCHOOL

Time Period: 08/24/11 – 02/02/12 ❶

Total Grades: 3
Total Students: 190
Average Lexile Growth: 102

Lincoln Middle School (190 total students)

GRADE	❷ TOTAL STUDENTS	❸ FIRST TEST SCORE (AVG.) IN SELECTED TIME PERIOD	❹ LAST TEST SCORE (AVG.) IN SELECTED TIME PERIOD	❺ AVERAGE GROWTH IN LEXILE
6	43	354	470	**116**
7	78	539	624	**85**
8	69	598	707	**109**

Grade 6 (43 total students)

CLASS	TOTAL STUDENTS	FIRST TEST SCORE (AVG.) IN SELECTED TIME PERIOD	LAST TEST SCORE (AVG.) IN SELECTED TIME PERIOD	AVERAGE GROWTH IN LEXILE
Bentley 1	17	398	541	**143**
Bentley 2	9	494	577	**83**
Dahlberg 1	13	313	382	**69**
Dahlberg 4	4	585	657	**72**

Using This Report

Purpose: This report measures Lexile growth over time, between two SRI test dates in a selected time period, by district broken down by school, and by school broken down by grade and teacher/class.

Follow-Up: Identify schools, or individual grades or classes within a school, that are not showing adequate growth over time and provide extra help to optimize SRI performance.

How It Helps

I use this report to monitor reading growth and provide additional support in areas that are not showing adequate growth over time.

Understand the Data

❶ **Time Period**
Default time period setting of This School Year displays results from most recent SRI administration. Customize time period settings to compare results between any two SRI tests.

❷ **Total Students**
Total number of students in each school, grade, or class who have taken at least two SRI tests within selected time period.

❸ **First Test Score (Average) in Selected Time Period**
Average student Lexile measures for the first test within the selected time period.

❹ **Last Test Score (Average) in Selected Time Period**
Average student Lexile measures for the last test within the selected time period.

❺ **Average Growth in Lexile**
Average increase in Lexile score between the first test and the last test for all students who have completed at least two SRI tests within the selected time period.

Use the Data

Who: Administrators

When: After at least two SRI tests have been administered

How: Apply the information in this report in the following ways:

Monitor Progress

- Establish and communicate expected annual growth goals. In general, one year's growth is between 50 and 100 Lexile points, depending on grade level and initial SRI results.
- Monitor growth rates to ensure that schools or classes are on track to meet annual growth benchmarks.
- To track growth for specific groups of students, apply applicable student demographic filters on the SAM Reports screen.

Acknowledge Success

- If students in a particular school or class are doing especially well, explore the instructional strategies being used and share them with other teachers or schools.

Provide Additional Support

- Investigate results for classes or schools whose data indicate that they are not meeting expected growth benchmarks.
- Provide additional implementation training and in-classroom support for classes or schools who continue to fall below growth expectations.

Review Related Reports

- SRI Growth Goals Report (p. 112)
- SRI Demographic Growth Summary Report (p. 182)
- SRI Demographic Proficiency Report (p. 184)
- SRI Proficiency Summary Report (p. 192)

Data in Action

Appropriate Growth Expectations Total SRI growth for the year depends on the students' grade level and initial Lexile. Review the SRI Growth Goals Report to see individual growth goals.

Proficiency Growth Report

Purpose

This report tracks changes in performance standards over time by district, school, grade, and teacher.

Proficiency Growth Report

SCHOOL: LINCOLN MIDDLE SCHOOL

Time Period: 08/24/11 – 02/02/12 ❶

Total Students: 190 ❷

Lincoln Middle School (190 total students)

❸	❹ FIRST TEST IN TIME PERIOD		LAST TEST IN TIME PERIOD	
PERFORMANCE STANDARD	STUDENTS	❺ PERCENTAGE OF STUDENTS	STUDENTS	PERCENTAGE OF STUDENTS
Advanced	0	0%	5	3%
Proficient	12	6%	24	12%
Basic	82	39%	94	48%
Below Basic	116	55%	72	37%

Grade 6 (43 total students)

	FIRST TEST IN TIME PERIOD		LAST TEST IN TIME PERIOD	
PERFORMANCE STANDARD	STUDENTS	PERCENTAGE OF STUDENTS	STUDENTS	PERCENTAGE OF STUDENTS
Advanced	0	0%	0	0%
Proficient	1	2%	4	8%
Basic	22	51%	22	51%
Below Basic	20	47%	17	40%

Grade 7 (78 total students)

	FIRST TEST IN TIME PERIOD		LAST TEST IN TIME PERIOD	
PERFORMANCE STANDARD	STUDENTS	PERCENTAGE OF STUDENTS	STUDENTS	PERCENTAGE OF STUDENTS
Advanced	0	0%	1	1%
Proficient	9	12%	14	17%
Basic	30	38%	30	38%
Below Basic	39	50%	41	53%

Using This Report

Purpose: This report shows changes in distribution across performance standards over time by district, school, grade, and teacher.

Follow-Up: Identify schools (or grades within a school, or classes for individual teachers) that are not showing adequate growth over time and provide extra help to optimize SRI performance.

How It Helps

I identify schools or classes that are not showing adequate growth and provide extra support to optimize SRI performance.

Understand the Data

1 Time Period
Default time period setting of This School Year displays results from first and most recent SRI administrations. Customize time period settings to compare results between any two SRI tests.

2 Total Students
Total students for each class, grade, or school who have taken at least two SRI tests within the selected time period.

3 Performance Standard
Students are grouped into four performance standards based on SRI test results and grade level: Advanced, Proficient, Basic, and Below Basic. Lexile ranges for performance standards vary based on grade level.

4 Students
Number of students in each performance standard. Only students who have taken at least two SRI tests within the selected time period will appear on this report.

5 Percentage of Students
Percentage of students within each performance standard.

Use the Data

Who: Administrators

When: After at least two SRI test administrations

How: Apply the information in this report in the following ways:

Monitor Progress

- Establish expected annual proficiency growth goals. Communicate expectations for students moving from lower to higher performance standards throughout the year.
- During the year, track performance standard changes to ensure that students' reading results are improving.

Acknowledge Success

- If students in a particular school or class are doing especially well, explore the instructional strategies being used and share them with other teachers or schools.

Provide Additional Support

- Investigate results for classes or schools whose data indicate that they are not meeting expected benchmarks.
- Provide additional implementation training and in-classroom support for classes or schools that continue to fall below expectations.

Review Related Reports

- SRI Demographic Growth Summary Report (p. 182)
- SRI Growth Summary Report (p. 188)
- SRI Proficiency Summary Report (p. 192)

Data in Action

Tracking Growth The total number of students in Basic and Below Basic should decrease throughout the year as students move to higher SRI performance standards.

Proficiency Summary Report

Purpose

This report displays the reading performance of students within a district, school, or grade.

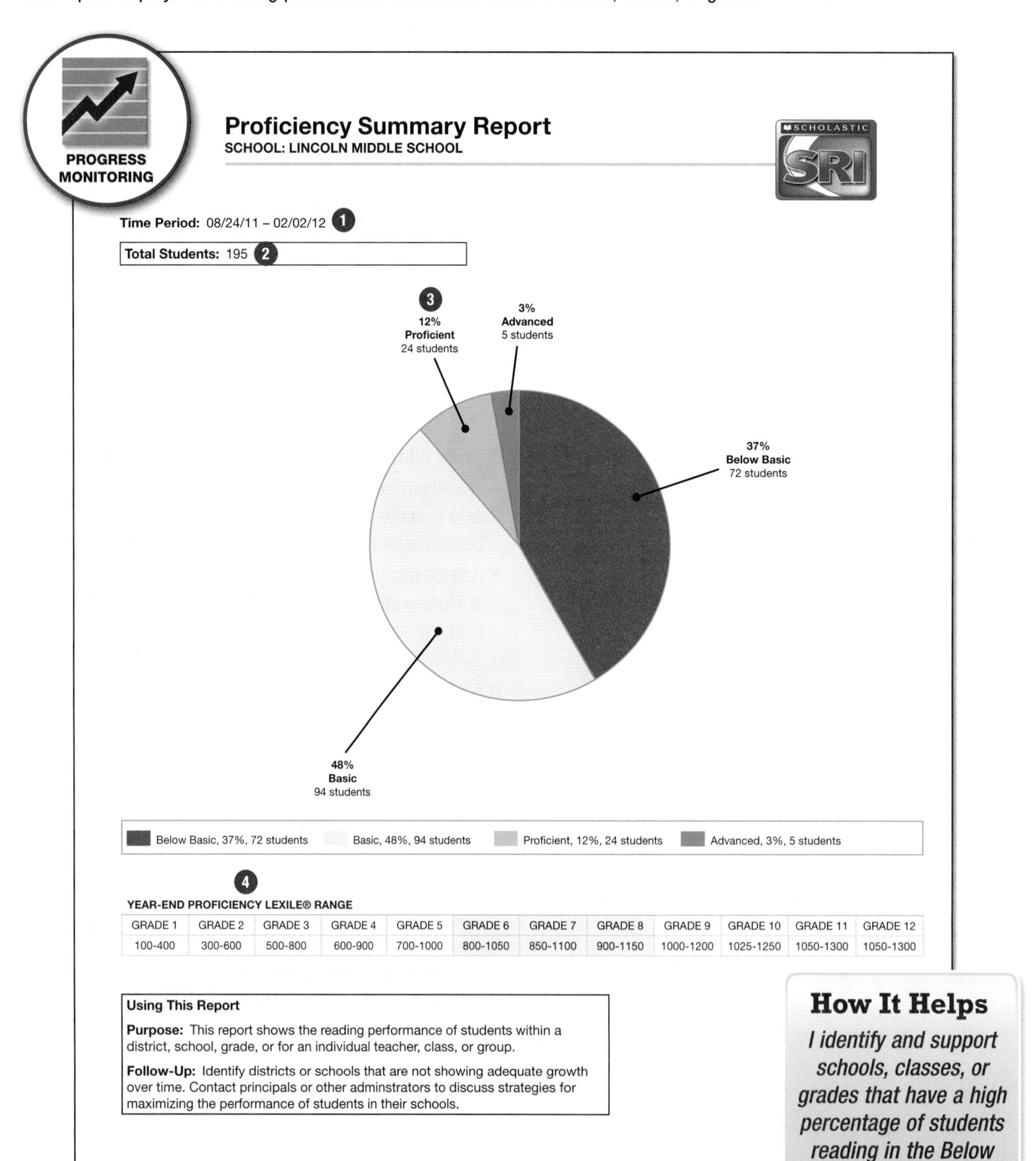

GRADE 1	GRADE 2	GRADE 3	GRADE 4	GRADE 5	GRADE 6	GRADE 7	GRADE 8	GRADE 9	GRADE 10	GRADE 11	GRADE 12
100-400	300-600	500-800	600-900	700-1000	800-1050	850-1100	900-1150	1000-1200	1025-1250	1050-1300	1050-1300

Using This Report

Purpose: This report shows the reading performance of students within a district, school, grade, or for an individual teacher, class, or group.

Follow-Up: Identify districts or schools that are not showing adequate growth over time. Contact principals or other adminstrators to discuss strategies for maximizing the performance of students in their schools.

How It Helps

I identify and support schools, classes, or grades that have a high percentage of students reading in the Below Basic and Basic Range.

Understand the Data

1 Time Period
Default time period setting of This School Year displays results from most recent SRI administration. Customize time period settings to review results from previous tests.

2 Total Students
The total number of students who have completed at least one SRI within the selected time period.

3 Percentages
Percentages of students within each SRI performance standard: Advanced, Proficient, Basic, and Below Basic. Lexile ranges for each performance standard vary by grade level.

4 Year-End Proficiency Lexile Range
Expected year-end student Lexile ranges for reading proficiency in each grade. Lexile ranges vary by grade level. Grades included in the data are highlighted on the chart.

Use the Data

Who: Administrators

When: After each SRI administration

How: You can apply the information in this report in the following ways:

Monitor Progress

- Establish expected annual proficiency goals. Communicate expectations for students moving from lower to higher performance standards throughout the year.

Acknowledge Success

- If students in a particular school or class are doing especially well, explore the instructional strategies being used and share them with other teachers or schools.

Provide Additional Support

- Provide additional implementation training and in-classroom support for classes or schools who fall below expectations.

Review Related Reports

- SRI Demographic Growth Summary Report (p. 182)
- SRI Growth Summary Report (p. 188)
- SRI Proficiency Growth Report (p. 190)

Data in Action

Monitoring Progress The information in this report can help you assess proficiency progress and track trends across an entire school or district.

Teacher Roster

Purpose

This report shows SRI usage by teacher. Correlate the results from this report with district testing windows to ensure that all classrooms are following established testing procedures.

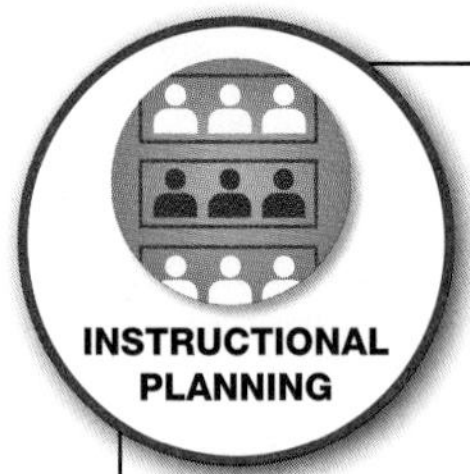

Teacher Roster

SCHOOL: LINCOLN MIDDLE SCHOOL

Time Period: 08/24/11 – 02/02/12

TEACHER	GRADE	STUDENTS ENROLLED IN SRI	STUDENTS TESTED ONCE	STUDENTS TESTED TWICE	STUDENTS TESTED THREE OR MORE TIMES	STUDENTS NOT TESTED
Bentley, Elizabeth	6	30	0	5	25	0
Dahlberg, Bill	6, 7, 8	52	0	6	46	0
Greene, Sarah	7	29	4	2	23	1
Kravitz, Elaine	7, 8	43	0	1	42	0
Schirmer, Margaret	7, 8	42	1	3	36	0
TOTAL TEACHERS = 5		**195**	**5**	**17**	**172**	**1**

Using This Report

Purpose: This report shows SRI usage by teacher. It lists the number of students enrolled per teacher and how often students have been tested.

Follow-Up: Use the report to review SRI usage per teacher. Investigate instances where SRI is not being implemented according to the district or school plan.

How It Helps

I use this report to monitor test activity during and after SRI testing windows. Then I follow up if the report indicates that SRI use is not meeting expectations.

Test Activity Report

Purpose

This report provides information on how each school or classroom utilizes SRI. Correlate the results from this report with district testing windows to ensure that all classrooms are following established testing procedures.

Test Activity Report

SCHOOL: LINCOLN MIDDLE SCHOOL

Time Period: 08/24/11 – 02/02/12

TOTAL STUDENTS: 195

GRADE	TEACHERS	STUDENTS ENROLLED IN SRI	STUDENTS TESTED ONCE	STUDENTS TESTED TWICE	STUDENTS TESTED THREE OR MORE TIMES	STUDENTS NOT TESTED
6	2	43	0	8	35	0
7	4	83	4	5	73	1
8	3	69	0	4	64	0

Using This Report

Purpose: This report provides data on how each school in a district is utilizing SRI.

Follow-Up: Contact principals or other administrators in schools where student SRI use is not meeting district plans or expectations.

How It Helps

I review SRI usage for teachers within a school or district and investigate instances where the SRI is not being implemented according to district or school plans.

Books Read Summary Report

Purpose

This report provides data on *Scholastic Reading Counts!* quiz success rate by grade, class, or group.

Books Read Summary Report

SCHOOL: LINCOLN MIDDLE SCHOOL

Time Period: 08/24/11 – 02/02/12 ❶

Grades: 3
Students: 195

Lincoln Middle School ❷ ❸ ❹ ❺ ❻ ❼

GRADE	NUMBER OF QUIZZES PASSED	STUDENTS	AVG. STUDENT LEXILE®	AVG. BOOK LEXILE®	AVG. BOOKS PER STUDENT	TOTAL WORDS READ
6	189	43	470	513	5.0	1,120,462
7	322	83	549	546	3.4	2,632,037
8	450	69	707	573	6.4	4,243,536
TOTALS	**1,031**	**195**	**567 (AVG.)**	**533 (AVG.)**	**4.6 (AVG.)**	**7,996,035**

Grade 6

TEACHER	NUMBER OF QUIZZES PASSED	STUDENTS	AVG. STUDENT LEXILE®	AVG. BOOK LEXILE®	AVG. BOOKS PER STUDENT	TOTAL WORDS READ
Bentley, Elizabeth	168	30	380	484	7.0	735,663
Dahlberg, Bill	21	13	600	738	1.5	384,799
TOTALS	**189**	**43**	**470 (AVG.)**	**513 (AVG.)**	**5.0 (AVG.)**	**1,120,462**

Using This Report

Purpose: This report provides data on the number of books read by a district, school, grade, or class.

Follow-Up: Identify groups that are performing less than optimally in the SRC! program and intervene accordingly. Congratulate and offer further encouragement to groups that are doing well.

How It Helps

This report provides an overview of Scholastic Reading Counts! *performance in my district.*

Understand the Data

❶ Time Period
Time period settings can be adjusted to view year-to-date or month-by-month results.

❷ Number of Quizzes Passed
Total *Scholastic Reading Counts!* quizzes passed, shown numerically and graphically.

❸ Students
Total students who are enrolled in *Scholastic Reading Counts!* in each school, grade, or class.

❹ Average Student Lexile
Average current SRI Lexile scores for students who are enrolled in *Scholastic Reading Counts!* in each school, grade, or class.

❺ Average Book Lexile
Average Lexile of all books for which students have passed a quiz. Students should strive to read books and articles within 100 Lexile points of their current Lexile level.

❻ Average Books per Student
Average number of *Scholastic Reading Counts!* quizzes passed per student.

❼ Total Words Read
Total words read for all books when each *Scholastic Reading Counts!* quiz is passed.

Use the Data

Who: Administrators

When: Monthly

How: You can apply the information in this report in the following ways:

Acknowledge Success

- Establish and communicate quarterly or annual goals for quizzes passed per student. Congratulate teachers or principals on quiz success rates.
- Hold reading celebrations. Visit classrooms to congratulate students who have met or exceeded reading goals.

Monitor Progress

- Ensure appropriate reading goals.
- Monitor quizzes passed, average books per student, and compare average book Lexile with average student Lexile. Follow up with teachers or administrators whose students are not taking or passing quizzes.

Review Related Reports

- *SRC!* Books Read Report (p. 138)
- *SRC!* Participation Summary Report (p. 198)
- *SRC!* Points Summary Report (p. 200)

Data in Action

Progress Monitoring This report shows independent reading progress, as measured by the number of books read. For classes or schools using points to motivate students' reading performance, run the *SRC!* Points Summary Report.

Participation Summary Report

Purpose

This report provides district- and school-wide data on *Scholastic Reading Counts!* participation.

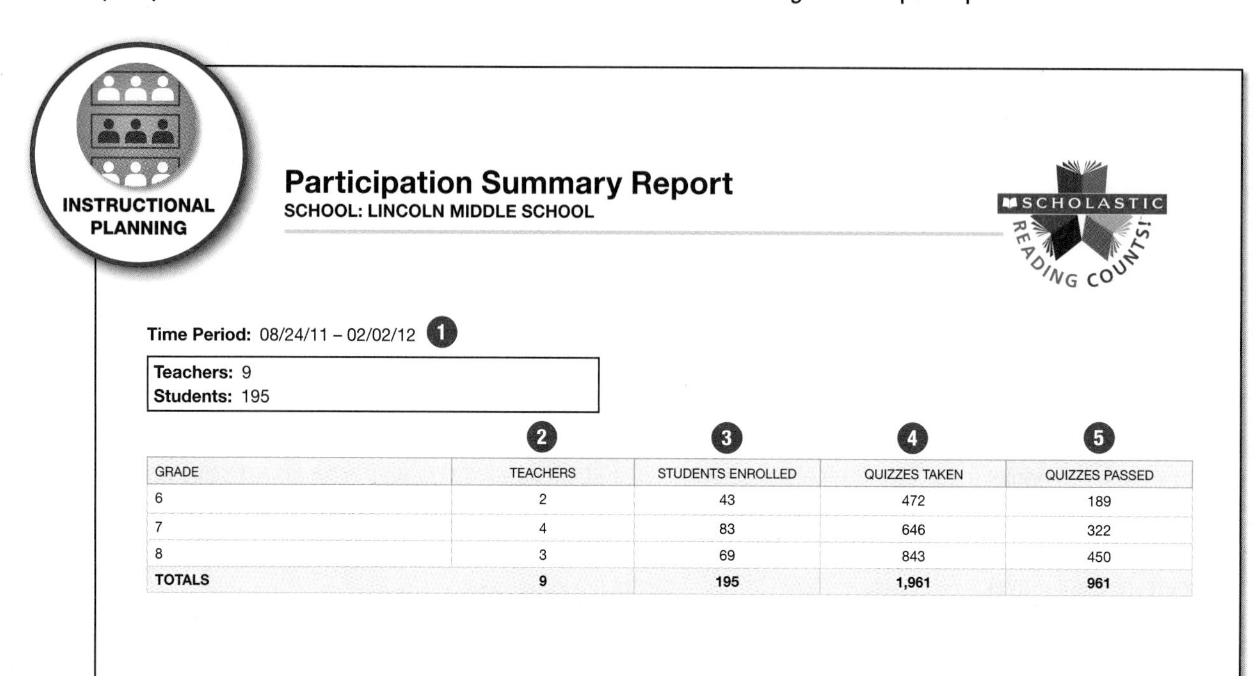

Participation Summary Report
SCHOOL: LINCOLN MIDDLE SCHOOL

Time Period: 08/24/11 – 02/02/12 ❶

Teachers: 9
Students: 195

GRADE	TEACHERS ❷	STUDENTS ENROLLED ❸	QUIZZES TAKEN ❹	QUIZZES PASSED ❺
6	2	43	472	189
7	4	83	646	322
8	3	69	843	450
TOTALS	**9**	**195**	**1,961**	**961**

Using This Report

Purpose: This report provides district- and school-wide information on the number of teachers using the program, students enrolled, quizzes taken, and quizzes passed.

Follow-Up: Identify schools or classes that are not participating in the program according to expectations.

How It Helps

This report helps me quickly track SRC! *participation across the district and within individual schools—including total quizzes attempted and passed.*

Understand the Data

1 Time Period
Time period settings can be adjusted to view year-to-date or month-by-month results.

2 Teachers
Number of teachers in each grade with students participating in *Scholastic Reading Counts!*

3 Students Enrolled
Number of students enrolled in *Scholastic Reading Counts!*

4 Quizzes Taken
Total quizzes attempted in each grade. Students may attempt a quiz on the same book up to three times, with different questions presented in each quiz attempt.

5 Quizzes Passed
Total quizzes passed in each grade level. Optimally, the total number of quizzes passed should be close to the total number of quizzes taken.

Use the Data

Who: Administrators

When: Monthly

How: You can apply the information in this report in the following ways:

Monitor Program Implementation

- Establish quarterly or annual participation goals for grades, classes, teachers, or schools. Communicate expectations and celebrate successes.
- If a particular school, teacher, or grade level does not appear to be fully using the program, investigate further by running the *SRC!* Books Read Summary Report.

Address Needs

- If quiz pass rates in a particular grade, school, or class are low, schedule a meeting with teachers and program coordinators to discuss methods for optimizing program use.
- Ensure that all classrooms have the technology and print materials necessary to maximize usage.

Review Related Reports

- *SRC!* Books Read Report (p. 138)
- *SRC!* Books Read Summary Report (p. 196)
- *SRC!* Points Summary Report (p. 200)

Data in Action

Celebrating Success Encourage teachers to print customized certificates from the SAM Roster to recognize reading achievement. Recognize successes by reading with students during Modeled and Independent Reading.

Points Summary Report

Purpose

This report provides data on *Scholastic Reading Counts!* quiz points earned for quizzes passed.

Points Summary Report

SCHOOL: LINCOLN MIDDLE SCHOOL

Time Period: 08/24/11 – 02/02/12 ❶

Grades: 3
Students: 195

Lincoln Middle School

GRADE	NUMBER OF POINTS ❷	STUDENTS ❸	AVG. STUDENT LEXILE® ❹	AVG. BOOK LEXILE® ❺	AVG. POINTS PER STUDENT ❻	TOTAL WORDS READ ❼
6	942	43	470	4513	21.7	1,120,462
7	1,430	83	549	546	15.1	2,632,037
8	2,250	69	707	573	32.1	4,243,536
TOTALS	**4,622**	**195**	**567 (AVG.)**	**533 (AVG.)**	**20.7 (AVG.)**	**7,996,035**

Grade 6

TEACHER	NUMBER OF POINTS	STUDENTS	AVG. STUDENT LEXILE®	AVG. BOOK LEXILE®	AVG. POINTS PER STUDENT	TOTAL WORDS READ
Bentley, Elizabeth	701	30	380	484	29.2	735,663
Dahlberg, Bill	122	13	600	738	8.7	384,799
TOTALS	**823**	**43**	**470 (AVG.)**	**513 (AVG.)**	**21.7 (AVG.)**	**1,120,462**

Using This Report

Purpose: This report provides data on the number of points earned by a district, school, grade, or class.

Follow-Up: Identify groups that are performing less than optimally in the SRC! program and intervene accordingly. Congratulate and offer further encouragement to groups that are doing well.

How It Helps

The number of points students earn in SRC! *is a good indicator of their progress in Modeled and Independent Reading.*

Understand the Data

1 Time Period
Time period settings can be adjusted to view year-to-date or month-by-month data on program usage.

2 Number of Points
Total *Scholastic Reading Counts!* points earned, shown numerically and graphically.

3 Students
Total students who have passed at least one *Scholastic Reading Counts!* quiz.

4 Average Student Lexile
Average current SRI Lexile scores for students who are enrolled in *Scholastic Reading Counts!* in each school, grade, or class.

5 Average Book Lexile
Average Lexile of all books for which students have passed a quiz. Students should strive to read within 100 Lexile points of their current Lexile level.

6 Average Points per Student
Average number of quiz points earned per student. Students earn points only for quizzes passed. Point values for each book vary based on word count and interest.

7 Total Words Read
Total words read for all books when each *Scholastic Reading Counts!* quiz is passed.

Use the Data

Who: Administrators

When: Monthly

How: You can use the information in this report in the following ways:

Acknowledge Success

- Establish and communicate quarterly or annual goals for quizzes passed per student. Congratulate teachers or principals on quiz success rates.
- Hold reading celebrations. Visit classrooms to congratulate students who have met or exceeded reading goals.

Monitor Progress

- Monitor quizzes passed and average books per student, and compare average book Lexile with average student Lexile. Provide additional support to teachers or administrators who are not optimizing program usage.
- Ensure appropriate point goals. Points earned for passing quizzes vary by book.

Review Related Reports

- *SRC!* Points Report (p. 144)
- *SRC!* Books Read Summary Report (p. 196)
- *SRC!* Participation Summary Report (p. 198)

Data in Action

Recognizing Reading Success Students enrolled in *System 44* may have experienced reading challenges in the past. Help build confidence and reading success by implementing awards or celebrations for success in *SRC!* Establish goals for points earned, books read, or quizzes passed. Celebrate students, classes, or schools who meet or exceed these expectations.

Index

Appendix 1

The chart below displays the correlation between SRI Lexile levels and their equivalent grade levels. These performance bands are established by the Scholastic Achievement Manager (SAM).

Performance Bands and Lexile Correlation

Grade	Below Basic (Far Below Grade Level)	Basic (Below Grade Level)	Proficient (On Grade Level)	Advanced (Above Grade Level)
1	N/A	0L–99L	100L–400L	401L and above
2	0L–99L	100L–299L	300L–600L	601L and above
3	0L–249L	250L–499L	500L–800L	801L and above
4	0L–349L	350L–599L	600L–900L	901L and above
5	0L–449L	450L–699L	700L–1000L	1001L and above
6	0L–499L	500L–799L	800L–1050L	1051L and above
7	0L–549L	550L–849L	850L–1100L	1101L and above
8	0L–599L	600L–899L	900L–1150L	1151L and above
9	0L–649L	650L–999L	1000L–1200L	1201L and above
10	0L–699L	700L–1024L	1025L–1250L	1251L and above
11	0L–799L	800L–1049L	1050L–1300L	1301L and above

Districts or schools that wish to adjust these Lexile performance bands to match district or state performance standards, including the Common Core State Standards, may do so in the SRI Settings of the SAM Roster.

Appendix 2

State Assessment
Arizona's Instrument to Measure Standards (AIMS)
California English-Language Arts Standards Test
Florida Assessments for Instruction in Reading (FAIR)
Georgia Criterion-Referenced Competency Test (CRCT)
Georgia High School Graduation Tests (GHSGT)
Hawaii State Assessment
Illinois Standards Achievement Test (ISAT)
Kansas State Assessments of Reading
Kentucky Core Curriculum Test (KCCT)
Minnesota Comprehensive Assessments (MCA)
New Mexico Standards-Based Assessment (SBA)
North Carolina End-of-Grade (NCEOG)
North Carolina English I End-of-Course (NCEOC)
Oklahoma Core Curriculum Test (OCCT)
Oregon Assessment of Knowledge and Skills (OAKS)
South Carolina Palmetto Assessment of State Standards (PASS)
South Dakota State Test of Educational Progress (DSTEP)
Tennessee Comprehensive Assessment Program (TCAP) Achievement Test
Texas Assessment of Knowledge and Skills (TAKS)
Virginia Standards of Learning Tests (SOL)
West Virginia WESTEST 2
Proficiency Assessments for Wyoming Students (PAWS)

Teacher's Notes

Teacher's Notes